WRECKING BALL

WRECKING BALL

Race, Friendship, God, and Football

RICK BASS

HIGH ROAD BOOKS ● ALBUQUERQUE

© 2025 by Rick Bass
All rights reserved. Published 2025
Printed in the United States of America

ISBN 978-0-8263-6856-0 (cloth)
ISBN 978-0-8263-6857-7 (ePub)

Library of Congress Control Number: 2025932270

Founded in 1889, the University of New Mexico sits on the traditional homelands of the Pueblo of Sandia. The original peoples of New Mexico—Pueblo, Navajo, and Apache—since time immemorial have deep connections to the land and have made significant contributions to the broader community statewide. We honor the land itself and those who remain stewards of this land throughout the generations and also acknowledge our committed relationship to Indigenous peoples. We gratefully recognize our history.

Cover photograph courtesy of Trevor Paulhus
Designed by Felicia Cedillos
Composed in Adobe Garamond Pro

FOR KIRBY

CONTENTS

Introduction 1

1. Last Year 23
2. Court 33
3. Winter Practice 41
4. The Rock 55
5. First Game 63
6. Dogcatcher 87
7. Ass-Whipping 111
8. Practice 153
9. Bison 193
10. Dreams 219

Acknowledgments 223

INTRODUCTION

TO TALK ABOUT FOOTBALL with passion, wonder, and appreciation is to exercise the talents of denial. A casual observer would and should recoil, as when one hears a military person espousing combat, or even a boxer speaking of the sweet science of devastation.

Football damages bodies and, make no mistake, minds. It is a difficult sport to defend, but in my opinion, not impossible. I am intrigued by the complicated, the contradictory, and the paradoxical. I do not care for symbols any more, preferring instead the organic, shifting vitality of metaphor. The way a thing *is*, but also the way it *isn't*. I'm interested in the way football is changing its own self, the players and coaches, and the fans who watch it. Metamorphosing.

To me, football is a living system, and what I love best about it—where the addiction comes in—is that always, first and foremost, the game is about problem-solving. It's like writing a novel, except you get to use your body, and you have a clan, a loyal family, helping you.

I see and understand all the bad and dangerous stuff. But when I say that I love football, what I'm thinking of is the incredible meld of the physical and the mental. It's also like the world's best soap opera: from the official beginning of the season in early September, until the culmination of the 32 teams' journey, the Super Bowl—one winner and one loser, happening sometime in early February—the storylines and plots change daily. Coaches and players who were fired from one organization meet back up with their mentors and former teammates. Star players who have spent months or even years battling their way back from the most gruesome injuries make their way back out onto the field, achieving the sole focus from their long isolation and estrangement, the long rehabilitation. Future Hall of Famers play on the road in what will be the last game of their career, to applause.

On any given play, the most amazing things can happen. A Hail Mary, an Immaculate Reception, a Music City Miracle. The Catch. There is no end to it, except it's not soap opera; it's real, not made up—and the offensive, defensive, and special teams coordinators plot and scheme, chess masters all. They adjust game plans on the fly, in real time, and no one ever knows how it's to turn out, other than perhaps gods high atop a mountain, looking down. The rest of us simply have to wait and watch for time to reveal all—which it always does.

I even love the hoary clichés—each containing kernels of life wisdom that transcend far beyond the 60 minutes of any one game. *You are what your record says you are*, and, *Father Time is undefeated*.

In 2015, I did a story for *Texas Monthly* magazine about a semi-pro football team, the Texas Express, in the once-upon-a-time small town of Brenham, famed for being the locale of Blue Bell Creamery ice cream, of which vanilla, perhaps unsurprisingly, is their flagship product. And justifiably so. If there is a better store-bought ice cream sandwich, I have yet to encounter it.

That was the nature of the world, I think, for white middle-class Americans, such as myself, having finally been lifted out of the whipping over the last recession, lifted up by the Obama administration's years of economic policy. It had been a long scrap, but there was light ahead. It was possible even to get a freelance assignment covering such irrelevancies and insignificances as a semi-pro football team. It was possible to think summertime thoughts about *Who makes the best ice cream sandwich?*

MY BEST FRIEND since high school, Kirby Simmons, was volunteering as trainer for the Texas Express: wrapping players' ankles and wrists, treating their sprains, icing muscle pulls, splashing hydrogen peroxide on their wounds. He told me stories of each week's exploits, the heroic and the humorous—and of the tempestuous passions, the pride and the fury of the coach, Anthony Barnes, then 50 years old, an ex-player whose tough love most of the players had looked for all their lives, and which they craved. No small number of the players were refugees from the gang-grip of a city—usually Houston. Coach Barnes worked three jobs: garbage truck driver, dogcatcher, and city water inspector. A devout Christian, he was also a voluble and creative curser.

I was teaching at Montana State University as writer-in-residence at the time, and the position included a robust special project budget. That spring, then, I flew down to Texas a couple of times each month after teaching my Thursday night workshop. I'd arrive Friday, rent a car, and drive to wherever the Express were playing.

The year before, they'd been magnificent, advancing to the playoffs. Coach Barnes had never had a losing season in 17 years of coaching, and he'd had success helping various players get scholarships to four-year and community colleges around the country. One of the bull-necked fireplug running backs, Jarvis Brown, was the brother of an NFL Super Bowl star, Malcolm Brown.

To call them semi-pro, however, was a misnomer. In their best moments, when all the parts of the offense or defense whirred and clicked into place, the Express looked professional, or partly professional. That was a rarity, however, and despite being a long-time fan, it was fascinating for me to see how interconnected the parts were, yet how a failure to execute by even one part of the puzzle rendered the whole thing awkward and ineffectual. At which point Coach would lose his mind.

In theory, the players would share some ghostly percentage of gate receipts and merchandise sales, but there were no receipts.

The games were played in the spring—like a shadow league—seen by almost no one, making me think of the way the Southern Hemisphere's springtime is our autumn, and of the way too that at any given point in time, while half the earth is bathed in light, the other half lies in darkness.

Something I had noticed in covering the team, that year when they were winning so many games, was how small many of the players were: almost slight. The linemen, of course, were massive, but players in the skill positions that involved speed were not big at all. I had played for a year as a walk-on at Utah State University, first as a flanker and then, when they realized how slow I was, as a tailback at the very bottom of the depth charts. The Fighting Aggies. It occurred to me how nice—how wonderful—it would have been to know about this league as a young man, just after college, instead of waiting 40 years.

But what most got my attention about the Express was that this was not a recreational league, but instead, in some ways, a life-or-death league. The players loved the game, but did not need it. What they needed, I think, was Coach.

And how much pressure would that be for any one of us, even if it was what a person asked for—to be of service to the poor and broken in spirit, the long suffering? Be careful what you ask for. When one is strong in any way—physically, or otherwise—one can become accustomed over time to shouldering more and more of the thing one seeks to carry, or the thing that seeks to be carried.

Here's another football truism that's applicable to life: *Winning makes everyone get along fine.*

For whatever reason, the year I started traveling down to Texas, the Express began losing. Maybe it was the retirement of their star cornerback, David "Florida" Hallback, who, with his fiery passion, had clashed with Coach often. Maybe it was the loss of nimble-handed Doran Toussam, with his full-ride scholarship to Texas Tech. Sometimes even the slightest smallest perturbation can be a tipping point, in football as in life. With so many moving parts, there are always unintended consequences radiating in all directions. Once that tipping point is crossed, trouble can compound quickly; not unlike a contagion. Another football-and-life truism: *When in trouble, simplify.* Go back to the basics. *Block. Tackle. Run the ball.* Three yards and a cloud of dust. Don't get fancy. Fancy will get you in trouble every time.

So Coach was carrying a lot. It always impressed me that while he could cite you his win–loss record in any given year, when it came to his players' lives—the young men who were holding onto the rope he had thrown them—it was the ones he'd lost that he tallied, not the successes or victories.

The victories—with his indomitable confidence—were to be expected. I think in Coach's mind, the losses were what graveled him. "Nine to the penitentiary, two to the Grim Reaper," he said. "Only two."

Implicit in his use of the word "only" the high number of near-misses. The ever-present danger. And again, the accumulating stress of that responsibility.

●

I ENDED UP playing, that first year. Injuries had decimated the Express's ranks. I don't recall precisely how it happened, but I do recall in shuttered, fractured vignettes, suiting up with the ever-diminishing number of the team. Walking in my cleats across the tile floor of the bathroom at The Rock, the ragged field and stadium in Brenham—the locker room door torn off the hinges, rust-stained sink, power and water shut off years ago—putting my contacts in, in the dimness, then going back out into the bright light, tottering in my cleats as if wearing high heels.

I remember running downfield on kickoffs, angling to throw a block—squaring up and hitting, and being hit, for the first time in more than 40 years, at the somewhat desiccated age of 60. I remember how, as I sailed through the air, I was surprised by how light I felt—like a styrofoam glider—and realized it was because I *was* lighter, by 25 pounds.

It was a year of pulled hamstrings, calves, and groin. After a home game, I'd gimp back to Kirby and Jean Ann's house, barely able to walk, yelping sometimes as a stab of pain gripped me, even as I tried to do the most mundane tasks: sitting down on their couch, for instance, and leaning forward to receive a plate of food, or a glass of wine. This would prompt a look of concern from both of them, though as the season wore on their expressions of compassion would be unable to be held long, and would invariably give way to mirth and then outright laughter, which I could not argue was in any way undeserved.

My recollections of that time are that I spent vast stretches of it either atop a lumpen miscellany of ice packs, or floating like a pale frog in a steaming tub of lavender-scented Epsom salts, existing in a not-unpleasant fog of limbo as twisted old muscles loosened their swollen knots. Too wracked to sleep the night following a game, I'd eat a banana and a handful of Naproxen, then drive in my little rental car to whatever airport had been nearest the game that week, and fly back to Montana, to my secret life as a college professor.

Why?

Friends and family were concerned, but the mind, for better or worse, is powerful. I craved the problem-solving pathway, the neural pathway and body memory of those shifting plates of light—shuttered, fractal gaps and gashes of discovery, which the runner, in synchrony with his blocker, perceives but also helps create. I wanted—needed—to know it one more time. Not to talk about it, or write about it, I realized, after 60 years, but to do it, however awkwardly. To be in life. And, as well, the players were struggling. It would be fun. It is, after all, or should be, a game. I wanted to show I cared enough about them, and their efforts—their gambit—to show up.

●

MY FATHER AND his wife Maryanne drove up from Houston for one of our games at The Rock. They were nervous, I could tell, and puzzled, but accepting. As I ran onto the field with my teammates, running our pregame drills, our stretches, and then our pass routes—our dedication to a larger purpose—I wondered if they thought it was as if I had joined the armed services. Did it appear to them I had been scooped up by a cult?

Up in the stands, they visited with other families beneath a single umbrella, in a cold, hissing rain. Out on the field, we began to crumble.

The slippery grass was dangerous. One of our immense star defensive linemen, David Bratton, went down writhing and gripping his knee, and play ceased—we could hear his groans—and it took Kirby and Coach Barnes, as well as Coach's friend, come-and-go Coach Eddie, and two other players, to help David off the field, his leg dangling gruesomely, with David unable even to let his foot touch the ground.

An ambulance was summoned. After some time it arrived and carried him away, with his patella torn all the way off; and when I looked back up in the stands to see how Dad and Maryanne were faring, I saw they too had left, following David's family out to the ambulance to offer what consolation they could, and then driving back to Houston, having seen enough.

•

ANOTHER GAME: CHANDLER'S shoulder separated, Wyatt (our quarterback) concussed and then—playing through the concussion, but loopier than shit—a sprained ankle. Ernie twisting an ankle, Big David Fontenot twisting his back—we had to suit up Coach and Coach Eddie at halftime, so that the second half was as surreal as any dream. It was plug-and-play at any and every position, just to get 11 players out on the field at any one time. At one point I was the only person on our sideline and still we had but 10 on the field; Coach Eddie had come out with a broken finger.

He pointed me toward the huddle where we were backed up, defending our goal line. I ran out and lined up on the defensive line to rush the passer—in no way did I want responsibility for covering a speedy receiver.

I adjusted myself to fit between the two giants facing me, like a slip of paper through the mail slot. And it worked. They lunged at me, but I was too small; their aim was off. I was crawling under their legs, and then up and running again, and then into the backfield, chasing their quarterback, hot on his heels as he ran a bootleg. I was *so* close to catching him, and my pursuit forced him to throw early and high and on the run, an incompletion, and we held them without a score on that drive, though the game was already out of hand. The goal was merely to finish, and with pride, and to stand in a struggle with friends.

During the last winning season with the team, Coach had gathered the team around him after a particularly close and hard-fought win. The team was much larger then, and there was a lot of clowning around—the specific good camaraderie just after a game when it's still so fresh in the players' minds that it's almost as if the victory is still happening. They can remember every play, every gesture within each play, the incandescent lighting of those details having a photographer's flashbulb quality to them. The game is over and won, but the body is still feeding, nursing, on the adrenaline. There is joking and, already, a retelling of the battle, complimenting, praising each other, as I'm sure it was for our kind, our species, after battles and long hunts.

"Gentlemen," Coach said, trying to quiet the swarming hubbub of post-game sideline celebration, the crowing and strutting, the pantomiming of tackles broken, hits delivered. Coach himself had raged and howled throughout the game, had known both agony and ecstasy in the cauldron of his own soul—and he, too, was still riding high.

"Gentlemen," he said, wagging his finger at them. A coach still, even as a celebrant. A teacher. "*Gentlemen.* Tonight the Ugly Thing reappeared. You won—you men played hard—but the Ugly Thing reared its ugly head. It came back. It must not come back."

The players, still jubilant, looked at one another, the carbonated fizz of their joy starting to dissipate.

"We will not speak its name," Coach admonished. "But it came back."

He was definitely in his preacher mode. Which of the seven deadly sins was it? Rage, sloth, envy? I didn't know. I don't think any of us did.

Whatever it was, it seemed to me it might be the only thing in the world Coach could be cowed by. It's said that all anger is fear, and if that's true, he was often a most fearful man, though the word anyone would use to describe him would be fearsome, not fearful. And yet, there on the sidelines, watching his players celebrate another championship—another year in the playoffs—I thought I detected a flicker of nervousness, and of *caution*, in this most intemperate and passionate of men.

"We do not speak its name," he whispered, now that he had their full attention. "Now then, you are to be congratulated. You men did a great number of things well on the field. In the fourth quarter, when they were trying to come back, you kept your foot on their throat. Yes, *sir*," he said, "you kept your foot on their throat." Smiling, now, with the pride of a craftsman, pleased with the immaculate aesthetics of his work.

He gathered them around in a circle, heads bowed, and gave a heartfelt prayer, raising and then lowering his voice in cadence with the tempest within; and the players, now meek and humbled, nodded, eyes shut. Some murmured *Amen* at certain points, while others shouted it. The heart of the prayer was gratitude for being alive—at one point, Coach went into graphic detail about all the things that could have happened to us. But the theme that resonated most was when Coach spoke of the unbridgeable gap between the Lord's goodness and our own irredeemable (except through the blood of Christ) unworthiness. A distance too far. A distance so vast as to seem to be the definition of sorrow, alienation, estrangement, loneliness.

But the game!

That night after the game and the midfield prayer gathering and debriefing, the players released from the huddle and ran across the field like children, carrying their duffel bags again like grade-schoolers coming back from a sleepover. Shed of their helmets and shoulder pads, they looked smaller. They *were* smaller. They chased one another across the field, zigging and zagging beneath the stadium lights. They had won, *and* they had been saved, baptized yet again by the spit and spray of their snarling, howling, whispering coach. All in all, a good night. All in all, a good year.

●

THE FIRST TIME I carried the ball for the Express was also the last. I'd been practicing with the quarterbacks, taking pitches on sweeps, catching screen passes from out of the backfield, and taking handoffs on straight-ahead dive plays.

I don't know why Coach sent me in, nor why he called the play he did. In the intervening years, I have forgotten the name of it. It could have been something like 24 Blast, where the tailback, the 2-back, lines up deep behind the quarterback, takes the hand off, and tries to sprint through the theoretical crease between his left tackle and tight end—the 4-hole.

We were backed up near our goal line. It was third down. It was a night game. The lights at the end of the stadium were brilliant, almost hallucinogenic.

"Get out there, old man!" Coach said suddenly, slapping me on the back. To this day I don't know what he was thinking. You can ask him the same question three times and get three different answers, a quality in him that's all the more endearing for the fact that each of the three answers will be mostly or even all the way true.

Little Dooney—muscled like a bowling ball, and the only other player who wasn't a 20-something—having just turned 40 years old, and our best and most reliable running back—was who I would be replacing. The team was already in their huddle when I dashed out there.

There's really not that much to think about: helmet, mouthpiece, receiver's gloves. Remember to buckle the helmet's chin strap so that when you're hit, the navy blue helmet doesn't go flying off, which is always a sight that demoralizes the team whose player lost the helmet, and fires up the other team, as if the player's head has been separated from his body.

But oftentimes during the season, it would seem like too much to remember. I'd be called out onto the field for special teams, or to fill some gap here or there, and would be in a panic, searching for one part or another like a man looking for his car keys. Complicating my situation was the tiny notepad and pen I kept tucked in my game pants, surely an illegality.

I ran out onto the field, tapped Dooney on the shoulder pads—he saw me coming and appeared puzzled for only a moment, then nodded, gave me a low five and sprinted off—and Wyatt, the quarterback that year, reconvened the huddle, called the play, "*On two*," and we clapped our hands in unison and broke the huddle, trotted into our positions.

It was strange, seeing my teammates in a real game. Their faces were recognizable, but not exactly the same. Inside the helmets, their faces looked smaller and more gaunt. They looked more businesslike. It's hard to describe, but the unity of purpose around them was a real thing, the way a cloud or an echo is a real thing. But it was more than that. We were like one swirling organism.

Things were happening so fast. I could feel my heart in my throat. I was hungry for the ball. Wyatt checked behind him to make sure I was lined up at the correct depth, waved me over a nudge to the left, then turned his back to me, ready for the ball. I could feel his joy as he waited for it. I could feel each of my teammates' joy, as each prepared to do his one assignation.

Across the line, the defense: a roving, malignant mass. Preposterously, it had not yet occurred to me that all 11 of them would be focused upon annihilating me. I had not known there would be such fury. I knew it logically, of course, but I knew also that I would have pretty much my whole team either blocking for me, or pulling away some of the defense through the deception of their pass routes, which the defense would be forced to cover.

But there would be little deception, here.

The play clock was ticking. I had no idea how many seconds were left—less than a handful—but the defense could read the melting numbers on the scoreboard behind me, and they knew also I would be getting the ball. Such a tiny and ancient specimen as myself had not been summoned for no reason.

The ball was snapped and I lunged forward, my arms open to receive the ball. Wyatt spun and was running back to meet me, his eyes focused intently on my arms as he reached the ball out and into the basket I'd made. He extended the ball to me in the way of a man touching a match to a mound of wood that's been soaked in gasoline.

I took the ball—*hold on*, I thought, *don't give it up*—and veered toward the 4-gap, even as I saw, not at all in slow motion but instead very fast, my offensive line swinging to the right while I went left, in what would afterward be called, mildly, a miscommunication. Only Wyatt and I had it correct.

I did not see who hit me until he hit me. The player truly seemed to come from out of nowhere.

Just before he hit me square in the chest, up high, I did see one player hurtle past me, the timing of his launch thrown off, perhaps, by him thinking I'd be moving much faster than I was.

But the one who came in at me straight was tall, long as a javelin. It was a lovely hit, not a wrap-up-and-wrestle-to-the-ground tackle, but a rocket launch, a spear into my chest with all the force he could muster.

I remember going to the ground. Rather, I remember being on the ground, and chagrined it was so, for it meant I was no longer running, and that the play was over. I was aware that I had held onto the ball, had not fumbled it. I was aware also I was still alive.

On the film, the sea of white that is my team is largely absent. I'm running along resolutely, chugging, bobbing like a little tugboat into the swirling sea of the other color, navy jerseys. The one place, the one direction, toward which I should *not* be running. *Here be dragons.*

And then—in the film, and I have to believe my eyes how it happened—comes the part where I am uprooted and—miraculously, really—am sailing through the air, recumbent, laid out perfectly horizontal upon an imaginary flying carpet that's four feet above the ground. It's like the scene in *The Big Lebowski* where The Dude has been knocked out and is dreaming, flying through the clouds with a bowling ball outstretched, weightless, a big old goofy grin on his face while Bob Dylan sings "The Man in Me."

I'm still perfectly parallel to the ground, stiffened as if with rigor mortis. I am still clutching the ball in both arms—again, the grip of rictus—flying past other players at their shoulder height, and they are watching as I sail past them.

When I finally land on the ground, I do not fumble, and the contact with the earth is what awakens me. I bounce a couple of times, then reach a hand up to two of my vanquishers, asking for a lift back to a standing position. *Good hit*, I say.

They do not take my extended hand. Instead, they are dancing in a circle around me, whooping in a caricature of the war whoops on the Saturday morning Westerns I would watch as a child, more than half a century ago.

I roll over and get to my feet, toss the ball to the ref, pat one of the linemen on his shoulder pads, and trot unevenly off the field, my head not feeling connected to my body, and my upper back feeling glass-shattered.

Over on the opposing sideline, their entire team was still whooping and hollering, and across the wide field drifted the jubilant yet also dismayed cry, "They killed Papa!"

Coach, busy sending in his punt team—fourth down—looked at me quickly, as if seeing either a miracle or a ghost, or both: "You all right, old man?" And when I nodded and said *Oh yeah*, he shook his head and turned his attention back to the game, aware, I think, of how close both of us had skated to true disaster—ambulances, or worse.

Another truism: players must have a short memory. Learn from the mistake, but keep moving forward. There's no time to look back. Forget about it. The clock is always ticking.

●

I DID NOT go back in at tailback the rest of the game. I played some on special teams but remember nothing. I do not know how I made it back to Kirby and Jean Ann's. I do not remember flying back to Montana the next day. It was as if a slab of iceberg had fractured and slid away into the cold Arctic: *calving*. Later that night a screenshot from the game film, the picture of my horizontal self floating high in the night sky, through and above the sea of other players, would circulate through the Texas United Football Association domain, with the comments "They killed Papa" and "Oh, it looks like he needs some *milk*."

The bulk of our offensive line—unpracticed, having missed our Thursday night sessions—had pulled the wrong way. One by one, in weeks subsequent, they would come up to me and tell me they were sorry, and that they would do better the next time. *Team*.

●

I KEPT PULLING muscles in practice. It was no way to prepare for a game—flying—and I wondered how the bodies of the pros stood up to it—getting hammered on Sundays, then flying home immediately after a game, then often getting back on a plane to fly again, sometimes cross-country, and sometimes on a short week, to play again on Thursday night. Another truism: playing a game is like being in a bad car wreck—afterward, every part of your body is sore from the traumatic radiant energy released in the collision.

The pros crawl into ice baths as soon as possible. They have physical therapists rub oil into them and separate the inflamed muscle tissues by hand, stretching everything to make it pliable again. They bask in hyperbaric chambers so that the broken body can be convinced it is not broken, and they can go back out there and be broken again. It's why the great Andrew Luck retired, though still in his twenties: he had rips and tears in his calves that simply would no longer heal. Achilles, the fleet Greek hero, felled by a similar stab; tragedy, and yet in tragedy, victory. *Survival.*

MY CLEATS WERE too substantial. When I was running and planted suddenly to make a cut, my joints and muscles were no longer strong enough to absorb even that once-simple shock. My drying-out twisted fibers, latticed with scar tissue, popped, stretched, separated with microtears again and again, evincing mysterious bruises even when I had not been hit. But my God, what fun, running up and down the field with the *fellas*, chasing the ballcarrier, or running about, looking for someone to block, in the high-speed flowing pulse, the ever-changing geometry of the return: trying to help spring one's teammate into open space, and victory. I spent that spring swaddled in ice and reeking of Tiger Balm, always burning and tingling, until I seemed to myself an unfamiliar specimen, perhaps even a different subspecies. The goal was no longer to feel good or to be strong, but instead, only to stop hurting enough so that by the next Saturday, I could at least get back out on the field.

The long, joyous, addicting diminishment.

The game in San Antonio was the most brutal yet. An immense team, whose every player towered over us, the talent of San Antonio (seventh-largest city in the United States) rivaled that of a team in the NFL. We had no business being on the field with their aerial circus, and their gigantic stadium with all of its fans—another night game— but we went through our drills with the belief that we could yet win.

On the very first series, I popped a hamstring and had to come back to the sidelines and stretch it out. Michelle, Big Quincy's girlfriend, was helping Kirby with the fallen in that game, like a battlefield nurse, and gave me this new kind of magic ice bag that wasn't ice at all, but when activated, generated through chemical reaction a great and satisfactory numbing. I shoved one up under each pants leg, right against my hamstrings, and within 10 minutes or so, knew no pain: a miracle.

During a game, you're hyperaware of every little thing that happens. Your receptivity to the five senses blossoms as if to flame; everything is indelible, and, immediately following the game and for days afterward, unforgettable. You replay it again and again.

Then, one day, it is gone, as if it never really happened.

I can no longer remember the play in question. I remember running way downfield, chasing the runner; the ragtag band of us were all chasing him, but he was faster than we were. It was strange that we were kicking off rather than receiving. We were getting drubbed. At some point someone knocked me flying—I skidded across the Astroturf like a rock skipped across calm waters—and after the play was over our kickoff team hurried off the field.

It was the end of the quarter, so there was a tiny break before the two teams went back out onto the field; and when I looked out at the great green perfect lawn, dazzling emerald beneath the space-age intensity of all the high halogen lights, and at the stadium seats on the other side of the field, not entirely filled with people, but with what looked to me like a thousand or more—I saw a strange glowing blue object out on the middle of the field, about the size and shape and color of a beached jellyfish, or, I realized, an adult diaper. One of my contraband ice packs had squirted out from my pants when I'd been hit.

Calf-hobbled, hamstrung, groin-tweaked, and back-aching, I had to trot out there, the sole player on that momentarily empty field—the referees and umpires were down at the other end, readjusting things for the beginning of the next quarter—and pick up the blue object while what felt like an entire nation watched.

Desperate for the ice's healing properties, I shoved it back down into my pants and gimp-trotted back toward my sidelines far away: an old gray beard, a halftime entertainer.

●

WE HAD NO business playing these professional teams from San Antonio, Houston, or even Austin. Once again our tiny band of warriors began to splinter and fall away, broken like balsa wood gliders. Kirby was busier than ever on the sidelines tending to the damaged.

I must've been a little out of it, because once again, in a panic, when Coach turned to scan the sidelines—"We need another!"—his eyes fell upon me, a body, and he put his hand on my back and told me to get out there, and to hurry.

Our team once again was down at the farthest end of the field, our own end.

Because I was a tailback, I assumed that was the position I was to fill. It was a long way down there. I was a little out of breath by the time I arrived, and the play clock was melting down. Our team was already lined up, and there was only one player in the backfield, a player I had never seen before. And I wondered where Wyatt, our quarterback, was.

"Where do you want me?" I asked. The new player looked as confused as I did, and because he was already more than seven yards back, it made no sense for me to line up 10 or 12 yards deep. I positioned myself by his side. He still looked confused, and said, "Move out a little bit." So I took one step to the side. The new player gestured to me again, then motioned to the line of scrimmage where all the other players were.

"I'm a running back," I said. "I can't go up there."

Our new player looked toward the sidelines, exasperated. Perhaps instructions were shouted to him, which, being hard of hearing, I did not discern. At any rate, he changed position, went up to the line of scrimmage himself, so that I was the sole player remaining in our backfield; the quarterback now, or so I thought.

There was so little time left.

I moved two steps back to the right, so that I was directly behind the center, seven yards deep. I figured I would take the snap and just run with it, and see what happened.

Over on our sideline, I could now hear Coach howling, as were the players next to him.

I didn't even know the snap count. I held my hands up, ready for it, then called for the ball silently—gave the hand movements of *now*.

Ernie did not snap it. Would not snap it.

A yellow flag flew high up into the night sky as if from a flare gun—*too much time*, a five-yard penalty—and seeming relieved, all of our players relaxed and stood up from their crouched and ready positions, and another player from our sidelines, Isaiah, the big offensive lineman, came hobbling back out; told me I could go back to the bench.

It had been fourth down, and we'd been in punt formation. I simply hadn't been paying attention. I'd been watching the game, but not seeing. Dreaming. My own little private Lebowski-fest, once again.

●

FROM THAT FIRST year, I remember one particular evening practice on the field at Jackson Park. We'd finished a great practice. There'd been a fair size smattering of us—a dozen or so—and everyone had run with fresh legs, powerful in the lingering light of spring dusk, and then into the night. There was the scent of our fresh sweat, all of us shining in it, and the scent of the fresh-mown grass, the clippings coating our shoes, our ankles. We'd all had good stretches in the evening's warmth, and only now was the night beginning to cool. I could hear crickets. I could hear a distant train rumbling down in town, passing through. I found I'd wanted to build a bridge, wanting to be part of a clan, a tribe, in my home state, and so I'd walked right on into the middle of a group with whom I had nothing in common, young Black men, and had asked to be admitted—asked if I could cross that bridge—and they'd welcomed me in, placed their arms around me. They would fight for me and I would fight for them, and we'd laugh, and all fight for Coach, and his approbation, hard-gotten and rare. And for our own, just as hard-gotten.

The next week's game was in Austin, less than two hours away, but a world away from Brenham. A land of affluence, with a robust city and county police force, and the road between our town and the big city dense with highway patrol.

There were players on the Express who had never been to Austin, the state's capital. And why would they want to?

After the practice, and after the prayer ("We could be dead, oh Lord! Thank you, thank you Jesus, for the gift of life! We could have died in terrible accidents or shootings. Thank you for choosing to let us keep living, so that we can continue to praise your name!"), Coach addressed the team with an intensity beyond even that which he used for explaining defensive adjustments and offensive philosophies. His most important lesson yet. And the team ceased all joking, stilled themselves so they could hear his every word, and watched him without blinking.

Wyatt was not there that night, nor was Chandler, who rarely came to practice, only showed up on game day. I was the only white on the field.

"You must not have *anything* illegal in your car," Coach said. "And you *must* not get stopped. You men will be passing through a *gauntlet*. It's just a short distance," Coach said, "but it's the most dangerous journey you will ever take. *Do not get stopped*," he said. "Do not do anything illegal. Travel together," he said. "And if you do get stopped, it's all *Yessir* and *Nosir*. Keep your hands where they can see them," he whispered, his eyes searching those of each and every player, who were still rapt, as their elder handed them the keys and the code to survival: and as he gave them, his beloveds, the rarest thing—a vulnerability I would not have guessed was within him. The lion, the warrior, counseling his proxy warriors to be meek this time, to be submissive. That was how much he loved them.

And as they—as we—walked off the field that night, our steps were slower, our heads tipped down as we—as they—considered the gravity of the upcoming situation. Of the invisible wall that lay between them and safety; between them and joy. The veil, in every next breath, between living and dying.

Following George Floyd's murder, *Sports Illustrated* investigated the statements of 57 major college coaches who spoke to the issue. Wrote Chantel Jennings (August 15, 2020), "The common word was *change*, while other top keywords were things like *team*, *country*, and *coach*. The phrase *Black Lives Matter* appeared three times. *Police brutality*, *systemic racism*, and *inequality* appeared only once each . . ."

But acknowledgment of the brutality—the clear and ever-present danger—began finally to appear in football, as elsewhere. Patrick Mahomes helped reverse NFL commissioner Roger Goodell's longstanding opposition to Colin Kaepernick's return to football (along with white NFL team owners and the then-president of the United States) through a powerful montage of video statements.

University of Texas student-athletes succeeded in changing the name of the football stadium from Darrell K Royal-Texas Memorial Stadium to Campbell-Williams Field, unarguably the two greatest players in the school's long history, both Black. Texas A&M University quarterback Kellen Mond and receiver Jhamon Ausbon helped remove a statue of a Confederate general from their main campus, and a tweet from Mississippi State running back Kylin Hill led to the state legislature's removal of the Confederate flag from the state banner. And in the NFL, after the longest period of handwringing, the Washington Redskins—also disgraced for epidemic sexual harassment within the organization—changed their name to "Washington Football Team" and, later, "Washington Commanders."

●

THE SPECIFICITY OF the sport is fascinating to me: the elliptical shape of the pigskin, inflated taut to somewhere between 12.5 and 13.5 psi, with stitched lacings for the grip (to be a successful quarterback in the NFL, one's hands must measure at least 9¾ inches wide). I love the intimacy of familiarity with that stitching, and the shape and nature of the ball, more deeply ingrained than that of a catechism—the way the ball seeks to be held tightly in one hand, or both hands, or carried by the self, or handed to another, or passed forward or backward to another.

In remembering practices, and the games—their pageantry, when all of us were paradoxically more alive, and filled with, or overflowing with, purpose, passion, and even compassion—it feels important to me to capture details of how it all went down: a season in which we would not win a game, when we'd felt we might win them all, or at least any of them.

And a year later, I still have dreams in which we are playing, and winning. They are long, detailed dreams that last half the night—as if the dreaming is as real, and takes up as much time, as the doing, or having done.

We came together in what seems now a kind of innocence. It was the last wedge of time—like the last of the night's darkness, at the edge of daylight—before the Black Lives Matter movement would finally have its legitimacy, its necessity, illuminated for all by the cries of a dying man who kept repeating that he could not breathe. We wore face masks on our helmets to keep out other players' hands and cleats, but we breathed in each other's shouts of despair and ecstasy; we held our bare fists in the air and chanted, shouted, "Express Your-self!" And we gathered in a huddle before every play, reuniting each time. We bled together, fought our enemies, then met them afterward on midfield to commune, to rejoin with even those who had been our enemies.

And then it came: undemocratically, at first—the Angel of Death seeking the meek and the broken, first. And in some ways we were ready, and in other ways, not. And as ever, we consoled ourselves over our shortcomings with the eternal phrase, the coda, of *Next Year*.

Nothing will ever be the same, and in so very many ways that is the greatest news, the best story possible. Not next year. Now so many of us think, this year.

1

LAST YEAR

MY FAMILY THOUGHT IT was a terrible idea: to suit up and run around and hit and be hit. Kirby had been managing the team for a few years and had gotten to know Coach Barnes, who up until the time I joined the team had never had a losing season. I traveled with the team during the spring of 2018 and played in almost every game, usually on kickoff returns, though also whenever and wherever they needed me, which, as the season wore on without a victory—indeed, without an offensive score—became more and more often. Some games we'd have only 14 or 15 players, so that everyone had to play both offense and defense. Coach himself suited up in a too-tiny uniform, which had the effect of making him look like a large child, and played linebacker, sweating wildly and, it seemed to me, forgetting, for a little while, that he was a coach at all. Running, chasing the ballcarrier, leaping into the air with verve to swat at a wobbly pass like a cat after a butterfly. His timing was a little off in nearly everything he did, but he was out there.

Even Coach Eddie hurried onto the field to spell whichever player was puffing the hardest. This left only three of us on the sidelines, and as the sideline players returned in increasingly depauperate condition, they began to tag me, as if in a child's game, telling me where to fill in. Once, I ran out onto the field to spell an injured offensive lineman, but

Coach nixed that, called an injury timeout, and shuttled some other players around creatively. It wouldn't do to have a 155-pound left tackle; it would be dangerous for me, but also to the quarterback I was tasked with protecting.

The more we lost, the fewer players showed up for Thursday night practices. Some nights there might just be the four of us—Coach, Kirby, big Neil Mathis—a lineman—and myself—and I'd feel badly for Coach, who would have loaded his truck with duffel bags of gear, cases of disposable bottles of drinking water that flashed under the overhead park lights when a player tilted his head back and drank deeply, draining the slender little 16-ounce plastic bottles, which crumpled as the players guzzled them. The sound of the wrinkling plastic was loud, as were the heaves of breath from the sweating, glistening players, and the water vanished quickly into them, as if the players had *mined* it.

And if they'd been sitting on an ice chest, or kneeling, or even, late into the practice, lying on their backs, they'd heave back to their feet and reconvene for Coach's next drill, and time would be lost to them— to us—for no one wore watches. There were no clocks. To someone watching from a great distance, our movements might have seemed as graceful as those of skaters within a snow globe.

Those losing evenings, however, Coach would drop his tailgate— as if, were he to pretend to start offloading all the equipment, the other players might begin appearing, like cattle coming to the sound of the feed truck—but, realizing no one else was coming, he would sit down on the tailgate, not quite defeated, for that was a state of mind he could never allow in himself, but for sure wrestling with some inner demons that were not hard to parse, nor singular to any one coach, or any one person: rejection, doubt—*Is my path the true one, does my work matter, why do I give so much when so little is received or returned?*

He would force a cheery smile and affect a nonchalant attitude. He would try to make lemonade from lemons, lecturing Kirby and Neil and me about the importance of coming to practice. About how we couldn't expect to improve or pull together if we didn't commit. About how that was what was wrong with the young men of today.

As he talked, the facade of his positivism began to disintegrate, but it seemed important to me that we—the choir for whom no preaching was needed—hear him anyway. That we were helping him practice being a coach. That no work was ever wasted, and that even the rolling soliloquy of his haranguing might somehow still be valuable to us as well; as if, by having it delivered to us in excess, we might be able to store it as capital for a time when what was once easily available and unquestioned in its permanence might one day begin, incredibly, to diminish.

With all of the unutilized gear in the truck—the giant tractor tire, which he challenged us to flip, end over end, huffing and chugging down the field, using every muscle in the body; the smaller tires, which he usually arranges for agility drills; the huge leather medicine ball; the battered blocking pads, looking like rejected crash test dummies, misshapen and leaking tufts of fiber speckled with the blood of players' noses, knuckles, and forearms from across the decades . . .

All that gear remained in the truck, on those underrepresented evenings, giving the semi-disconsolate Coach—dressed up in his athletic sweats, hooded sweater, ballcap, and whistle around his neck—the look of a large boy at a birthday party where no one had showed up.

That's what losing will do to you, and it was hard to witness its effects on the players as well as on Coach. It was a feeling that everything good had left us, much of it through the bittersweetness of talent drain. We were happy for Toussam, an emigre from Cameroon who'd never played organized football but received a full scholarship to Texas Tech, with his speed and ability to run precise routes, with his great "sticky" hands—I never saw him drop a pass—and his ability to time his jumps to win contested throws.

But it bothered me, once the idea of losing set in, how quickly in each game the team's loss of confidence would begin at the first sign of trouble: our secondary giving up a long touchdown pass, or our quarterback crumpling, being sacked, or throwing an interception.

We'd had confidence the previous year, when we either won or were close to winning, but then the next year we did not have it. Out on the field, we could feel the doubt immediately, as could the other teams. On television, the announcers refer to these shifts as *momentum*, and any fan invested in the game can identify the precise moment, and precise gesture—a single penalty, a dropped pass—when the tide turns.

Seen on television, these shifts and reversals seem nuanced. As a viewer, sometimes you recognize them in real time, though there are also instances where the moment occurs undetected and is recognizable only after one has traveled some distance ahead and can look back at all that happened subsequently as the result of some choice made, or not made. An opportunity missed, unseen or otherwise unexploited. A regret, perhaps.

On the field, however, these markers of extreme importance can sometimes be harder to discern. On the field, there are no slow-motion replays, where time slowed is made to go backwards: not half a heartbeat backwards, as sometimes happens in dreams, but farther back in time—15 seconds, even half a minute.

On the field, time skitters, pushes ahead as if seeking something; on the field, we have manipulated a structure in which time is *forced* to seek something—some discovery, probing and reaching as if into cracks and clefts in the mountainside.

On the field, we are encased in the centerstream of time; not like a fossil in a seam of stone, but instead, the living, as time itself is living.

We have tapped into the live-wire electricity of real time, and only the most experienced players who have spent some significant percentage of their adult lives in this exhilarating and addictive vein have the ability to recognize, on the field, the infinitesimal harbingers of fate changing.

One must trust the coach, then—the one who has designed and choreographed our movements. One must trust that if one executes the dream, the treasure will be reached. On offense, that treasure is the first down, or ultimately, the holy land of the end zone. The coach therefore is the intermediary between heaven and earth; between free will and fate; a prophet, describing to us the ways in which we can reach that sacred space.

There on the tailgate, Coach seemed some nights not to be speaking to us, his few remaining acolytes, nor even to himself, but instead to the future—to that island not of this year or some year past, but to next year; and of how, through the muscular force of will alone, he strives to correct our imperfections, as well as his own.

Coach's ability to motivate extends, I've come to see, to either sides of the game: the days preceding, and the days following. There's really no other way to say this: he meddles in their lives. He gives them dating advice, work advice, spiritual advice, life advice. He is not tender in his counsel. He is fierce in all matters.

He gets good production out of them at practice. The receivers blaze with speed on their routes; the quarterbacks zip the ball with great velocity and accuracy. All the players, even the behemoth linemen, dance nimbly through the tires in agility drills; and the running backs are fast and powerful as they line up in the I-formation and then surge at the snap of the ball, taking the handoff from Wyatt, or Shaun, or even Coach himself, galloping ahead with cleated feet, tearing up clumps of black soil and green grass.

The fragrance of that newly cut wet earth and the adrenaline of the runner is so pronounced it seems that for a little while, before it ultimately dissipates or evaporates, a cartographer could map the precise route of each river of scent, with the traveler following perfectly the same route, same destiny, charted by Coach's pen on the index cards that comprise his playbook.

The semi-pro game seems skewed toward speed. It surprises me how easily power—the brute power of mass—can be negated or at least neutralized in the scrum that tends to occur at the line of scrimmage. The season that big Lloyd "Phat" Turner—our 300-pound quarterback—played, he was sacked several times in a row, crumbling like a gingerbread man on three plays in a row.

From what I have seen, determination can be an effective replacement for power or mass, and few exhibit this more clearly than little

Last Year   27

Dooney, a gnome-like man who, though not bulging with muscles, possesses no fat, and though not skinny, could be viewed as slight.

When he runs the ball, however, it's another matter. He's got the ability to compress and get small in a crowd, knees churning as he bounces this way and that; careens off tacklers like a Superball, energized and feeding off the contact, rather than being impeded by it. You watch him slash his way quickly into the scrum and are tempted to look away, thinking, *Well, that's the end of that*, but before you know it, he's gotten seven, eight, ten yards.

He's good in practice, but great in games. He's quiet in practice—seems almost detached—but I realize now that likely stems from the fact that at the age of 40, he's seen it all before and is saving his real fire for those incandescent 60-minute intervals that occur for him only eight times per year—*the season*, weekends in March and April.

Most of the players, however, are better in practice than in the game, which is to be expected. Wyatt, last year's hard-luck quarterback, is certainly one of these, though Wyatt's is such a complicated position, with success dependent upon so many other factors—beginning with the blocking of the offensive line up front, but including also the running backs' ability to run the ball effectively, so that the defense is forced to allocate more defenders to the line of scrimmage.

The quarterback's success also depends upon the ability of the running backs to ascertain and block any blitzing defenders who burst through the line of scrimmage; the ability of receivers to run the routes the quarterback is expecting them to; and of course the ability of a receiver to catch the ball.

I don't recall us scoring an offensive touchdown all year. I know that we must have, but I don't remember any. Something always stopped us—as if there were some invisible force field, unseen but shimmering, which always prevented that success.

●

IN THE TOUSSAM era—one of the players left over from the year before's championship run—there was a *fleet* of tall, rangy receivers with more speed than seemed natural or necessary. There was no way anyone could keep up with them, and their ability to glide into or out of a break was also peerless, at least in our league. They reminded me of cheetahs.

Evan was one of those receivers. When I asked him who his favorite receivers were in the NFL, he named Michael Crabtree, ironically a former Texas Tech Red Raider, which was the school that would subsequently offer Toussam a scholarship, but not Evan.

I remember watching both Evan and Toussam practice, and giving much more notice to Evan's leaping showman catches: his arms and legs splaying out wide as he elevated to reach the high ball, rarely dropping a ball, making contested catches off the top of a defender's helmet with elan and wild glee. Whereas Toussam, a bit smaller, was more compact in his movements and catches: efficient that way, pulling in with his strong hands any ball in his vicinity, and never breaking stride.

I should've seen it coming. But my eyes were on Evan.

Toussam rarely spoke. Evan, on the other hand, often had chatter ready for the defense in practice, or instructions for the offense—gesticulating to Wyatt that he was open, wide open, on almost every play. He even talked trash to Coach, who seemed, in Coach's way, to be liking it, until he didn't.

I'm not sure what was going on between Coach and Evan, only that a frustration was growing. For a long time I thought it had to do with the way Evan underperformed in games—dropping passes that hit him right in the numbers—and, on defense, getting torched again and again for big plays, giving the deep sudden touchdown strikes that are a dagger to the entire team. For a long time I thought these lapses were something that might not be fixable—a subconscious disposition, calibrated to failure—some childhood remnant of self-loathing, shame, fury, what-have-you, so that in a pressure situation, he short-circuited.

It made me sad for Evan whenever it happened; I lamented, with each stupendous drop, the slipping away of what in practice had seemed to me like really good chances for a college scholarship and, who knew, if he worked at it with the ferocious drive required, a look at the pros. Hell, who could say how these things would turn out? He might go on to be a star for a couple of years, or even three or four. Stranger things have happened. He had the talent, if nothing else; though, without that "else," he was just a strand of thread blowing in the wind.

I'd see Coach talking to him one-on-one after practice some nights, off at the edge of the lights, a hand on his shoulder. It was unusual for Coach to give such an extraordinary amount of attention to just one player. Usually, Coach bounced around all over the place, checking in with everyone—and from both men's postures it was evident there was some serious shit going down, and serious advice.

Still, I was surprised when, less than a year later, Evan was in court for a really, really bad decision: storming over to his ex-girlfriend's apartment, where she was living with her children, and shooting a gun through the wall a number of times.

No one was hurt and I know nothing of the circumstances—drug-altered, or "just" rage—but even in Texas, that was a bad thing, and he's in the penitentiary now for a long time. He writes Kirby letters expressing his remorse—pretty amazing letters, actually, about love and God and justice and his understanding of how he needs to serve his time. Kirby and Coach, as they have with so many others, attended his trial, but it appears to have only made the judge angrier, for she pretty much threw the book at him; and no one, not even Evan, could disagree.

The next year, our best new linebacker, Jabaar—a young clone of Coach, definitely college or even pro material—was also arrested for domestic violence. This was a side I did not see of either man, only heard about afterward, and it was disturbing that they could be so carefree out on the field, and considerate of each other's feelings and predicaments, only to get physically violent in their relationships. I couldn't know how any of them were in the intimacy of their relationships—only how they were with me, and their teammates. But in time

I learned that some untold number existed as if in a shadow world. A lesser and darker world than the sweet illumination of the game.

I wished Coach, their spiritual adviser, could make it stop. But the bombs kept going off, one or two each year, and it was always a surprise. I could never really guess who had it in them to strike a partner, and who didn't. You'd think you'd be able to tell; that you could see a thing like that. There wasn't ever any boisterous high-school swagger, never any denigration of their partners to the rest of the team.

I couldn't help but wonder if the violence on the field carried over: if there was yet another unaccounted, associative cost to this most American of pastimes.

I don't believe there is. I don't believe the shape of the football or the rules of the game have anything to do with it. That that violence in men was here before a football ever first flew through the air. But certainly, how wonderful it would be if football players—the large and the small, the white and the Black, the brown and the red—spoke out against it when it happened. For football is, or can and should be, always about problem-solving.

②
COURT

WE'RE SITTING IN A crowded municipal courtroom in Brenham. One of the Express's players, Darion, is being sentenced today, for having been found guilty of cattle theft. He's a player of extraordinary talent, far and away the fastest player on the team, maybe the fastest player in the entire town. "He's used to getting away with stuff," Kirby says, "because he's so good. He's never had any accountability. Every team he plays on, he disrupts it, does what he wants, comes and goes when he wants. He lives with his aunt. Both his parents are in jail, as is his older brother."

It's a story so ancient it seems a cliché, rather than what it is: a young man with *maybe* the opportunity for one last chance—though it is also likely that in his blazing speed, he has already skated past that one last chance. That he has an idea this is what it is, and that all he can rely on here, now, today, is luck.

Darion hasn't even shown up yet. The thing about good luck, I have noticed, is that once it stops, it sometimes does not come back.

I sit next to Kirby on the wooden pew near the front. At first I can't quite identify the atmosphere in the crowded room—it's definitely not a church service—and then I recognize it. A downtown bus station, crowded with delays. Everyone is going somewhere, they just don't yet know when, where, or for how long. There are no swaggering outlaws, no unrepentant gangsters refusing to cede even a shred of their self-bestowed authority to the judge.

Instead, it seems a confused placidity with which the defendants await their reckoning. Sometimes they seem easily identifiable, with their concerned or harried support team—girlfriend, attorney, mother, brother?—though other times, particularly in the larger pods and clusters, it is more difficult to guess who is the defendant and who the supporters; as if all are so entangled that what happens to one happens to all.

It occurs to me that dressed as Kirby and I are—black pants, white button-down shirts, dress shoes—we are mistaken for attorneys, just as the people we're observing are likely to be mistaken for defendants.

There's a big round analog clock on the wall with an immense second hand, reminding me of the classroom clocks of my elementary school in Houston. The demographic in the room is mostly Black or white, evenly split; there are very few Hispanics. Any other nationalities, I cannot parse. The parity between Black and white reflects the Brenham populace and somehow reassures me a little, though that is not quite the right word, for there is nothing really in this crowded room to feel good about. I'm here to help Kirby support his team and Coach, but I feel panicked; that I've gotten trapped in a place where I do not want to be, and I'm at the mercy of the clock, the mercy of time, waiting for the judge to move down the docket, perusing a registry that is not available to the rest of us.

It makes no sense, but my agitation continues to grow. I'd rather be doing *anything* in the world. The young man is a stranger to me. I know Coach and Kirby, but Darion is like a fly caught in a web, and now I have been pulled into it. He is a young man but I am an old one, whose slight quiverings in the web are attracting the enormous spider whose appetite is not for blood, but time.

I have little time left to squander.

How long do any of us have? Not even the judge knows.

●

DARION APPEARS WITH his attorney just moments before his case is called. I'm struck, as I am so often with members of the Express, by how normal they appear physically—even small. Darion could be a young man selling shoes in a Foot Locker, in his first job. None of the players have time for the middle-class indulgence of becoming gym rats—of knowing the deep and at times mesmerizing pleasure of throwing one's self into a thing wholeheartedly, 24/7—though it is true that in the games, within the organic sphere of that carefully curated 60 minutes, even the poorest among us, with regard to the availability of time, become rich again, with all the senses illuminated with the incandescence of a purity once known in childhood, and rarely again.

Darion is little removed from childhood: a wisp of a boy. If one didn't know better, it would be hard to believe he is as fast as people say he is—and his luck, if it can be called that, holds, for now Kirby and the attorney and Darion approach the judge, who studies this mildly curious scene, and in quiet respectful tones the two white men (the attorney is a small man himself, wearing blue jeans and a clean pressed rodeo shirt with pearl snaps) describe to the judge how much potential Darion has.

The white judge peers down from her high desk lectern and appears momentarily interested, and in that moment looks as if she does not want to be a judge. Perhaps wants to forget she is a judge. There may not be much she has not seen, but she is giving us what we wanted and came for, what we asked for. She agrees to delay sentencing on Darion if he can commit to 20 hours a week of community service.

The judge looks at Kirby, then the court-appointed attorney. "You two will need to get together to determine the work." She then looks at Darion like a hawk.

She knows he is going to fail, I think.

She doesn't believe it; she *knows* it.

I want to argue with her unspoken assessment, her countenance. I want to dare to hope, dare to believe. There are underdog stories everywhere, and they are wonderful, I want to tell her. But the courtroom is hot and stifling, with its muted sounds of coughs and murmurs, and the big second hand on the clock is chewing up space, yardage, as it always does; and I see that although the judge at first thought Kirby was a coach, trying to keep a talented player on the field for his own interest, she understands now he is but a do-gooder: one who will be disappointed.

"If you miss one work appointment," she tells Darion, "you will be incarcerated."

We're dismissed. We go out into the hallway.

We convene more like surgeons than barristers. Elsewhere in the poorly-lit hallway—were all our nation's courthouses built in the 1950s and 1960s?—other clots of people are huddled similarly, trying to decide whether to take a deal. As if they have any choice. Restructuring, reorganizing, their lives. Scraping together the funds, reallocating the time-sharing: who will babysit, who will give a ride to work, who will take care of grandma now?

Next man up, they say in football, when a member of the team goes down to injury; but what if there isn't a next man?

●

THERE'S A LITTLE country cemetery outside of Brenham near the tiny community of Independence, where Kirby and Jean Ann's daughter, Payton, is buried. She passed away 13 years ago, at the age of 13, following complications from an injury sustained while riding her horse.

Kirby keeps the little cemetery immaculate. It was once out in a meadow with a shady grove of juniper, pine, and oak, providing a shield against the summer sun: a nice place to sit and listen to the lowing of cattle. No child, no young person, loved animals more.

In the distance, subdivisions approach; the prairie feel of the place is changing. Civilization encroaches as the past recedes, but the trees and their shade are still there, as is the space, the Payton-space; and Kirby tells Darion's attorney that there's definitely 20 hours of cemetery maintenance each week: mowing the lawn, keeping flowers watered, trimming and piling and burning branches, sweeping the sidewalks leading to the little plot, picking up windblown garbage. Withered, crinkly helium balloons, sun- and rain-faded from Grand Opening auto events and children's parties, unknown miles distant.

Kirby volunteers to be Darion's ward—that is not the right word, but there is no word—*point of contact,* or *keeper of hours? Sponsor? Boss man?* None of it is accurate, but Kirby agrees, and they make their first appointment for that weekend.

"Twenty hours a week," the attorney says to Darion. "That's a lot. Are you sure you can do this?" Half a full-time job, when to the best of our knowledge Darion's never had any job. This is it: the job of staying outside of jail, and outside of the system. As he uses his speed to get out past the edge of the defense, so too here he is being given a good blocking scheme, at least four different linemen working to spring him to the outside, to the sweet green openness of space, at least one more time. Maybe only one more time.

●

IT IS NEITHER an original nor inaccurate observation that in Texas, football is a religion. And if time is the deity of our era, then our ritualized engagement with it, in the groomed and sculpted confines of the level playing field, takes our abstract idea—that all units of time are equally valuable, each identical to the other—and heightens, to ridiculous disproportions, the role of humans within the equation of time.

The four quarters of a game, like the four seasons, and the splendid 60 minutes, replete with the ability to stop even the greatest force, *time,* in its tracks, through certain rituals—running out of bounds, or throwing an incomplete pass, or, most magically of all, calling "time out!"—are able to freeze the clock and all forward activity in its tracks.

This is the preserved incandescence that is achieved in games and, because we are good at compressing and packaging ideas, we create playoffs, championships of divisions and conferences, and finally crown, with a golden trophy, the champions of the world.

In football, time is no longer an abstraction. Time transmutes into the steam coming off the players' heads, the torn-up turf left in the wake of their battles. Time—in becoming hyper-compressed and hyper-manipulated—creates a physical residue every bit as distinct as the sediments that are the remnant of a boulder's, or an entire mountain range's, erosion.

The concentrated desire—the communal prayer of millions on one side, and millions of others on another side—resides surely as some kind of silent vibratory artifact in the seats and stands and goalposts within the silent but not empty confines of the stadium, which back in the day were not named for corporations but instead teams—*Arrowhead*—or individuals—*Lambeau*.

The players are warriors, gladiators pitched against each other, but in battles where all are mindful also of the larger opponent, the idea of time, so ever-present as to be elevated to the status of worship.

One needn't win completely; one needs only to win: to score more points and to hold the opponent to fewer points, within that glassine envelope of 60 minutes.

This ritualization of time renders the warriors, the players, as demigods; the referees, umpires, back judges, and linesmen (and now lineswomen) as striped, anonymous, and impartial judges and arbiters of the fates of all who enter the arena; and the radio and TV commentators as the storytellers of ancient myths.

The coaches are like ancient gods—Zeus, Pan, Thor—and the valor of an individual's struggle against time is given, again, ridiculous disproportion—more, not less.

The game is won or lost in the trenches. The largest players, the offensive and defensive linemen, are paradoxically the hardest to see: the most invisible. They exist as a coordinated whole, an entity that is no more effective than its weakest link.

Because they take such a battering on every play, as well as for the fact that they are so immense, well in excess of 300 pounds, linemen's relatively small joints—feet, knees, hips, wrists—are always battered, sprained, or sewn or taped back together.

The linemen play with broken fingers and broken hands. The job demands much mentally. Five or six huge men must choreograph at quickest possible speed to align against an infinitude of possibilities in blitzes, stunts, and twists, with the 11 players on the other team representing the permutation of 11, which is 39,916,800 different arrangements in each given second.

They must slam their bodies against other giants on every single play, time and again—usually 75 or 80 plays generated from the line of scrimmage per game. The force of hitting or being hit by one of these giants, has been likened to being in a car wreck. This is an accurate comparison.

The chain of them—in theory, the unbroken chain—is dependent upon unity. When one lineman is having a bad day, the man next to him will slide over and help with the blocking, even as another player (a running back, perhaps) will step up to guard against the new weakness exposed by the adjustment. The men have to be committed to each other and to the notion of remaining unbroken as a group.

In the locker room, the linemen's lockers are always next to one another. They take their meals together and travel together, but because they rarely ever touch the ball (if they do, it is almost always by accident—diving onto a fumble, as if onto a hand grenade), their existence is predicated not so much on their individual talents but on how they work together. They are rarely noticed except in times of extreme failure, catastrophe, disaster.

Our fan's eye is trained to follow the ball, carried always by only one person at a time—to look past the efforts and achievements of all the others who work to get the ballcarrier "into space." But without the concept of team and teamwork, the game would be no more interesting than a swordfight or a boxing match.

Athletics can often have this effect of reducing things to the lowest common denominator. The extreme compression of scale can render a thing—humility and gratitude—dense as a cube of cobalt: elemental, primal, easily seen and understood.

The borders and boundaries of the game—the intense desire compressed into those 60 minutes—yields fascinating, intriguing fruit, every game, every time. It is addicting, alternately beautiful and awful, and there is no way to know, really, which of the two will emerge under pressure.

A game of stars and stardom can, paradoxically, illustrate the importance of teamwork, and its various necessary components, trust and accountability. *Do your best. Do your job*, and yet believe in grace, luck, and miracles, which can flow both ways—to your team, or to the other team.

It is a passion play. How can anyone who has ever been a part of it willingly step away? Few, if any. Most end up being banished by time—discarded. How frustrating to see a young man like Darion be offered, time and again, a second chance.

●

HE DOES NOT call. He does not show up. He blows it off. He goes to jail. His life may yet turn around, but he is down by much, and for him already, it might as well now be the second half, or later, while others his age or older are only just now stepping out onto the field.

3

WINTER PRACTICE

I DISAPPEAR DURING HUNTING season: five weeks of nonstop physical bliss, rigorous as boot camp; awaken long before dawn, disappear into the snowy mountains, and climb straight up for two-thirds of the day, looking for tracks, carrying my rifle and heavy pack. Each autumn, I work through the pain and scar tissue and reduced lung capacity of middle age until a kind of incandescence is reached and it all melts away—is burned away—and one feels young again, powerful and pure of mind and spirit and body. For me, it's no longer about whether I find an animal or not.

Watching from the top of a mountain as the dull bronzed disk of late autumn sun starts to sink, and, wistfully, turning around and starting down the mountain, taking a different route. My knees start to burn and swell again, so that every hour or two I have to stop and rest for a minute. Or rather, I don't have to, but it feels good to take the weight off for a few moments; though other times, if I've gone too far or stayed too long and darkness is hurrying, I hurry too, pushing the discomfort aside.

Then: a nighttime bicycle ride down the narrow lane of the old logging road that I used to get so many miles deeper into the mountains. Back home by seven; a bite of cold leftovers, a shower, then in bed and asleep by eight—but ready to crawl out again at four the next morning and do it all over, one day after another melding into a continuous scroll of time.

By the end of the five-week season I'm in good shape. *That which does not kill us makes us stronger,* said the philosopher. I know he was speaking to young people, not old. But teetering somewhere in the middle, or on the back side of the middle, it seems I can still feel the faint breath of that truth.

●

AFTER THE HUNTING season, I try to keep it going, but without the intensity, the urgency of securing the year's wild meat, it's just not the same. Still, there is an obligation of fidelity to the team, which, though separated by the miles, I am connected to. They message back and forth about practice times, each query a pain to the chest that I am not there yet to practice with them. Wyatt: *Anybody want to go throw the ball around at the park this Sunday?* Neil: *Yes sir. What time?* and Ray: *Hey fellas, I'm going to go run a couple miles tomorrow morning; anybody down?* This year, they are going to win.

●

FOR A LONG time. I've been dreaming of the team—REM dreaming, where I'm running down the field on kickoffs, trying to pick my way through blockers to get to the ballcarrier; or running routes, catching a quick pass over the middle before turning upfield.

In the dreams there is no contact, and in the dreams I am running cleanly, with neither limp nor diminishment.

In the huddles—gathered as I imagine wolves gather before their launch on a quarry—our breathing is slow and our minds are clear; we are unified. The quarterback, usually Wyatt, calls the play, but we know what he is going to call before he says it.

We each know our assignments, and in the dream we execute them with precision. It's a cliché, but it's like when the tumblers within a lock fall back and away from the key's entrance into the slot.

The defense falls away. Each of the 11 opposing players are surgically addressed, leaving only one of ours, somewhere on the field, unattended, so that whoever has the ball is running free and clear, and he is not caught. Coach's elaborate scheming has been applied perfectly.

Was it this way for our species when we hunted in bands, chasing deer or antelope, caribou or, I suppose, buffalo and mastodon: hazing and harassing them toward a gated weir or the nearby cliff?

The village hunters, indeed, perhaps much of the village, might've engaged all the week before or longer, carrying and stacking stones in an intricate drive line. The curved boundaries of the rocks and low walls built to force the animals' movements into an increasingly constricted space, with the journey culminating in a final confluence of time and space that results in meat.

In my father's house, says the scripture, *there are many rooms.* The best metaphors are those that are true at any scale. I have long thought of this verse as describing human consciousness more than any physical structure of stone and timber. I imagine the mansion of the brain possessing neural pathways of bliss—winding, hyper-illuminated trails through the coils of the various chambers of the brain, glowing with life like streets lined with gold.

What was it like for those Paleolithic hunters when their unity of purpose was achieved, and their force of will—as real and passionate as prayer—was realized? What was it like when those same ribbons of light ignited simultaneously in the minds of all involved?

One of the beauties of football is that it has evolved, and continues to evolve, into a ritualized endeavor where this illuminated state of mind can be achieved by the players.

One of the great tragedies and paradoxes of football is, of course, the near-total prevalence of chronic traumatic encephalopathy (CTE). In no way have we evolved as a species to keep up with the demands of this ritual, this game—this lifeway in which our proxies, the players, continue performing well past what once and not so long ago was a natural lifespan of approximately 34 years.

In no way was or is it an evolutionary advantage to bang our heads—repository of the self and architect of our destiny—against anything, much less one another. I've been hiking in the mountains in October, when the air is a deep shade of blue and is cold and dry, and have heard startling pistol-crack sounds coming from the other side of a deep canyon where there cannot possibly be a human, or pistols. And looking across the chasm, I'll see two bighorn rams only a few yards away from each other, facing each other, lowering their heads and charging, and colliding.

It's a full two beats before the sound drifts across the canyon, so that by the time my mind registers it, the rams have already absorbed each other's blow, each knocked backwards some distance, staggered by recoil but not beaten. And then, silently it seems, with no consequences whatsoever from the past collision, they launch themselves at each other again, with only the wash of silence between me and them.

I wait for the sound waves to reach me at some point in the not too distant future: one-Mississippi, two-Mississippi . . .

There in the mountains, the sound is exactly like the sickening crack heard throughout the stadium when two players collide in a helmet-to-helmet collision.

The bighorns have evolved with ever-thicker skulls; four inches of solid bone protects their forehead. How long did it take, and what was the mortality involved with that evolutionary journey?

Four inches seems to be enough. One of the most specialized animals on the continent, they are adept at tightroping along ledges with nonchalance and a grace that would be the envy of any NFL receiver trying to not let his feet touch the white line of out-of-bounds. Some bighorns do succumb by slipping and falling to their death, but they have cast their lot—have chosen to occupy mountaintop peaks that almost all other mammals deem unsuitable habitat. Here is where they have made their stand, and though their populations are small, in those few places where they are found, they are regal in their chosen habitat.

Their orange eyes, splintered with radial flecks of black zodiac streaks, are crazed, burning with an intensity not seen in other animals. It could be argued they live in a state of constant addlement and head-knocked confusion; or conversely, that theirs are eyes that have seen so much they are no longer connected to the lower world others inhabit.

In a bank of freezers at Boston University's medical school are the brains of former football players who played at the collegiate and professional levels, preserved not like JFK's or Einstein's brain tissue in the hopes of somehow saving something singular, but instead retained so they can be sliced paper-thin and examined, across the years, beneath a microscope, where the various miniature chambers of cells light up like stained glass in a church on a sunny day early in spring.

The brains are no longer growing or shrinking, living or dying, but instead are frozen in time: each in the stop time of a personal confused agony that was surely specific to each victim yet also catastrophically communal.

The plaque of early onset dementia was shown to be overtaking the brains of 96 of the 97 specimens in the hospital. Even the brain of a field goal kicker—a player who is hardly ever in harm's way, is almost never tackled, and who never blocks—was riddled with the disease spreading through his brain like the creep of flooding wrought by a rising sea.

What is more amazing to me than the fact that nearly all of them are affected is the fact that one exists which is not. It seems impossible; miraculous. Was his skull thicker? Did he possess an enzyme in his blood that helped to repel the protein accumulation that is the signature of the disease?

What was his diet? What was his exercise regimen? What was his lung capacity? Did he keep his brain bathed constantly with oxygen, as if in a hyperbaric chamber? At what elevation did he reside? What was his genetic makeup? Did he meditate, consciously or subconsciously? What was his resting heart rate? Did he dream, and if so, what were his dreams?

To peer too closely into these men's miseries is to inspect with nearly unbearable accountability the price of one's own pleasure and passion. To watch the game is, at the farthest extension of logic, to support or otherwise enable the grown men, who have grown more powerful each generation, rendering their collisions more destructive in prolonging their deadly—and I do not think that is too strong a word—pursuit of what was once a child's game. To view a commercial, whether for a Bud Light or the US Army, is to help fund the system that destroys men's brains and bodies.

But is not this handwringing misplaced in a species of free will? By this same logic, if one is to read the poetry or novels of a man or woman affected by alcoholism or a similar addiction—if one is, say, to buy the books of such a writer—is one not enabling a similar downward trajectory? *Ah*, a reader might say, *the alcoholism is not about choice; it is a chemical disease and addiction.* But I would suggest that so too is football. And that unlike, say, alcoholism or other chemical dependencies, which destroy not only the individual, but relationships—the invisible threads that keep us, as social creatures, tethered to this earth—football is complicated by the fact that there is so very much about it that enriches, strengthens, and inspires a life, and lives.

Force, power, speed, and mass in collisions will continue to take their toll. There will always be accidents. Knees will be damaged, joints set out on a premature journey to arthritis, just as surely as are those of the farmer on his or her tractor jouncing on stony ground to coax the wheat in our bread or the barley in our granola. The tractor's fumes disappear invisibly into the heated ether; the world grows warmer; we all leave enormous footprints; none of us are pure . . .

You get my drift.

Perhaps poetry is to be consulted here, in this conundrum. Writes Mary Oliver in "The Wild Geese":

"You do not have to be good
You do not have to walk on your knees
for a hundred miles through the desert repenting
you only have to let the soft animal of your body love what it loves."

I know I sound like an apologist. I know I sound like I am in denial. I suspect that I am in denial.

Professional football is as much a transaction of finance as it is passion. How rare is it, how fortunate are any of us, to retain some love for a thing with the simple purity of childhood, at any distance, into our adult lives? Each day into the future in this regard is always a negotiation.

The body is bartered for time and, in any culture, compensation. Is it not just as inappropriate or improper for me to judge a player who follows the slippery slope from joy to commerce, exchanging the unknown specificity of future health as it is for me to frown at the executive who stays late at the office, bartering one's time at the desk in a direct exchange of time spent away from one's children, or spouse, or friends, or other relationships? Regret seems to me to be one of the cruelest and saddest in the portfolio of complicated—that word again—human emotions.

Moderation in all things counseled the Greek poet Hesiod, more than 2,700 years ago. It's ridiculous to think how spacious the world was back then; how much more relaxed were our perceptions of space and time.

How compressed things have become, since. Our tempers are shorter. Anxiety radiates from us with such intensity it can be measured in the hair follicles of the domestic dogs we've bred for companionship. *Moderation in all things* is still likely good advice. Yet I think we might have been pushed to the entire other end of the spectrum, so that our grayscale range of emotions now resides only between moderation and benumbedness. That with so much fear and anxiety in the world, crowded together as never before, mere moderation can seem like the new passion.

In a time of no-emotion, almost any emotion can seem like big emotion.

I think of moderation as being somewhere around midfield. Not necessarily the 50-yard line, but maybe in the 20-yard span between the two 40-yard lines.

I think of passion—the electric, heated roil of anticipatory joy, or joy-in-the-moment—as being down near the opposition's goal line when you're on offense, and striving, *yearning*, to get the nose of the ball across the goal line.

Once your offense has the ball inside the opposition's 20-yard line, you're in what's called the red zone. The place where scoring is imminent, if only because a field goal becomes a likelihood, so long as you don't fumble or throw an interception, or get sacked for a big loss, or commit a penalty (*holding, false start, illegal man downfield, illegal formation, face mask, etc.*) that sets you back.

Within this final 20 yards, all the senses are compressed to an incandescent blooming. The best teams are cool and calm, yet when the ball is snapped, block and run with heightened determination. Passion *blossoms.*

And at the other end of the field—defending your own red zone, once the enemy is within it—you're trying just as hard now to keep something from happening. Defending, at the other end of the field, with ferocious resistance.

Moderation. Coaches say games are won or lost in the trenches, in that midfield area: how one team's line imposes its will on the other's, marching and grinding across that midfield marker, or stops the other team's advance, there in the middle ground, and forces the other team to give the ball back up with a punt, or a takeaway.

●

SO I DIP into the game with moderation. Perhaps the Texas Express, with their once-a-week practices, and their 10-game schedule is something that should be the future of football, even as we all know it won't be. The NFL is a $75 billion industry. No one's going to give up that kind of money. The NFL, which currently has four preseason games, 17 regular season games (and is considering adding an 18th), plus if one goes all the way to the Super Bowl, four more post-season games)—well, that's not sustainable. As fans, we love it, but the chances of any one player making it all the way through a season are incredibly slim.

I listen to some NFL games on the radio. I watch the playoffs and, on rare occasions, a regular season Monday-night game with friends when the matchup is epic—two undefeated teams, midseason, or a traditional rivalry like Packers-Bears, or Seahawks-49ers, or Steelers-Ravens, or Dallas-Washington . . .

But for the most part, I've pulled back. The pros run too fast, their collisions are too violent; the torque and twist they place upon their bodies never ends well. Sooner or later—usually sooner—the magnificent athlete is destined to lie writhing on the field like a thoroughbred on the racetrack with a shattered tibia.

The player will hobble off with his arms around the supporting shoulders of two trainers, or will ride off on the golf cart, taken to the locker room for X-rays, or will disappear into the blue tent to be evaluated by the league's concussion protocol: quizzed as to who the president is, what city they're playing in—even what the player's name is. And we call it a game.

●

I FEAR IT'S becoming harder to unfurl one's fullest passions into an ever-more-crowded world. That there is no longer sufficient safe territory to be one's largest, most rambunctious self. *This is what is wrong with us*, wrote D. H. Lawrence, *we are bleeding at the roots.*

What is the value of a brain whose chambers alight, now and again, with the brilliance of passion? Does such interior illumination scald and scrub and purify the tangled dull accretia, the plaque of no passion? Does it—the electricity of the passion-rivers in the mind—burn away the accumulated and numbing detritus of the mundane, allowing us once again to be our best and most interesting selves?

Perhaps this is the same principle by which art has endured and evolved within us as a species: that it is good for all chambers in the brain, all rooms, to be lit, illuminated, glowing from time to time. The burning.

IT PLEASES ME to introduce women to the game. Often they've shied away from paying any attention to football, put off by the seething violence and ferocity. It is not irrational to consider that nurturing such violence of spirit on the field might bleed beyond the boundaries of the game.

Indeed, there seems no end to each season's litany of awful off-the-field behavior: more than enough to wonder at the possibility of cause and effect. To deny the pandemic of domestic abuse that strikes victims and families every year is to do a disservice to those who suffer. This is one of the dark sides of human nature: that bullies can reside anywhere. The toxic American narrative that *Might makes right* can, in such a ritualized pageantry, take full flower in an individual already disposed to such a belief.

This can happen anywhere that power is concentrated: in the church, in the entertainment industry, in the family, in the government, in the military, in the law enforcement industry. That it does so again and again is one of our species' many stains. It is not going to go away soon or easily.

And complicating things—tempting the apologist to look away—are the anecdotes of weight and counterweight. For every story of a running back punching a girl at a party—the horrific yet not singular story of Ray Rice clubbing his wife unconscious in an elevator—there is a story of a young man buying his single mother her first home; of enormous offensive linemen reading books to inner-city children during story hour; of visits to children's hospitals.

We look away from the domestic violence and assault and remember Drew Brees holding the Super Bowl trophy and his toddler, his whole family, around him, the year the New Orleans Saints delivered the world championship to a city bent but not broken by the ravages of Hurricane Katrina. We remember the Houston Texans' star defensive lineman, J.J. Watt, raising a quarter of a billion dollars for people affected by Hurricane Harvey in Houston.

They're not gods, but neither are they like you or me. They are demigods, receptacles and reservoirs for our fears and desires; and with our fears and desires, we help shape them. We customize them with baroque hopes and expectations, as if we own them, like property. Like something we, or someone, has bought and paid for.

And when they crumple or break, we walk away and get new ones. When one goes bad, corrupted by a violence within, we look away. When they break their bodies, we forget them immediately. When they break the law, they are removed from sight for a game or two, or maybe three or four—sometimes almost an entire season—suspended until the crime has been forgotten.

Power corrupts, and absolute power corrupts absolutely. There must always be checks and balances, and to say a conversation of power and culture has nothing to do with football is as dangerous as it is untrue. If we are to enable an excessive cultural power that approaches the status of worship, we must hold ourselves accountable in this transaction, as well as the actions of our Sunday proxies, our part-time gods and demigods.

Our culture, and the culture of the NFL, has the ability to impose its muscular will upon the opposition; the NFL just needs to look up from the business of making money and do the right thing. To wait for leadership in these matters is to be complicit in the interim.

Talk is cheap. Coach Bill Parcells: *You are what your record says you are.* No excuses.

To criticize from the inside is so much more effective, I think, than from the outside. This is what terrified the NFL about Colin Kaepernick's resistance to police brutality against people of color. It's astonishing to me that the league, composed as it is of players of non-white color—72 percent of the league—has only 3 percent non-white ownership.

What if a player was to begin taking a knee in support of domestic abuse? Ownership's blackballing of Kaepernick would surely give future players pause with regard to exercising free speech on any non-league-supported issue, no matter how unjust.

The greed—the pressure to win—comes from the players and coaches, but it comes from us, too, the fans and consumers, at least as much.

If you don't love football, by all means, continue to stay away from it—avoid it. But if you do love football, work to change it.

●

I DIP NOW with relative reserve into what was once a boilermaker obsession. Out on the field, I run a play or two at tailback—no longer so thrilled to be out in the space in the flats, in the backfield, a guppy awaiting the sharks—catch the ball and then tuck in behind the giant David Fontenot or Neil Mathis. Twenty Dive: lean forward, go down in a pile. I line up for special teams—receiving and delivering kick-offs—six, seven, eight times a game. I run as fast as I can down the field with the braid of the other players onrushing, and I try to block, or evade blocks, to get to the ball.

I spell my team on defense when one of them staggers with fatigue, and we simply need a body to line up and rush, to occupy a blocker, so that another defensive lineman can shoot through a gap and achieve success. Terry Tempest Williams writes, *How will I survive my affections?*

It's extremely unlikely I'll help them win any games, but I love the community, the familiarity. I love the Facebook Messenger posts, love supporting them.

And so like a religious novitiate, I train, up in Montana, back in the cold dark forest, up on the Canadian border, with the days so short that darkness, not daylight, is the default setting of my hours, while down in Texas, in the languor of near-eternal spring, the rest of the Texas Express go on without me. They run and cut and leap in cleats and pads on green fields beneath the blue skies, or in night practices on the same green fields of Hohlt Park beneath the dazzle of overhead halogen lamps.

Up in Montana, waiting to rejoin them, I stretch on the bare wooden floor of my home in front of the woodstove, then lace up my boots and go outside to run up and down the driveway in the ankle-deep snow, which cushions the jarring on my knees. I run with high knees, as we do in our drills—backwards, sideways, scissoring, with my headlamps strafing horizontal through the darkness, the falling, swirling snow diamond-lit by my light, and my own trail up and down the driveway bisected sometimes by the thread of tracks from wolves and lions, which I do not fear—they want nothing to do with humans.

Far more dangerous and formidable than any wild animal is the unstoppable passage of time.

4

THE ROCK

THE PLAYING FIELD AT The Rock is not level. To an out-of-shape individual, it might seem the field is almost as treacherous in its topography as are the giant bodies that swoop and thunder through its hills and valleys. They batter, slice and slash, hand-fight and high-point, crack-back and hurtle.

When the field has just been mown, the casual eye perceives levelness. The center of the field is actually quite a bit higher, to help it drain in this quasi-equatorial land of thunderstorms. The field is grass, however, increasingly an artifact of the past, as most playing fields have been converted to the easier maintenance of Astroturf.

Being tackled on Astroturf is like being tackled on a city street. When players' helmeted heads strike the turf, they bounce like a basketball: *thump, thump,* or *thump thump thump.* And even the act of running up and down a field of artificial turf jars knees, spines, and foot joints.

The soil, or what was once soil, at The Rock, is packed tight as marble from nearly a hundred years of cleated battles. But it is still earth; it still has a pulse and a rhythm running beneath it, with the whispered breath of those who have run up and down its length countless times, their spirits and enthusiasms, as well as their athleticism—their vitality—surely still vibrating just beneath the taut old skin of The Rock, as an old guitar is said to retain in its wood always the unheard tremblings of chords played a hundred years ago.

When I was teaching for a semester in Indiana, living in a campus apartment on the edge of an old highway which, despite its battered condition, was one of the major transport corridors to and from Chicago, I slept on a bed so narrow my dog couldn't sleep on it with me. And if I opened my eyes in the night I would see the crazy flash of headlights sliding across the ceiling, so that it felt I was turned upside down, looking up at the streaming traffic from below.

Even in my sleep, I heard and felt the pounding of the loaded trailers as they hurtled north, the bent and broken road absorbing every slamming shock and casting the violent energy in all directions, so that the sound splashed across me like an invisible rain. And over time, my own body absorbed the steady beating until I, too, felt deep in my bones, the vibratory thrumming, the ceaseless echoes in me even when the trucks were gone and there was brief silence.

While I was in Indiana, the great quarterback for the Indianapolis Colts, Andrew Luck, formerly of Stanford, came to campus to speak to the DePauw football team as a courtesy to a friend who knew the DePauw coach.

There are some players who look larger in pads, uniform, and helmet, while others look larger in person. Luck was definitely the latter. I sat in the team's film screening room. (It was essentially a tiny theater; gone are the days of sitting in a coach's office in tiny plastic chairs or even elementary school desks, the wood creaking, watching the grainy flicker of dark jerseys surging amid white jerseys flowing in the other direction, trickles of white surf braiding and unbraiding across a volcanic beach, seen from a thousand feet above.)

At DePauw, we sat back in the movie theater seats—it was easy enough to guess which student played which position, as they settled in bands and friendly cliques into certain regions of the little theater—the lithe receivers; the burly running backs; the thick-necked linebackers; the towering defensive linemen; and the rounder offensive linemen. The quarterbacks, with their keen confidence, even arrogance: perhaps earned, perhaps not.

Some players sat waiting for Luck with the attentiveness and manners of good students, while others perched on the arms of their seats or leaned back with long legs and feet propped up on the seats in front of them, so that the difference between, say, a college sophomore and a fifth- or sixth-grader seemed indistinguishable. And it was all the more so when Luck, dressed in knit slacks and a close-fitting white short-sleeved sports shirt with the Indianapolis Colts insignia on it, came into the theater, not like a star appearing from the stage, but a visitation from Olympus, coming through the same double doors through which they themselves had entered.

He came not with a bodyguard or press crew—the Most Valuable Player in the National Football League—but alone, almost like a student himself, if a large one.

As he appeared a man among boys physically, so too did he in his poise and articulation, as he greeted them.

Their questions where those of children. *What is the difference between college and the NFL? Who was your favorite player when you were growing up?* They twisted in their seats, as suddenly shy now as they had been boisterous just minutes earlier.

Luck was diplomatic in his answers; truthful—the NFL game surprised him with how fast it was: he'd heard about it, but never experienced it; it wasn't anything a person could really prepare for. The questions they were asking were no different than the old chestnuts asked of thousands of other NFL players. (Someday I hope one player will punk the media and say something like *The NFL is slow, man, compared to the Southeastern Conference*). And yet Luck was deft in answering the old questions with a new spin—loving the sport so much as to seek to honor it by breathing new life, his own life, into the answers.

"My locker was right next to Dwight Freeney's," Luck was saying. Freeney was the Hall of Fame defensive end who had helped revolutionize defensive schemes, giving rise to the "hybrid" position that coaches now so love to employ. Freeney was short for a defensive end (generally, taller is better, for swatting down passes at the line of scrimmage), but was extraordinarily powerful with his strange fireplug stature. His arms were preternaturally long, so he could still swat. He was adept at also dropping back in coverage to work as a linebacker. He was a dervish, a game-changer, an undersized legend—but still a big man, just a bit smaller than the rest of the defensive linemen with whom he played.

He was definitely larger than even Andrew Luck, outweighing him by maybe 40 or 50 pounds, and so much older; haggard with the scars of a dozen or more surgeries; a man who'd seen a lifetime's worth of complicated defensive schemes and alterations. A chess master, as Luck would soon himself become.

Luck said what surprised him was how much *larger* the players were in college. "I used to be one of the biggest guys on any team," he said. "But when I introduced myself to Dwight, he looked down at me and said, 'Well hello, little one.'"

The son of former NFL quarterback Oliver Luck, Andrew grew up in Houston and picked Stanford as his college of choice, where he studied architectural engineering with the hopes of someday, after football, designing and building a football stadium. (Something I imagine would rival the Coliseum in Rome. I imagined him spending the middle part of his life traveling to all the major stadiums in the world, taking notes and dreaming a lifelong dream of ways to construct the perfect stadium.)

Oliver had not been the talent Andrew was—had ended up playing some years in pro and semi-pro leagues in Canada and Europe—but had trained his son to be the best of his generation.

I'd followed Luck's exploits since his Stanford days, where he'd competed for a national championship. My oldest daughter Mary Katherine, schooled with him, said he was geeky and sweet, an admirable assessment I found corroborated by his choice to stay in school for his senior year, rather than leaving for the NFL draft after his junior year. By doing so, he gave up tens of millions of dollars—he was a surefire number one pick. His reasons, however, were well thought out. He had grown close to his teammates, he said, and wanted to come back and compete for a national championship. He wanted to finish his degree and, most endearingly, said his younger sister would be an incoming freshman and he wanted to stick around and help show her the ropes.

Plus, he said, he really liked the college game.

There in the DePauw Tigers' film room, he rolled with every question, as graceful in the attention paid to the questioner as he was on Sundays, shuffling up into the protected pocket of time and safety—an invisible bubble with a shifting lifespan of somewhere between three and four seconds—afforded to him by his offensive linemen, aided sometimes by a chip block from a running back.

None of these DePauw players would ever see the NFL. Their game was essentially intramurals. It was still football, however, beautiful in its logic—but Luck was essentially performing a community service, like visiting a children's hospital, or a retirement home.

He was talking about something he'd noticed in his first NFL game, a thing he couldn't have expected or prepared for, which was the way the field itself buzzed, he said, with electricity.

It was the plasticized filaments of Astroturf, he said, each strand made into a conductor, absorbing the sound waves generated by the roaring of the fans. It made the hair on his neck stand up, he said, like there was some kind of a force field. "I could feel it tingling in my bones," he said. "The tips of my fingers, and in my teeth."

I'd never heard of this phenomenon and yet here he was, making the world anew for all of us.

It reminded me of the stories from West Texas, where the strands of tightly strung barbed wire would sometimes pick up and conduct, even transmit, radio signals from far away: an evangelical station in San Angelo, or in Mexico. Or of the way, up in the snowy mountains, on blue sky sub-zero days, the air is so dry and cold that what little moisture exists in the atmosphere turns to shimmering flakes that glint and shimmer in the sunlight. Those crystals can, I imagine, spiral amid and among each other, making the most delicate, barely audible sounds, more imagined than heard, like the tinkle of wind chimes a thousand miles away: and yet, it has to be measurable; it has to be more than nothing.

One more thing about Luck. He was famous for congratulating opposing players after particularly hard hits. On himself! He's a big man, but nowhere near as large as the defensive linemen who were chasing him down, sometimes crushing him from behind, other times from the side, and still other times traveling at high speeds and planting their enormous shoulders directly into his sternum. Uprooting him, driving him backward and then down into that tingling Astroturf. Those hits were like a sledgehammer delivering the final blow to a railroad spike. And after he bounced back up, he thanked them for that play.

He stayed with us for the better part of an hour, until questions and conversations were exhausted, and for no reason other than a favor to a friend. He was simply being an ambassador for the sport, the idea of football, a thing he loved.

And after he left us, and the rest of us dispersed into the bright spring sunlight, the players chattering like teenagers again, I studied further on what had happened, and why. And the best I could come up with, again, was that he was just doing a favor for a friend.

Does football build friendships? I believe that it does. Working together with others toward any common goal can build friendship. But in an age of disconnection—an epidemic of disconnection—how ironic that a sport in which helmets collide and brain trauma occurs, a thing as simple and yet as great as friendship can be cultivated, and grown.

This is not an apology. This is an observation.

I would not want any child of mine participating in the sport. I could not stand to watch it, were the players my beloveds. And now that I'm getting to know the Texas Express, I wince with even greater empathy when I see an especially hard hit. It's different inside the game, rather than outside. On the inside, time behaves differently, even within the already different bubble of football time.

One's eye is hyper-attuned to the body of the teammate; able to detect, with the acuity of a physician, the slightest favoring of a muscle, limb, hand, or foot. One definitely is aware of the state of mind of every other player. Each and all of you are compressed into a closed system. You're aware of an electrical circuit—almost a buzzing—that connects you to them.

You know immediately what has been damaged and how badly. When the player is lying on his back, looking up at the blue sky, knees drawn up, writhing slowly, you know. *Get up*, you're thinking, *get up. Take a breather. Come to the sideline and gather yourself. I'll go spell you for a while.*

It's strange, but it shouldn't be. I think it's the way things used to be, back when we were new in the world and all we had was each other.

Even when the field is not level—even when it is in a horrible, tilted condition of inequity, as is the case at The Rock—the structure and essence of the game itself summons and creates an equality of spirit and purpose that is as exhilarating as it is uncommon.

Such connectivity is a very close relative of empathy.

⑤
FIRST GAME

AS WITH A WEDDING day, it takes forever to approach. The preceding emotional currents are those of languor, anticipation, and preparations both tedious and grand. Matthew 25:6—"A midnight cry goes up, the bridegroom approacheth!" The final hours collapse to kaleidoscopic fragments of imagery, a tiny component of a larger whole that is coming soon.

The other team—the Houston Ducks—has arrived, luminous in their fluorescent yellow T-shirts. Many of them are immense. One man is so large he is having trouble getting out of his low-slung four-door sedan. His muscular teammates gather around him and pull. His teammates likewise are brutes, swollen with muscle and youth.

It takes forever for everyone to get ready. You'd think otherwise: how difficult can it be? A few of us go out onto the field early, pitch and catch tight 20-yard spirals. I make the mistake of looking back over my shoulder while falling into line for receivers' drills. One of the tall men for the Houston Ducks is running a route in our direction. The ball, thrown by his quarterback, is already in the air as he comes out of his break; it looks like the hill will surely be out of his reach. But his rangy receiver betrays no concern, only that all is as planned. Somehow the receiver picks up speed without evincing any extra effort, and casually—like a man reaching for one and only one grape, sunlit and on the vine—reaches his hand up and catches the ball in that one hand as might a centerfielder.

The big receiver doesn't even pull the ball into his body for safety, but continues loping, the ball seemingly stuck to his hand like a burr. I look away quickly, but too late, the knowledge is in my brain. And back in the line, I see a few of my teammates similarly trying to not look back.

Why is it always this way? I know the answer, but I do not want to accept it. Houston is a city of 3,000,000-plus. Brenham is a small town of 16,000. The Houston team can practice every day, can draw from an immense talent pool of physical wealth. And their coaches are passionate, too. But we've got a slugger's chance, I tell myself. At the end of the day, it's just 11-on-11; it's not 16,000 against 3,000,000.

And as the battalion of the perfect row-and-column phalanx of butter-yellow jerseys executes their jumping jacks in perfect shouted militaristic cadence, I'm grateful for the elliptical shape of the football, which is always capable of bouncing strangely, randomly, disorderly. We can find a way to beat them.

Coach calls us together for a group prayer. Despite being the home team, we've dallied with the taping and the dressing, and with our staggered arrival. Ernie, our center, leads us. His beard has gone gray in the last couple of years; he looks like a chunky Fidel Castro. Our time is abbreviated; the referees, dressed in perfect zebra uniforms, come trotting over to tell us we have 10 minutes.

Ten minutes! I've been waiting two years to return. So much has happened in that time, and yet, here on the spring-green grass of The Rock, nothing has changed, only Ernie's beard. I've been stretching a lot, and feel like Gumby this year. It feels good, and it feels good to be running on lush green grass, and I can see the joy—the thing beyond happiness—sparking in my teammates' eyes, as we gather, finally, for the start of another season.

In their eyes, and the energy of their pregame banter, they carry the excitement of boys. *They get past you*, Lou is lecturing a new safety, *pull 'em down by their shirt. Don't let 'em get past you.*

Coach's eyes burn brightest. His demeanor is a strange mix of deep pleasure and a calm, practical wisdom. I can tell he's trying to keep us focused, but he's struggling; he wishes he could be back out there. Coaching is second best.

It's so damned good to be alive. I'm so grateful to my teammates for making a space for me.

Here at The Rock, our players are still trotting willy-nilly in various stages of unreadiness. Kirby is taping players one at a time, using the back of Coach's truck as a training table. Players are trying on helmets from Coach's and Kirby's random collection. Kirby peruses e-Bay several times each day, looking for and bidding on various used helmets. It's impossible to say how much he spends on the team each year. He goes through $50 of athletic tape each week alone. It would be nice to secure a local business sponsor, nice to have jerseys with players' names on the back. That's a nonstarter for now, however, with several players coming and going for but a few games, and still others in and out of jail. As it is now, Coach takes all the jerseys home in a giant duffel bag for his wife, Mattie, to launder the next week.

We pick and pluck through the sweet-smelling neatly folded jerseys to select either our favorite number or the number we had the previous week, or—as if betting on horses at the track—an entirely new number, in the hopes of performing better: a numismatic makeover, possibly channeling some NFL great of yore.

As such, our players' numbers can change by a few to several digits week by week, making it hard for us to sometimes identify one another by name and position.

Some are recognizable by their build alone: Shaun, a sprite; Kojo, with his lean frame and long arms so ebony they sometimes glint purple, like a raven's feathers in sunlight; Jeremiah Maxey, with his ridiculous trapezoid superhero silhouette.

Myself, certainly, I imagine: slender, crooked, minuscule.

Coach's wife, Mattie, does not come to the games. I've made a note to myself to get a thank-you card before the end of the season and have the players (whoever might be remaining) sign it for her.

IN BETWEEN THE hurried preparations, Coach takes me up into the "stands"—three rows of aluminum bleachers, only 20 feet long—just a bit longer than the length of, say, a canoe—and introduces me to an ancient white guy in a powder-blue short-sleeved knit shirt, a natty ball cap with gold trim.

"Cap'n Rick, I want you to meet my coach. This is Mark Chaffee," Coach says, then stands there still and silent for half a beat as if I should know who Mark Chaffee is. That I might as well be beholding Ray Nitschke, Mike Ditka, Dick Butkus.

The man in the lawn chair does not look as if once upon a time he might have been in the mold of the greats; though just as surely, too, it is apparent that time has wizened him. He looks more like the venerable godfather of the NFL, Gil Brandt, still evaluating players at the age of 89 and a member of the Hall of Fame than he does the husk of a former linebacker. As a geologist, I've spent my life observing how time can reduce a boulder of granite to a pile of loose minerals and pink sand in but a few decades—frost, sun, wind, water—as if even stone is animate, and privy therefore like all else to the contract between life and death. But not much fades faster than the youth of a once-young man or woman.

"Coach Chaffee taught me all of what I know about football," my Coach says, and the little white man sitting before me does not deny it. "Coach Chaffee, Mister Rick is my biographer," Coach says. "He's the one who wrote that article." Coach Chaffee beholds me with a reserved, civil, friendly distance. I believe that he is living in the past; living in the sphere of time that is football, only football. Or maybe there is nothing more to him than what I see: an old man sitting in the mild sun in a small town in late February, the wind ruffling his white hair. Though I don't believe that is the case, and what can he possibly have to say to me anyway? I was not there. I did not inhabit or play for him in the past.

Perhaps the game has changed so much from those days that it is not even fully recognizable to him—appears like some other sport, its rules as mysterious now as those in which middle Easterners ride horseback carrying a goat's head.

Coach Barnes has things to do, since we're the host team. He has to make sure we have a scorekeeper and timekeeper to operate the little electronic scoreboard that's set up under a tin-roofed hut. Pay the refs $100 per man per game; a minimum three refs and umpires, but preferably five. We each hand our secretary a crumpled $20 bill before being issued one of the clean jerseys.

"Captain Rick, you can ask Coach Chaffee anything about the old days. What were we called?" My Coach either forgets or pretends to forget. He grasps for the team's name, a wisp of cirrus whipping past. Then he remembers. "Sidewinders," Coach Barnes says, grasping it with satisfaction.

"Texas Sidewinders," Coach Chaffee confirms.

Coach Barnes leaves, and I'm caught flat-footed, with no time to think. I'd rather listen than come up with the questions. Sometimes I don't think of the questions I want to ask until years later.

"Will you be coming to all the games?" I ask.

Coach Chaffee shakes his head. "Just this one," he says.

I don't know what to say to this. Why would he drive all the way up here from Houston rather than waiting for us to come to Houston later in the season? It seems too personal a question.

"Coach Barnes gives so much to these young men," I say lamely. The wind is strong up there in the bleachers, and I'm not even sure he hears a word I say.

"What was Coach Barnes like?" I ask. *Damn*, I think, that's *lame*.

I think about all the miles of cracked and brittle orange celluloid game film stored in attics and film canisters—thousands or tens of thousands of useless, earnest data recording various Sidewinders through the decades as they raced up and down the green fields, chasing the ball, and running to catch, or to avoid being caught. Thousands of miles run, and thousands of miles of film, with those young men old now, or gone.

The wind is picking up and I'm not dressed for the game yet. I ask Coach Chaffee for his contact information—I know questions will come to me later—and thank him, and shake his hand to take my leave.

"Anthony was one of my best players," Coach Chaffee says, only now opening up as I am starting to leave. Isn't that always the way it is? But who among us is not that way—initially guarded in the first face of enthusiasm, and the attempted extraction of the past?

"He could have gone to the NFL if he'd had some breaks," Coach Chaffee says. Do I hear, in his voice, even 30 years later, some regret? "He had some bad breaks."

I've got to go. I want to hear more, but there's a game to play. The clock is melting. I thank him for his time. Anthony's past is interesting. But nowhere nearly as much as his present.

●

THE FACT THAT there aren't many of us, compared to the Ducks, becomes more evident when we gather around Coach for the prayer. I get the sense Coach has been working on this prayer—this first game prayer—for a while. It's overbrimming with praise, a psalm of thanksgiving for our lives, health, families, safe journeys, and the opportunity to serve the Lord. *Is he seeking to curry special favor?* I wonder, uncharitably.

Soon he segues into parable, describing "how when Eve looked back, she was turned into salt. That's what we're asking here, oh Lord, to help us smite the enemy. Not on the field," he is quick to add, "but rather to be good soldiers for Christ, and to allow our small band to have the passion and righteousness of 20,000 rather than 20," he says; and again I can't help but think he, too, has snuck a peek over at the other side, and been alarmed by the size of the army amassing.

"We want to thank you, oh Father, for your greatest victory on Cavalry," he says, and now he's definitely crossed over from lobbying into full-bore tampering. *He can't help himself,* I think; and if it's done out of love, how can that be bad?

"Help us, oh Father; do not let us forget we must put our foot up their asses! Forgive me today, but today we have to be bitter, not sweet."

"*Amen*," choruses the team.

And if there is a God or greater consciousness above, how are these earnest words being received? Will they be received before kickoff? It is not difficult to imagine the deity to whom they are sent smiling, taking some time away from various wars and pandemics to look down on the little green jewel of The Rock and smile, amused by Coach's and the team's pluck.

Leaning back in the celestial easy chair, even cracking open a cold one and tuning in for a while, taking his or her mind off the last 10,000 or so years of trouble over in this corner of the world, one of an infinitude of tiny blue drops of water under the microscope.

We're hurrying; there are only a few minutes now. I'm wearing my flashy yellow running shoes—not a color I would have chosen, but they were all that fit me from a footlocker of free shoes to be recycled at an Olympic training facility I visited in Vermont last year while teaching a writing workshop. The flashy shoes catch Coach's eye, and he tells me to put on my cleats—that they won't let me onto the field in the sneakers—and his response catches me by surprise as I realize he's serious about me going into the game, despite the critical nature of it: the first game of the season. It's one thing to go in and carry the ball late in the season when all hope is lost; but the first game of the year?

I start to tell him my theory about how I pop my groin when I plant my feet and cut with the deep cleats, but then realize how ridiculous it sounds—like complaining how the color doesn't match my uniform, or that I never could learn to run in heels—and anyway, he's already moving on, hurrying toward the sideline, reaching in his back pocket to consult his loose batch of index cards, his favorite plays highlighted in yellow Magic Marker.

I turn and trot back to the bench, kick off my lil' lemon sneakers, and lace up the horrible cleats.

On the sideline, just as we're about to go out onto the field—our uniforms pristine and unmarked by blood or soil, as were those of

Confederate and Union soldiers reporting for their first day of duty—a referee is speaking to the father of one of our players. "They're going to beat you down. They've got so many that in the fourth quarter they can just beat you down." He is speaking like a prophet witnessing the outcome of all things.

Vignettes: the quarters pass like seasons. The game's deliciously slow. Both teams struggle, tugging and pushing and pulling at one another in the cautious manner of sumo wrestlers. Shaun throws an interception, then the Houston Ducks bust a chunk play, a short sideline pass to one of their big receivers, who proceeds to break about 10 arm tackles, motors 70 yards into the end zone, and a hollow feeling fills our souls. The ghost of two years ago—*winless*—is back already, just like that.

I think each of us felt that the more time and distance we put between that winless season and now, the more immune we would be to the Ugly Thing's return. Our sideline is stoic, silent.

I think I glimpse the tiniest flinch even in Coach. It's hard to describe the eerie emptiness—as if we're each and all destined to be prey for the stronger teams, even when our hearts are beautiful.

The emptiness is like the moaning sound the wind makes in a storm, when the barometer plunges, and swallows and swifts begin flying erratically. That feeling is a measure of the distance between where we are and where we want to be. There's a terrible stillness, and all we can do is hope and believe it's a false reading, and dig deeper.

Jeremiah Maxey, the muscular superhero, is walking up and down the sideline, thumping his chest and exhorting us all, rallying, railing. The game has barely begun.

"Kickoff team," Coach shouts to us, clapping his hands. "All right. All right. It's a game now. Now y'all see what it is. It's a game now!"

And it is, for a while. Houston intercepts another of our passes, then busts another long play over the middle, wherein another receiver once again runs through our feeble attempts at arm tackles. Coach starts to go ballistic, but suddenly looks down as if studying something infinitesimal in the grass—an ant, I think—and smiles ever so slightly to himself. It's as if he's keeping some sort of commitment he's made with himself—something he's been thinking about these last two years.

Twelve-to-nothing. The Ducks have missed both of their extra points. You'd think with all the soccer players in the world, teams would have good kickers, but it's a skill often lacking on all the teams.

Ah, but wait. There's no quit in our team. Our *fellas*, as Neil calls us. Coach calls the play known as "Bo," a simple pass play where the wide receiver runs a go-route down the sideline—but Kojo improvises when he sees an empty space in the middle of the field and heads toward it: sandlot football. He catches a tightly thrown pass from Shaun and gashes that big empty green space all the way to the end zone untouched, and we're whooping and thumping each member of the offense as they come trotting off: the first touchdown we've scored in over two years, and it feels like a miracle. It feels godly, and it amazes me how easily joy can be gotten. We're boys again.

We go for a two-point conversion, and get it.

The Ducks are rattled. Jeremiah Maxey, our left defensive end, is getting into their backfield and harassing their big soft quarterback, who doesn't like this *at all*. And Chandler, on the other side, is closing in as well, so that we're really disrupting their passing game. The Duck quarterback scrambles, and with his big hands able to grip the ball securely, or so he believes, he keeps waving the ball around wildly. It looks like a scoop of ice cream atop a wobbly cone.

When the defense comes off the field, I tell Chandler, "At some point you're going to just take that ball out of his hand and run the other way with it." And Chandler nods and says, "I know, I was so close." It's a meaningful game, stuck at 12–8. It's there for us to take.

Now is the time to surge past them; we can all feel it. But our offense, like theirs, has turned suddenly sluggish—we're not able to run the ball up the middle. They've clogged the lanes with their giants. But our outside receivers are in man-to-man coverage and can get open across the middle, if only Shaun can see them quickly enough and get the ball to them.

One does not say these things to Coach in the heat of the game.

Opinions are like assholes, he says, *everybody's got one*, and when our offense is on the field, Jeremiah gathers his defense around him and sketches little routes and gestures in the green grass, looking each defender in the eye as he narrates what he sees happening, and tells them how to adjust. His entire defense is rapt, occasionally interjecting their own observations to improve and embellish his tale.

The offense feels it too: this evolving confidence also. This hunger so ferocious it seems almost like joy. There are two teams, like two sides of the brain: offense and defense working together but separately, each holding informal convocations on the sidelines whenever the other half of our team is on the field. (There's a third and somewhat hidden team, like a hidden consciousness—the "special" team—responsible for kickoffs, punts, kickoff and punt returns, field goals, and extra points, but their presence on the field, though often critical, is so much less frequent than the back-and-forth slugfest, back-and-forth gashings of offense-versus-defense, that they tend to be an overlooked or forgotten element.)

Shaun, our little quarterback, is speaking to his squad with every bit as much animation as the volatile Jeremiah Maxey, though Shaun's tone is quieter, almost stealthy, as he details what he's seeing; and like a good leader, he listens. Their conversations are much the same, however, each seeing what the opposition is doing, and adjusting, modifying, ever so slightly, Coach's plays—Redtail, 22 ISO, USC Pass-or-Run—to slip a player into one of those coveted ever-shifting zones of space, the freedom that is the green unbroken field.

"They're waiting a second before walking all three of their linebackers down after the ball's snapped," Dooney's saying. He's excited, because when they do that, it opens up those little temporary islands of open field.

Coach hears none of this, and I wonder, is this just teen rebellion?

The time to attack is now, and I'm reminded of what an elk hunting expert in Montana told me about the most valuable advice he ever got with regard to the moment when, after a long hunt, the elk was within final stalking range: *You put your ears back and go after them with blood in your eyes.* Meaning not rage or anger, but determination. Don't do it halfway.

Coach is pacing the sidelines, eagle-eyed on the game at hand, so that for the rest of us it's very much an example of what I suppose religious scholars would call free will. Coach has given his commandments, but we have agency to obey or amend. And how much improvising Coach will support, I imagine, depends to some large extent on the outcome—whether the improvisation was successful or not.

If there is a deity looking down on us, observing his or her handiwork in the ongoing passion play, I wonder what that Creator's thoughts are when we veer from a teaching or tenet and yet achieve success, however that might be defined. With those small adjustments of our hearts, do we, in our own small way, help sculpt the deity?

The shadow of all things, however distorted, resembles always the object that cast the shadow.

Out on the field, a Duck is running down the far sideline. Our players are falling, crumbling like origami cranes incapable of flight. The big Duck is casting them off like a man brushing snowflakes from his shoulders; the arms and legs of our fallen are all akimbo. He is moving through our scattered defense like the proverbial hot knife through butter.

Our remaining upright players are chasing him, trying to converge on him, but the runner understands the dynamics of the tightening net all too well, and is adjusting accordingly, picking a path between them that will allow him to travel the last distance unscathed.

I look over at Coach and see that his heart is breaking. He is *bereft*—he truly believed, or *hoped*, this year would be different—that his long hard good work, and the virtuosity of his patience, would be rewarded.

It occurs to me that this might be by far too big a job for one man—that he needs assistants to do what the captains, Shaun and Jeremiah and Ernie, are doing, crouched on the sidelines like boys at recess, improvising. If our players executed perfectly, all would be well, even though the other side would be testing and challenging them. But the system—his system of discipline, and his X's and O's—are not sufficient to withstand the unavoidable imperfections each of us possesses, even without the challenges thrown at us by a feisty opponent. For that, he needs at the very least an offensive coordinator, a defensive coordinator, and ideally a special teams coach. Heck, why not throw in an offensive line coach, a defensive line coach, and an assistant for the running backs, receivers, and secondary?

The other team has all of these things and more. In addition to their mesmerizing phalanx of bright yellow uniformed players—few of whom yet even have a trace of The Rock's grass stains on their white pants—there are also coaches all up and down the sidelines, each identifiable by their dark short-sleeved knit shirts and khaki pants.

I'm not bitter. If anything, I take a certain pride in our scrap, our feist, our hard-bitten renegade outlawry. I know it makes no sense. There's something about a hard road that feels authentic to me, in a world where so much energy is spent avoiding the hard route. I don't mean to suggest it's a virtue—only that I prefer this side of the line to the other.

I am not suggesting we're morally superior to the Ducks. Only that I feel more comfortable among the ragged.

It is not lost on me that among my teammates, I am far from ragged—tenuous middle class—and how grateful I am that not only do they avoid judging me, but they accept me.

Out on the field, the Ducks have seized the ball from us and scored another touchdown, and kicked the extra point. *Time just gets away from us*, says the protagonist Mattie Ross in *True Grit*. The score is 28–8. It's still a meaningful game. There's still a chance, I think. But Coach has found the calm center I think he has been striving to cultivate in his two year hiatus—*I will be a better man this year*—and I'm surprised when, after he's called for the kickoff team, I inform him that we have only 10 men on the field.

He doesn't even look out on the field to count or to see who else might be able to fill the slot. "Get out there, old man," he says. I have not yet taken my helmet off the whole game, for fear if I got called out there I might forget to put it on and run out there bareheaded.

I dash out as if into the sea, the surf, and join them.

I'm on the front line with three other teammates. It's all a blur. I don't recognize their numbers or who they are. All I know, when the kickoff goes over my head, is to turn and run back toward whoever on our team catches it—Little Melvin, this time, number 1—and to then turn and square up to block for him. To run forward again. Which I do.

Ducks are flying at us: incoming, small- to medium-sized wide-bodied mean and muscular Ducks. There are more of them than would seem possible. A swarm of yellowjackets. I search out one, but he is already seeking me out. He lowers his shoulders for the impact, and I throw a forearm at him. I'm not sure what happens to him, but suddenly I find myself bouncing, skidding across the green grass.

Behind me, other Ducks have gotten to Melvin and are twisting him down. I get up and run to the play in case he fumbles and a live ball hits the field, but Melvin goes down. I give him a hand up, congratulate him on his run, and we all trot off the field. On the sidelines Neil greets me and says *Big Rick*, glad that I've gotten real contact.

Was I helpful? I didn't change the outcome. I did my job, I suppose—inelegantly, yes—but one of the great things about football is that there's always another chance. Or almost always. There's at least the perception that there's another chance. And it's a strange comfort, too, small but disproportionately felt, to have a nickname—any nickname—as was the condition of childhood. Later in the year, they will choose Sick Rick.

Indeed, that evening there are many more chances. Each time the Ducks score, they kick off to us. So I get plenty of practice. Their coach calls for an onside kick in my direction, preying on the weak member of the herd, and I don't blame him; I'd have done the same thing, even though it gravels my ridiculous pride. But Little Shaun swoops in and catches the skittering kick on the high bounce, cradles it and falls to the ground, curls up to protect it.

I was running toward the ball, and like to believe I too would have fielded it cleanly, but I'm glad he got it. In lunging toward it, I twisted my ankle, but not too badly. I was able to shake it off, but how ridiculous that would have been, to be felled without even being touched.

AT HALFTIME, COACH is surprisingly calm. "All right, all right, gentlemen," he says. "Now we know what we need to work on. Now we know what our *deficiencies* are." One player, a giant of a man who I thought I might like for the reason that he wore tiny eyeglasses even beneath his helmet—the man weighing easily 300 pounds, slow-moving but powerful—walks off into the setting sun, carrying his shoulder pads and helmet. Kirby said later the man had come to him complaining after the first series that his kidneys, liver, and labrum hurt, but Kirby said he thought he was just out of shape.

Another unnamed player—one who hadn't been to any of the Thursday practices—departs early as well; just up and slinks away, his leave-taking not noticed by the others until much later.

And that's about all Coach has to say to us, at halftime. He pleads with us to come to Thursday practices. He says we need to learn to tackle. He says, by God, we *will* learn to tackle: that our next practice will be live tackling. "You all ever hear of the Oklahoma drill?" he asks. It traces its origins to Bud Wilkinson, a longtime coach at Oklahoma. In the drill, two players lower their heads and run into each other full tilt and head-on, the defender trying to tackle the runner as the runner tries to bowl over the defender. They're enclosed in a narrow lane created by tackling dummies or other players.

It's a savage meat-grinder drill picked up by thousands of coaches around the country at all levels of sport (except the pros, where the players are too valuable a commodity to heedlessly ruin in a non-game situation), and across the years it led to who knows how many hundreds of thousands of concussions and mangled knees.

The drill was outlawed by the National Collegiate Athletic Association (NCAA) just last year.

I look around. It seems no one knows the drill. There appears to be a dull sense of shame pervading the team—a sluggish mix of shame, denial, and silent stoicism—with the setting sun taking on a gold hue.

We still have an entire second half to play. Shaun excuses himself to go pee. "I'll be back," he says, as if the small raft of deserters has us questioning even him, one of our captains.

I make the tactical mistake of waiting a minute or two too long before realizing I also would like to pee; but now the grandfatherly referee is coming over, looking all earnest, thinking, I'm sure, *You boys ready for another round of this ass-whipping?*

The Ducks keep scoring. We do not. We are stuck at eight points and enter a nightmarish sequence of deep sacks, runs for no gain, and incomplete passes. On one sack, Shaun is thrown down like a rag doll, his arms not tucked in close to his body, but spread out wide.

He does not get up, and Kirby hurries out to tend to him.

Shaun lies flat on his back for a while, staring up at the February sky, the cirrus clouds shoaling like beachside sea foam, the world inverted and, other than the pain, perhaps it is a sweet little spot of time in which he can rest, can just lie there and study the sky.

I thought he'd separated his shoulder or damaged his rotator cuff, but after Kirby and some players have helped him to his feet and assisted him off the field, Kirby tells me he thinks Shaun might've fractured a rib. It hurts Shaun to breathe.

Injuries almost always hurt worse the next day. Shaun's sitting on the bench with his head down, out of it, and I wonder if he's also gotten a concussion.

Shane—a tall, powerful man whom I'd assumed was a defensive end—runs out onto the field after a hurried conversation with Coach about which play to run. I've never seen Shane take a practice rep at quarterback, have never even seen him throw a football, but then I realize it was he with whom Shaun and I were playing lazy catch out on the field before the game. I try to recall if Shane's throws were exceptional or singular. They were all right. I think they all were on target. Sometimes a little high—helmet-high, or even a tad higher—but good enough. Consistent. Powerful.

Quarterback's an impossible position. It takes a lifetime to learn. The prodigies like Andrew Luck and Patrick Mahomes appear to hit the pros ready-made and fully formed, or in need of only one year of adjustment, but it's worth noting that both of those players are the sons of professional players themselves, and groomed for the position since infancy.

Shane has a rough go of it. The Express is having a rough go of it. The Ducks are not. On every play, they storm our walls like a sea-surge breaching a broken dike.

Shane retreats, twists, runs left, then veers right, still running backwards, but always, the Ducks fall upon him like hounds, and it's becoming so regular that they don't even war-whoop or celebrate their sacks now, but merely trot back.

It's a little hard to reconcile the name of so innocuous a mascot—*Ducks*—with the severity of the beating we are experiencing.

Images: I recall, from the slow steady unscrolling of time in the second half, looking down at my old man's thin shanks and being startled that they were ghost-white, alabaster in the low-angled late-day light; whiter than even my game pants. The long Montana winter. Skeleton-white.

●

THE SECOND HALF elongates. They're punching us around the field in the manner of a giant helium-filled balloon. Again and again I'm called out onto the field to receive yet another kickoff—repeated exclamation points to the Ducks' never-ending scoring. I feel a good little surge of adrenaline when I run out onto the field, cleats biting the green turf nicely each time; but the feeling is muted by the fact that now each time I'm out there we are falling farther and farther behind.

And as the game wears on, more and more of our players develop injuries, some serious, others mild, until it is getting harder to find 11 players willing to go out and receive the kickoff.

Even our spirited defense is glum. And I don't fault them. That's one of the things I'm here for: to spell them for a play, give them a chance to catch their breath.

They sit on the bench unblinking, watching the game but not really seeing it. Shaun's feeling better, but not good enough to go back out on the field and get hammered again. The players' faces and arms gleam with sweat. The sun is orange behind us now. Coach wanders the sideline like a sleepwalker.

Deep into the third quarter, the game has ceased to be a game and has devolved into a scrum, a sloppy tug-of-war, uninspiring if not quite tedious. None of us are being our best physical selves. We definitely are not putting our feet up their asses.

So pacific has become the contest that one of the players' children, a small boy of perhaps seven or eight who has been photographing and filming with his iPad atop a tripod, has been edging closer and closer to the field, trying to get better shots of the action. And with the outcome no longer in question—35–8, then 42–8—the players are sitting on benches talking about non-game matters. (Kirby has come over to where I'm standing to inform me he's going by Whataburger after the game, and asks if I'd like him to get me anything. *A chocolate milk shake*, I think.)

The little boy is now very close to the action following with his camera, a miniature Cecil B. DeMille, seeing the game through the colorful frame of the iPad's gaze. I scooch closer to him, not wanting to be authoritarian, and tell him to get back, but definitely on high alert, ready to scoop him up if a play veers in our direction.

A few times a game, a play will yaw toward one sideline or the other with such velocity that a mass of players will come flowing over the painted white boundary. When this happens, there's a delayed scatter of coaches and bystanders, everyone jumping back belatedly in the manner of children at a beach leaping back from a surprising tidal surge.

The ballcarrier, taught to run through the whistle, doesn't let up until after he's crossed the white line. And the defensive pursuit sure doesn't let up, so that it's easy for their momentum to carry any number of them—hundreds of pounds of furious muscle, gashing cleats, and helmets as hard as bowling balls—directly into the mass of innocent onlookers. Woe to any bystander who might be looking down at a clipboard or back over their shoulder, searching for a fan up in the bleachers.

The violence of that onrush is always so much greater than what is represented on television, where by comparison it looks sanitized; and even out on the field, it is not until those final microseconds of closure—close enough to *scent* the player, and feel the radiant heat coming off him in the instant before impact—that the true violence can be perceived.

So I'm ready, watching the little boy closely, trying to anticipate each next play and the likelihood of the ballcarrier—like a wild horse breaking free of its confinement—switching direction and coming suddenly at us.

My fret is for naught. Corey, the boy's father, has been watching him all along. Up in the bleachers with other family members, Corey calls down easily to those of us standing on the sidelines. "Hey, does someone mind moving the little man back some?"—and Little Man, hearing his father, does not need to be told twice. He folds up his tripod and retreats to the safer distance from which he'd been operating earlier. Even Little Man has picked up on the diminished vigor of the game, as the energy drains from both teams as it might from a stranded great fish, gasping, with the end of the things so near now.

●

THEN IT IS over, and immediately we are crossing the field, slapping hands; the outgoing chain of us paralleling the incoming chain of them, like the teeth of a zipper coming together. *Good game, good game, good game, good game.* At first we just low-five each other in passing—a glimpse of a human face, no longer a warrior, and somehow surprising, for that—but then, as we near the end of the line, soul-brother grips, though other times, an old-school regular shaking of hands.

Then we come together, the two colors, navy and yellow, on the middle of the field, with the sun almost down and the evening growing cooler. "Mix it up, fellas," the coaches yell, and we do. We move into one giant huddle, heads bowed for prayer. Thanks are given that there were no major or serious injuries—a rarity and, to this participant, a jubilation. I want to shout *Amen!* but instead I nod vigorously.

Then the two coaches address us. As is the custom, the winning coach goes first. The coach of the Ducks is a big white man with a florid, almost orange tan. He's larger than most of his players.

"My hats off to you men," he says, addressing us with a graciousness and sincerity I do not find patronizing. "I'll say this, y'all never quit." (The last time I dared look at the scoreboard, it was 49–8). "I know we'll meet up again in Houston." (Each team plays the others twice—once at home and once away). "And I have no reason to believe the results will be the same next time. Your team has our respect."

Now it's Coach's turn, and given the generosity and humility of the victorious coach's comments, might I be forgiven, basking in the pleasure of the other coach's lukewarm praise, for believing for a moment—for wanting to believe—that Coach will respond in kind?

For a hot second, in the echo of the Duck coach's words, and with Coach Barnes's head bowed as if he's searching for equally diplomatic phrasings, compliments, and platitudes, I'm convinced that Anthony Barnes has changed completely. That he is a new man.

Coach Barnes lifts his head, looks toward the back of the giant two-team huddle, into the vicinity of a clot of yellow Ducks. "Is y'all's kicker out there?" Coach asks. "That old white-headed man?"

The player in question, beaming, lifts his helmet off, revealing a premature shock of silver hair. He's probably in his early forties—a rugby-looking dude who, it must be admitted, had a heck of a punt, 60-plus yards with the roll, and who kicked several extra points as well. It's rare for an individual player to be singled out like this, and I can't figure out why Coach Barnes is addressing so typically anonymous a position as that of the *kicker*, who, despite having played well, did not significantly influence the outcome of the game.

Coach Barnes jabs a finger in the punter's direction. "This social media or whatever they call it, all this *Facebook* foolishness, talking about how y'all were going to come up to Brenham and beat us a

First Game 81

hundred to nuthin'—that's a bunch of bullshit. That shit's gotta stop. We got no respect for that," Coach Barnes says, and a pall blankets all of us. This is a public shaming, as ill-timed as it is accurate. "That's just punk-ass," Coach says, his voice thick.

He can only talk to us *that way,* some of us are thinking, *not to another player on a team he doesn't even* care *about.* And the punter, dissed and outed, looks down, in a way knowing that Coach Barnes, for all his ill will, is correct, and that the punter's day of glory is gone.

I had not known the punter was a Facebook troll who'd been pronouncing such blandishments, but Coach had been keeping tabs; lying in wait, a middle linebacker staying low but then rising up to swat down the pass or to waylay a receiver or runner. And with his venom refined and distilled by the humiliation of our own play.

After an awkward silence the referee says, "All right, on three, *Family,*" and we raise our fists into the circle, our hands on each other's shoulders, and chant "One, Two, Three, *Family!*" and the day is over, or almost over.

We trot back to our sideline, where Coach gestures for us to line up in front of him and sit on the low cinder block wall that parallels the playing field.

It's an unusual seating arrangement. Usually we're gathered around him in an informal half-circle, some kneeling, others standing. This positioning feels almost corporate.

Coach starts out steady and calm, reminding us again that now at least we know what we need to work on. He raises again the necessity of Thursday night practices. "*Just one night per week,*" he says. "We can't win/if you don't/come to *practice,*" he says, and now the venom is hissing out of him like wisps of steam.

All anger is fear.

"Gott *dammit,*" he says, pacing back and forth in front of us. Our defense is sitting down at the far end of the bench, and most of his fury ends up slanting in their direction. He thumps his chest. "Live tackling, this week," he says, with a quiet smile now which, if one didn't know him, might seem malevolent. Well, actually it *is* malevolent—but it's so transparent that it seems somehow less harmful.

Now the Ugly Thing has found him, however, in his wild pacings—as if he has been searching for it like a man agitated at having lost his keys in tall grass—and whether the Ugly Thing has found him, or he has found it, is debatable, but it seems to me now he is standing on some one little certain place on the field where the wrath and fear are coming up into him from far below, flowing through and then out of him, despair unleashed. *Desire is the root of all suffering*, I think, *and he desires to win.*

The spit, the spray, is back; the high screech-voice of fury is back: a thing perilously close to loathing. "This is *ridiculous*. I could tackle better than one-third of you out there!" he shrieks. He says it again and then glares at the defense, daring them to disagree.

No one says anything. Nothing in anyone's expression suggests we disagree with him. To me it seems an irrelevance—we're competing against the Ducks, not Coach—and his choice of that particular fraction, one-third, seems random and curious.

We don't take it personally. We know we are united in our goals and desire. This loss was due to lack of craft and its execution, not any moral failing. We are united in our dedication to craft. Criticism is good. We understand his is delivered in service to our love of and belief in the goodness of the game.

"*Oklahoma drill*," he says again, and for the first time I feel a tickle of concern, for there seems an inestimable paradox here. He is beseeching us to come to practice, and yet he is also promising pain and punishment. I don't think he's thought this through. As well, with our numbers down now to but 19, and with so much of the season ahead, it seems an unnecessary and ill-advised risk. What if we lost more of our starters in this brutal, ferocious, and essentially illegal drill?

The physical distance between Coach and the players fascinates me. It's about five or six yards in the line-in-the-sand space that separates him from us. Coach stands. We sit. I experience that strange and taut empty area as a quivering dynamism: a throbbing, shimmering electrical field, which, despite being at hand, and finite, is also simultaneously impossible to cross or breach. That it is as if we are separated from the face and love of a just and angry God.

And being an artist and an outsider, there is a part of me—a tendril, and maybe my own Ugly Thing—that seeks to poke a finger at this quivering soap bubble of tension. I'm not sure why. Only that I'm uncomfortable with such an imbalance of power and authority. I respect and support Coach, and yet it's unsettling, being a grown-ass man.

I'm reminded strangely of an incident from Kirby's and my adolescence. We had committed one perplexing infraction or another—I can't even remember what it was. There were many, and Mr. Simmons was counseling us to the effect that it was high time we grew up, time we realized not all the world was a playground. We couldn't possibly think we would be able to sally through the world in such an irresponsible fashion, could we? And what in God's green earth had we been thinking?

Kirby, who'd been staring down at the tops of his shoes as if pondering suddenly looked up and raised his hand as if in a classroom to interrupt Mr. Simmons's broadside.

The strangeness of the gesture was enough to give Mr. Simmons brief pause. (I should mention that Mr. Simmons had an aging German shepherd named Waldo; the dog had spent almost no time in the outdoors.)

"Yeah, yeah," Kirby was saying. "I hear all that, but listen, what I want to know is, can we take Waldo coon hunting Saturday night?"

Mr. Simmons had certainly never been coon hunting. Kirby had never been coon hunting. Waldo definitely had never been coon hunting, nor was there any place in Houston where such activity could have taken place.

The question was only what it was: maximum nonsense, gibberish designed to puncture, deflate, and divert the rapid escalation of—what?—an accounting? Mr. Simmons just shook his head, disappointed by our mirth, and our resistance to his counsel. He turned and walked away. Beaten, it looked like.

I have a secret, wrote the poet H.D., *I am alive.*

He needn't have worried, but that's a parent's job.

Here at The Rock, with the cool of night pushing toward us like surf, there is no active intervention to prick and release the tension. Instead, Coach's rage must deflate at its own rate, like a thing born from far below and ultimately unsustainable, up in this green world of the hopeful, the hungry, and the living.

Satisfied that he's encountering neither resistance nor disagreement, Coach shudders for a moment, like a dog shaking off a spray of moisture. He comes back to a place more proximate, I think, to what he considers his better self. And not for the first time do I wonder at what titanic clashings might be going on within him—might always have been going on within him—and of what our part is in them, if any. What positions each of us play in that battle that is not a game.

He gathers us for the post-game prayer. If I'm not mistaken, I think we're all feeling a little fragile, a little off-kilter. I could be wrong. It's like we've just endured what could be, what *is*, a bonding experience, even if it's strangely a negative one. We've still got each other, right, and isn't that a victory? But now there's all this other Coach-disappointed-in-us stuff. It's strange.

"Lord," Coach prays, his body still swollen with fury not just at the loss, but that he had been unable to change things through his will alone. "Lord, please help these young men who are struggling find it in themselves to come to our practices; help them, Father, to learn that we must take the bitter with the sweet. Help them to learn their plays and to not arm tackle. Help them to be men, not boys, so that when they look in the mirror, they can be proud, Oh, Lord. And as always, thank you; thank you for letting us serve you and be your soldiers, for we know that though the few make many, the dead make none. Amen."

Already, I'm starting to realize something beneath the surface that I had glimpsed but not understood in previous seasons. It had been easy to recognize the strivers: the players whose ambitions bubbled with effervescence.

But those most ambitious players had for the most part gone on.

They had either clawed their way into the next level, or had been plucked, swept up by the winds aloft that sought and seek such things.

Those who were left after the others had been broken, jailed, or recruited, are somehow like the finer-grained nuggets who've fallen through the miner's mesh screen. I think we-the-remnants are less aggressive, less motivated to win, and here more for the community and the process, and, again, for the sheer interest, the curiosity of hearing what Coach will say or do next. Several of the players wear T-shirts with his cryptic weekly prayer offering, the inscrutable koan: "The few make many, and the dead make none" emblazoned across the back. (Indeed, stretched across the backs of our larger players, the words appear ominous, even badass.)

We-the-remnants, I'm realizing, are like a throwback to childhood, when winning was not paramount nor losing insufferable, but instead the joy of the game and the sweet surprise of how each next play would unfold was simply a thing that made life more fun and interesting. The game was but an addition, a component, a richness—rather than the thing, life itself.

Of course we signed get-well cards for our teachers. Of course we said *please* and *thank you* and participated daily in the slow accruing work of becoming better: doing our homework, volunteering in the community, mowing lawns for spending money.

The grass kept growing, and we kept mowing. The days and nights were a steady, lulling tide, as we were carried so slowly toward adulthood. Football was a coda or ethos, much as I suppose were our churches—a world unto itself with rules, guidelines, strictures. Football was a world we stepped into when playing as if stepping into a cathedral or chapel on a Sunday—but then stepped back out of, after that hour's service.

Coach, however, has gotten lost inside it—the world of service. *In my father's mansion there are many chambers.* And now he wanders from empty room to empty room with a lantern, searching for what he may no longer even know—*all anger is fear*—and with a few of us following behind him, following the glow.

6

DOGCATCHER

ONLY NINE SHOW UP for the next practice, counting myself. I've gone back and forth about whether I'll throw myself into the grinder, the recently-outlawed Oklahoma drill, though as I draw closer, driving the Prius from Marfa to Brenham, I realize I probably haven't been driving 600 miles to say *No*. You're either in or you're out. On the drive, I spent no small amount of time thinking about how to protect my old knees in the drill. Twisting, trying to get skinny at the last second, and to slip past in a three-foot wide alley, could be super-risky if the tackler went low; not only might I take the blow on my knee, I might take it on the side—the dreaded anterior cruciate ligament tear, $10,000 and 12 months of rehab. Goodbye, autumn hunting season. And at 62, how many are left?

Getting low, trying to deliver a blow with my shoulder rather than taking one—such delivery being the object of the drill for both participants—would only work as long as my tackler didn't do the same thing at the same time, in which case both of us would collide head-on, helmet-to-helmet.

Even once I reached the practice field and was lacing up my cleats, I didn't have a plan, and had only cursorily thought about how to tackle one of our wild runaway running backs when it was my turn to be on the other side of the drill. Going low works, except you need to pick your angle when the runner's coming straight at you. If you go low at the wrong time, all you'll get is a knee to your helmeted head.

There's a reason the drill was outlawed. Truth be told, that windy spring day, three of the other eight are new players; essentially, only five other regulars have willingly shown up for Oklahoma. Lou, of course. Neil, of course. And Kojo, who I can't get a fix on—he's a curious mix of lassitude and earnest ambition; big Ray, and implacable Ernie. If we were playing basketball, we'd have a team, but we're not playing basketball.

Late winter games can be as brutal as they are beautiful. The slow-falling ragged snowflakes obscure the parameters of the game—the painted white stripes that are the underlying logic—so that the game evolves into something far more basic and primitive: surge, push forward, tuck one's shoulder, and lean in farther, legs churning.

Said an old political activist mentor of mine, US Representative Pat Williams: *It is a pleasure to struggle when the cause is just.* The ball is slippery, and hands are cold. When you're cold, it hurts to hit and be hit. The forward pass becomes but a fancy experiment. Time tilts. It's like going from being in your teens or twenties to somewhere in your sixties in but a single day.

But overlooked, I think, is the least traditional season of football, the spring, when for traditional fans and players, there is attendant to all things football the universal motif of the second chance. The old fall season is over, and the preparations for the new season are only beginning. There's the steady solace of the weight room, where no work is ever wasted, and the more time one spends beneath and amid the iron, the more powerful one becomes.

In the spring, there are no external forces pounding one down, and it is not just the body that is being reborn, but dreams, too.

It's a small thing, way down near the bottom of all the things that will be lost in the great burning of climate change and the Anthropocene—the attachment of our rituals and ceremonies to what was once the rock-solid solace of the four seasons—and I feel it strongly there, the day of the Oklahoma drill, as the small band of us gathers with our full armor—helmets, shoulder pads, cleats, gloves, mouth guards—not knowing if we will be thrown to the lions.

Ernie and Nathan are visiting in subdued voices with the concern of parents puzzling over the recent behavior of their teenager. They're trying to figure out how to inspire or motivate more of the players to show up for practice. "We aren't gonna win if they don't know the plays, man," Ernie says, shaking his head, as if this is the most basic truth of human existence.

At The Rock, the birdsong, the scent of the green grass not yet trammeled; the cool breeze and blue sky, with the swelling buds of new leaves burning green in all the trees. And in these last moments, as we gather, waiting on Coach, who's running late, our conversations and demeanors are reflective, even gentle.

There is no fuming, no fury—no outrage at having been whipped by the Ducks.

Ridiculously, through no more taxing an act than getting out of the little car, I've pulled my calf—I didn't get out and stretch often enough on the long drive here—and Lou shows me tricks on how I can stretch it out and get it to stop hurting long enough to practice. Kirby's brought some horse liniment, and Lou shows me how to do toe raises, and even how to walk. A pulled calf is notorious for lingering; it's thought to be what influenced Andrew Luck's decision to retire so early rather than remain trapped forever in the cycles of pain, rehab, injury, pain, rehab, injury.

It's been two years since Kirby and I attended Lou's father's funeral, and in that time Lou hasn't messed around. He's gone back to school, gotten a degree in sports medicine and rehabilitation, and is working at one of Houston's most prestigious hospitals, Memorial Hermann. He's got insurance, a good steady paycheck, and a girlfriend, Lacey, who he tells us he wants to marry.

He walks me through the stretches; tells me he'll put together a plan for me, as other players visit quietly. There's no nervousness, only a great and steady calm. Ray has brought his boombox and it's playing his strange and eclectic mix: some unrecognizable rap song, which several of the players sing along with quietly, sometimes just mouthing the words, the song as familiar to them as might be a nursery rhyme from their childhoods. And then, surprisingly, a country-and-western barroom saga of lost love. And then Lynyrd Skynyrd's "Sweet Home Alabama."

Coach drives up and gets out of his big new truck, weary but inscrutable, deflated but positive, if it's possible to be all of those things at once. I try to read his body language to see if the Oklahoma drill is still on. He's carrying an armload of orange traffic cones and two footballs, and so it seems to me it is.

He is avoiding looking at us, which could definitely be another tell—that he is not happy about what is coming; that it hurts him more than it does us.

No one has put on pads yet. We're waiting for the newly laundered oversized jerseys, which need to go on with the pads; like putting a pillow into a pillow case.

He does not have the duffel bag of clean jerseys.

Coach sets the cones up—it does not occur to me to wonder how he came by them—in an arrangement that is not overly complicated, but in the abstract interior of which might yet reside significant pain. And only then does he look up at us, gathered there waiting on his instruction, his commands; and even as he ambles over to us, still poker-faced, he is distracted but not appearing overly tormented or disheartened. Projecting a business-as-usual vibe—*I'm a coach; coaching is what I do.*

Only now, when he reaches us, does the old familiar kindness begin to manifest. Where does that kindness go within him when it leaves, I wonder? Is he in control of the ability to turn it on and off, or is he merely a vessel and conduit for it? Does it surge in spurts and plumes like Old Faithful, at various hours of the day—as unknown to him or us, in its presences and absences, as sunlight passing through the lazy drift of clouds?

"Oh, this crop of young men," he says to himself, shaking his head.

"What am I to do?" We don't know if he is referring to those who have gathered here before him or to those who are missing.

He repeats the phrase again, speaking to his God, but also to us—like being on a three-way conference call—and then we gather in a tiny circle, holding hands, while he leads us in a prayer which, as always, begins meekly, as from a supplicant, but which, as Coach warms, grows quickly more robust, even chippy, as he gets closer to what I think he considers the good part, which is often some variation on the idea of *Lord, let us be willing warriors for your way and your word; Father, just use us, use us*—the word *smite* is likely to appear—*in Jesus's name, amen.* And we chorus: *Amen.*

Despite the "Onward, Christian Soldiers" quality to parts of it, I like how the players acknowledge there's a thing larger than football, and that football, much less winning, isn't the dominant focus of our endeavor. I like how it unifies us, each man standing next to whomever happens to be there, each random time—all of us united, all of us together. I just wish there were more than nine of us.

"All right, men, get on out there for more warm-ups," he tells us. "Ernie, you lead 'em." And the word *Oklahoma* is not mentioned, nor does the bitterness of rage that afflicted him last week seem to be anywhere present.

We trot out onto the field wearing our helmets and padded pants, but still no shoulder pads, and for the first time I start to suspect we are not going to be pitted against one another; will not be called upon to destroy or even damage one another.

And this is as distinctive a feeling of grace as I have felt in a long time—so much so that I feel almost dizzy with relief and gratitude. I feel committed, too—recommitted—to helping this group of men in any way that I can. *It's just a game*, but really, what isn't? *Action is character*, I tell my writing students.

I love the familiar, lazy start of the warm-ups: Ernie's slow, soft cadence, launching us yet again. "All right, 35 jumping jacks on *move*, jumping jacks on *move*, ready? *Move!*" I love the first coming together, the physical lift of the boat shoving off into the waves yet again, as we chant in cadence, *one-two-three-four*. And even Coach is doing them with us, grinning, seeming again somehow as careful in his words and deeds as a man puffing the just-right breath, seeking to kindle the tiniest ember glow at the edge of darkness, and with colder weather coming on.

Someday I will ask Coach what combination of events transpired to lead him to reverse his decision to run Oklahoma, though I think I know already what it was: grace, and reason. *Why punish the faithful?*

For some reason the guys are still bantering about the brutal hit I took two years ago. "That was Tennessee who missed that block," Lou says, and there is robust confirmation, a general round-robin low renting of Tennessee.

Ernie has incorporated a new stretch into the routine, a yoga sort of thing; a modified hurdler's stretch where, after folding one leg out to the side and extending the other forward, we lie all the way back, as far as we can. I noticed immediately that the bulkier among us—Ray and Neil, notably—are unable to lean all the way back, while others swoon all the way back like swans, as if grateful for the ground to receive us. I'm reminded of Antaeus, who could access his great strength only by being in direct contact with the earth; and lying there on my back, feeling the full good lazy stretch, I watch wisps of cirrus clouds drift past the day-lit quarter moon, directly overhead.

It's a lovely feeling, lying there smelling the grass, listening to the birds, and viewing that elegant moon through the bars of my face mask. I have never beheld the moon in such a fashion; and for a little while time spins away from me, and is carried past with those clouds.

Later, we do cone drills, running intricate W and Z cover routes, linebacker drills. The drill makes Coach feel better, and I like it. Even if you play offense, it improves your craft to understand the defense better. And every member of the team is going to have to play offense and defense this year, and probably a multiplicity of positions within.

Best of all, I think the drill assuages Coach. Almost everyone missed tackles in last week's game, but as a former linebacker, that weakness graveled Coach the most. This, I think, is how he made his peace with not going forward with the Oklahoma business. He's still coaching, still teaching—walking us through the routes, explaining the thinking at each juncture, letting us see the route develop from the quarterback's perspective so that we'll have an extra half-step toward jumping the route, especially on those quick slants. Instead of beating up on us, he's building us up—doing one of the things I think he most wants to do: being his best self.

And watching him, I see more than a glimpse of the coach he was with his 19 consecutive years of winning seasons, and why his defenses were always top-rated. It's one of the hoariest clichés in football that the team that wins the turnover battle almost always wins the game. It's a mindset he's trying to build: you're not just trying to defend a space, but to actually take the football away. The offense has something that belongs to your team, and it's the defense's job to get it back. And maybe to even score. To take it to the house.

●

ANOTHER COACH PRAYER. "Man will let you down," he says, shaking his head, looking at the ground. It almost sounds like in his disappointment he's scolding even God. "Man will let *you down*," he repeats, lost in some dark memory, for now he's shaking his head as if in a trance. "Man will let you down, man will let you down. *Man will let you down.*"

Today, he has a parable. "Y'all know what the most dangerous animal in North America is?" he asks. He's pacing back and forth, challenging us, and though I can often be immune to social and facial cues, somehow I intuit that it is very important to him no one know the answer; that only he know the answer. I flash back almost 40 years. My wife, Elizabeth, and I were sitting in a truck stop diner in Alabama, at maybe two or three in the morning; I don't remember why. Two bleary truckers at another table were having a conversation, one educating the other about a nature program he'd seen on television.

"The *slyest* animal is the red fox," the man lectured. "But the *meanest* damn animal is the American wolverine." He said the word as if speaking the name of a saint or even a deity. As if he had personal experience, there on the interstates around Birmingham, with such a mythic creature, half a world and centuries away. For long years it was a punchline between Elizabeth and me.

I know not to answer, but I know the answer.

"Rhinoceros," Ray says, and Coach grimaces, yelps.

"*No, I said North America!*"

"Bear," says another player—I can't see who—and Coach can't help himself.

"*What kind of bear?*"

"Polar," the player says, and Coach shakes his head.

"Grizzly," says another.

"Nope."

"Hippo?" Ernie asks, from down at the other end of the bench, and once again, Coach is pained deeply.

"*No, I said North America!*" he all but screeches, as if the men are failing a citizenship test.

"Hyena," someone says—they are not jerking his chain; they're just eager to please. Disney animals, I realize—and Coach grits his teeth, hisses again, *North America!*

And now there are no more guesses coming, not for fear of failing, I think, but instead fear of guessing the wrong continent: double jeopardy.

I can't stand knowing the answer. "Wolverine," I whisper only to Lou, who's seated next to me. The first time I heard the word—five, six years old?—I thought it meant a diminutive wolf. Then I looked it up in a field guide: *Gulo gulo*, kind of a cross between a grizzly and a Tasmanian devil.

Coach lowers his voice to a conspiratorial register.

"I'll tell you," he all but whispers. He's still pacing back and forth. "It's the wolverine," he says. "Everything in the forest fears them. Arctic tundra, Canada, North Pole," he says. "Even a grizzly bear, a hundred times their size, is afraid of them. That's what you men need to be: wolverines." Now he gestures toward where Kirby is sitting, and then to a little ant pile next to him.

"And ants. You all need to be like those ants Kirby's sittin' next to. When it rains and the ants' nest gets flooded, they all make a single chain holding onto each other to keep from being swept away," he says. "A chain of little ants a mile long during the time of the great flood," he says. "Think about it. That's what you men are, supporting each other." It's as close as he'll come, I think, to acknowledging we're in a tight spot. That the Diluvian is upon us.

I'm certain he saw a nature special about the wolverine. I can see him crafting the parable of the wolverine, days in advance. A preacher devoted to his craft, shaping his gift to the team, teaching us the ways of wolverines. But the ways of the ant-people: that's improvised; just some common thing his eye fell upon, and which he picked up and converted to, well, love.

I think that's the end of the sermon, or the end of wolverine business anyway, but he veers back to it with a jolt. "What's the biggest, baddest bear in the world?" he asks, and these men, these grown men listen to him as they always do with curiosity and interest.

Sometimes I think he could be telling them almost anything and they would listen intently, taking it deep into their hearts and securing it there in some safe place. There is a school of thought, one to which I subscribe increasingly as I grow older, that you receive what you need only or most when you need it, and to therefore be always observant, noticing what you are being handed daily.

A few moments ago, we'd been ensconced in the snow globe of the four-three defense, where players were being reminded to keep their eyes on the quarterback and to raise their arms, to make the quarterback have to throw over them rather than through or past them. But then just a few seconds later, we're being quizzed on animal fun facts.

Again, the short list of possible answers is lobbed at Coach. Polar bear? Black bear? Grizzly? Even I am confused about this one. Is he referencing some prehistoric species, no longer extant?

"Ko-dee-*ak*," he says, relishing the pronunciation. "Eighteen feet tall," he vows, raising both arms high, and at first I have to stifle a laugh—it'd be like a damn giraffe, a *T. rex*. Where does he get these numbers? I don't argue with him on this point, nor the somewhat fine point that Kodiak *is* a grizzly bear, just a variety that lives on Kodiak Island, and which can get really large from the high proportion of salmon in its diet.

"Even the biggest bear in the world is no match for the wolverine," he says. He lowers one hand down near the ground to show the approximate height of the wolverine. A little larger than a beagle. It seems ridiculous, but later I'll look it up: the Kodiak grizzly is 12 feet tall. And who's to say bears aren't practiced at raising their paws over their head the way humans do? But if they did, well, they still wouldn't reach 18 feet. But in Coach-land, they might come close.

Such a drifty, lovely, tender spring day, approaching the first day of March. Lamb-like. I think of a random line from Walker Percy's great 1961 novel of existential angst, *The Moviegoer*. "Whatever do you all talk about?" asks one character. "Oh, larroes catch medloes."

We've been spared the Oklahoma drill, and we've had a good practice. I think we're better than we were before. Better than we were even this morning, in all ways. We're moving forward.

●

COACH AND I meet the next morning in Hempstead, bright and early. It's his third job, or his fourth, if you count the unpaid hours of coaching. I keep thinking back to Coach Chaffee talking about what might have been, if only Coach hadn't had bad breaks. I don't know many people who juggle four jobs, not at any age, and certainly not at the age of 52. Here, too, it tends to give credence when Coach offers workplace consultation to his players, urging them to go back to school, and to take the steady job.

His third job is that of dogcatcher. He'd had a hard afternoon a couple of weeks ago, having to lie in wait for a Siberian husky abandoned by its owners and which had gone quickly feral.

"I saw him walking by my house earlier in the day," Coach says.

"And that very night he went over to this neighbor lady's house and murdered her goat." His usually baritone voice rises an octave in his outrage and disbelief, and I marvel at what a strange and small world it can be: how in the autumn I can be in Montana visiting with a rancher who is indignant about grizzlies laying waste to his pigs, or wolves targeting his bleating herd of goats, only in winter to be encountering a variation of the same complaint, in the dwindling semi-rural landscape little more than an hour north of Houston.

This Sunday morning, Coach pulls into the parking lot a few minutes after eight, motions for me to climb in. His tinted windows are rolled up; I can only see the shadow of him within. Gospel music is blaring. He's got his iPhone plugged in and he's in an ebullient mood, singing along with bass harmony. A Bible is open on his dashboard, and the inside of his big truck reminds me of a shrine in India: pictures of loved ones gone by, and scripture pasted on the glove box. It's a lot to take in at once, and I regret I did not examine the Bible to see what page it was open to. Somewhere pretty much perfectly in the middle, it looked like to me. Psalms? Proverbs? Just before things turned bad.

He shakes my hand heartily—I've never seen him this happy, this *unfettered*—and he tells me he's getting in the mood for church, that we can visit in another minute, as soon as this song is over. He resumes singing along with it, more merrily than ever, and it surprises me. His is a deep, rich voice, practiced: another of his many talents.

He could be in a robe in the front row, leading the choir. He's the real deal, still singing as he drives, following a bewildering series of back roads and alleys, stop signs and neighborhoods, working his way toward the outskirts of town, the bottomlands of the Brazos River, where it floods so frequently that only the very poorest people can live there; and then a little farther, to the place where no one can live, right beside the lazy wooded river, where the dogs are kept.

He's never slow, it occurs to me. He's not frenetic, but he never stops to just *be*. For me to try to intervene in his daily flow, interrupting him to ask questions such as *What scripture is the Good Book open to there?* or *What song was that, and why does it speak to you?* would be a little like killing a mockingbird.

How many middle-aged men—stranded firmly somewhere in the socioeconomic geologic laminae of thin black earth that is the historical marker, the telltale seam between lower class and middle class—are singing their hearts out on their way to their third job on a Sunday morning before church?

He's on his way, it occurs to me, to go feed an imprisoned pack of cur dogs.

●

THE FIRST YEAR I played for the Express, my desires were to carry the ball. I envisioned plays designed where I could slash a quick gap, a sliver of daylight, into the end zone: the holy land for running backs. Now that I'm older and have spent more time with Coach and the players, my imaginings now are of simply remaining in the backfield, taking a fake handoff, and then cut-blocking a defensive end: protecting the quarterback.

At its best, the game is a microcosm of life writ larger. It enables some of us to see aspects of life we might otherwise have missed.

Me at 62, 63, wanting now simply to throw a good block, downsizing dramatically my ambitions from when I was spry and a mere 60, are a new sweet diminishment: wanting to serve my friends, my teammates; to spend some time once again and—suddenly!—late in life with my best friend, Kirby.

My partner, Carter, says often that paying close attention can be an act of love.

●

WHILE WE'RE DRIVING, a call comes in to one of the two iPhones Coach has plugged in that is charging. He turns the volume down on the one that's playing the church music and answers the other. It's his wife, Mattie. She's worried about their daughter, who came down from Dallas for the weekend but then left.

"I told her not to leave before I got back," Coach says. Mattie's on speakerphone. "I'm with that reporter I was telling you about," Coach says. His wife pauses at this, then parses her words.

"Well. Call me back when y'all are through."

"All right," Coach says, and hangs up. His voice is gentle, but his rapture is gone. In its place there's the quietude of parental fret, and he does not turn the music back on, just drives.

"I'm in no rush, man," I tell him. "I can get out and walk if you'd like to call her back. I'm sure she's stressed."

Coach thinks this over, nods. "Oh yeah, she's stressed." His voice is tight. But he keeps driving. He dials her back and begins the debriefing. "She's just acting up," Mattie says. "She said she didn't come home to talk about any of that. I told her she had to, but instead she up and left. So I told her bye. Tony, I don't know. Something is very wrong . . . No, she's already gone, driving all the way back to Dallas."

Coach says, "I told her to wait to leave till I got back." A silence, then he nods again. "All right, I'm going to talk to her. I'll call you later," he tells his wife. "We'll pray about it." He tells her it's all they can do. "Don't be worried," he tells her. "I know you do."

"I do," Mattie confirms. "I sure do."

"She's 30 years old," Coach says. *Tony.* "We've told her how to be and what to do and not do. We've helped her. I don't know what else to say, you know, just to keep telling her we love her."

Mattie says, "Uh huh."

"I'll call when I'm done," Coach promises. "Bye-bye," she says, and hangs up, and the distance between joy and the thing that is so often just a few yards shy of despair is back in the world and upon us. The reflexive response from Coach, the hot read, the checkdown, is prayer and faith. Big words, and not the kind of words I like to use or even talk about. *No ideas but in things*, I tell my writing students. If you can't paint a picture of it, don't use the word. Not what it's *like*, but the thing itself. You can paint a picture of a woman praying, or a man possessed by faith or lacking faith—but you cannot paint the picture of the thing, prayer, itself.

We turn down a long narrow caliche road, dazzling as bone as it cleaves a straight line through the green foliage of spring. The trees on either side of the road are still bare, but the vegetation on the ground is like a green fire. After my having been up north, in all the snow and all the gray, it looks edible.

We come to a locked gate and a chain-link fence: the Hempstead water treatment plant, a series of half a dozen giant tanks with catwalks spiraling around them. Rust blossoms on the walls of the tanks. Vines creep up the chain-link fences and catwalks. The road is straight as a ruler, and it strikes me that all over the world, this balmy spring day, parents in all walks of life, at all socioeconomic levels, are having these same conversations: these affairs of the heart that are always so much more vexing when they involve parenting—the one relationship no one can ever walk all the way away from.

I get out and open the gate. Coach drives on through, and I lock it back, then get in the truck and we drive on toward the wandering line of trees that tells me the river is just beyond.

Despite the lush green fields, the landscape is blighted—on our left, several acres appear to be used as a dump—a plastic tricycle, toy plastic basketball set, plastic water bottles crushed and cracked and graying in the sun. But at least it doesn't smell. As if it once was a dump, but that the dump has moved on somewhere else, and there are only these ghosts. An old barbecue grill, an ancient full-size fire truck fading to rust, wheelless and sinking down into the sea of brush.

We pass more water storage facilities with signs warning that the tanks are open and that people can fall into them: *Stay Away.* We drive to the very end of the road, at the edge of the forest, where the lost dogs are kept.

Upon our approach, they begin howling and wailing—equal in decibels to Coach's gospel song blaring through the glass just a short while ago.

The dogs hurl themselves against the chain link of their kennels.

They're all young and healthy, athletic, spirited—and being received with such enthusiasm, after having been prepared to see the depressed and listless state of the long-ago abandoned, feels remarkably like being needed, even wanted.

It's a job. How, 12 years after the fact, can the Great Recession still be so emblazoned in those who were nearly done in by it? Never say *no* again to the opportunity of work. There is no work that is not meaningful. Work is dignity. The absence of work, when it is what is most needed, is the absence of dignity. The absence of work relegates the one who struggles to the passive duty of victimhood, waiting and hoping, rather than acting.

As the dogs bay and yap, we pass through another locked gate—Coach has so many keys—and into an old shed that's filled with various medicines, like a vet's supply room, along with cleaning products and drums of dog food. All of this energy, and all of these resources, being spent way back at the end of a dead-end road, at the edge of the swamp, on a population of lost dogs.

They are not lost, Coach says. Instead, they simply have been turned out by their owners who no longer want them. Abandoned.

We scoop their food from a 55-gallon drum into buckets to carry out to the lost nation. Their clamant, ragged chorus is a little stress-inducing, but not as much as I might've guessed. Instead, it's almost a sound like exhortation, urging us to hurry, *hurry*. Almost like a kind of cheering.

These are nobody's dogs, will likely never be anyone's dogs. I don't have the heart to ask how long the expected stay is for each of the current residents. They look healthy and strong, every one of them; as if they've already been here a long time, and that each has become comfortable and familiar with the routine of their days.

Most of the dogs are pit bulls. The vast majority of them are males. Coach deploys me to work the high-pressure hose, spraying a nozzle of water into their buckets in each kennel. Each bucket has been depleted a similar amount; almost a gallon's worth. I guess they get thirsty from all the barking, and from a general nervousness; though I like to think too there are moments in each day where things slow and then are still for them—slants of yellow sunlight passing through the bare limbs of the forest, and the lull of birdsong. Time for them to think their dog thoughts, and look around at each other. This is where they are now.

One of them is not here, or not yet all the way here. Was here, but is no longer. A white dog, looking much like an Arctic wolf, was in one of the kennels but escaped. She pushed her way against a wire panel that another worker, a new guy, had done a poor job of fastening. That was three days ago. Rather than running for home, the white wolf has been hanging around, untrappable. I think of her as Blanca, the tragic mate of Lobo, King of the Currumpaw, the old bandit wolf who wreaked havoc on New Mexico's cattle herds a century ago.

She posts up at a distance, in the little copse of trees near the river's edge, inhabiting the space between her old life and freedom. Coach points her out to me, where she watches us from the woods, about 50 yards distant. "She's been trapped once," Coach says, looking over at her with a side-eye. "She's going to be hard to catch again."

Each day, Coach leaves open the gate to her old pen, fills her pail with fresh water, and puts food in her pan. She stands out amid the winter-killed stalks of cane and thistles, watching him, never coming closer, and never letting anyone approach her.

But each next morning when Coach returns, the pan is empty.

I think she is staying nearby for the company of the other dogs. That it is all she needs; she no longer has need for the company of humankind. She has seen and experienced enough of that. Though still, maybe she is torn. At one point, watching Coach and me feed and water all the dogs, she lies down in a strip of green grass out amid all the weed skeletons, and watches us. She does not wag her tail, nor does she look wishful in any way. But at least she is watching us, and observing Coach as he uses the high-pressure hose to spray the cement floors with a mixture of industrial soap and bleach, sending all the day before's shit and piss down the drain. All the dogs hide in their barrels during this brief cleansing; and afterward, the concrete floors are shining and sparkling, wiped clean.

From her repose in the mild sun, Blanca watches Coach—he's changed into his high rubber muck boots—work in service to her packmates. How important it is, I think, to the world's balance to have one out there who is unreachable, if not irredeemable. The two are not the same, Coach and Blanca, but at some point they might as well be.

It's a strange place to be. I feel not so much that I've stepped into the past, but some short distance into the future. The ragged weed-yard, the crumbling concrete water tanks housing the city's supply of water, even as eons of trash were once stored back here, with remnant archipelagos of refuse still lurking. And with the dog waste being washed back into the watershed and the downstream heavy metal detritus of the Brazos elevating into that same watershed—well, it's kind of a free-for-all shitshow. How can something so vital, *water*, be treated so poorly, taken completely for granted?

There is no money in this city for a system upgrade. Everyone is making do. There is barely the budget for a man to mow the grass around one of the tanks for a few dollars per hour. In the glittering cities that surround Hempstead and Brenham, there is now, briefly, a sparkling affluence reminiscent of the desert outposts of Middle East oil sheiks. The coronavirus is just starting to give wobble to certain socioeconomic assumptions that are proving now to be as vulnerable as almost any other myth-building.

How the elite will stamp their feet when or if, say, water is no longer available or usable. How quickly confidence and blind assurance will turn to fear. How cheaply society is getting by, hiring Coach for a few hours a week, and a few dollars per hour, to keep the roving packs of goat-murderers off the streets.

The dogs' howling has ceased; most of them, fed and watered and clean, are wagging their tails, now nose-to-nose with their next-door kennelmates. "These are the best-looking strays I've ever seen," I tell Coach, and he says, "Yeah, I do a pretty good job with them."

Vultures are roosting in the dying trees behind the water tanks. As the morning warms, their enormous wings become functional again; they lift off into slow, crooked flight. Dead branches break free from the force of the vultures' labored, initial thrusts, making it seem as if they're dropping bombs into the thorns and thickets. They wheel and flap in low circles around the dump, remembering the good times when it was up and running, eyeing the terrain for the return of trash, or some item overlooked, despite their daily gleaning and picking.

Coach and I carry the empty pails back to the shed. We pass through a series of flimsy gates and five-dollar padlocks, as if this is not the end of the world, but instead some high-security installation. Coach's key ring is so loaded it jangles like a jailer's.

He and I wash our hands with vinegar, then flap them to dry quickly as it evaporates; there is no soap, no paper towels. A redbird is singing as we walk back to the truck. We feel fuller by the simple pleasure of having done something. There's so much work to do in the world. How will it ever all get done? And yet, the world keeps turning.

We climb back into the truck—all the dogs watch us silently—and I'm reminded of a new thought in evolutionary biology regarding the relationship between dogs and their masters. Humankind has long promoted the story that we bred them for companionship—that a lonely wolf or coyote came up to one of our campfires, edged a bit closer into the throw of firelight, and allowed itself to be domesticated; that we went on to breed and select subsequent generations for various social attributes.

The new thinking however is that the wolves or coyotes came in from the dark and recruited us: that they trained us to feed and care for them; that they manipulated our sentiments to achieve a life where one of our primary tasks is to serve them. They were here first—preceding us by millions of years—and when we came along, they sought to find ways in which we could be useful, and allowed us to stay.

The dogs have manipulated our capacity for deep love, for deep emotions, much as the tropical fruit embeds its seed deep within the most delicious flesh. Do the dogs serve us, or do we serve them? Does it matter? If a dog is a god, doesn't the deity still need us to serve and worship it, in order to continue being a god?

I would so much rather be a player than a coach. The players serve the coach, and while it might seem the coach has all the power, it is the players I think who have all the freedom: the free will to serve the coach, or to not serve the coach.

And what a frightening feeling that must be for the deity at times, as the deity waits and wonders: are they going to love me, or not love me? Obey, or not obey? The god is powerful but without free will, the god might as well not even exist. Perhaps, even, does *not* exist, without that first blossom of love, or of need.

●

JUAKITA CALLS. COACH is achingly tender with her. He has some questions about different things, but Juakita evidently tells him she still doesn't want to talk about any of those. "You're not in the mood for what?" Coach asks. Juakita clarifies it again. "Okay," Coach says, practiced, as a parent, at meeting the child where she is, with a skill set he does not execute on the field. Apples and oranges.

"Well, all right," he tells her. "I'm going to get back to work—no, I'll talk to her later. Keep praying," he advises her. "That's all we can do." He listens for a moment, unblinking—hanging on her every word—then says "All right," and hangs up.

A crisis is averted, it seems. He's not jubilant, but feels better. These little victories, hour by hour. He swings by the old dumping grounds, which someone, perhaps with keyed access, is still using. He gets out and picks through the ruins: a crushed baby stroller, an armless plastic doll, a plastic bag filled with empty aluminum cans.

He picks up a splendid length of lumber, a 12-foot length of 2x4, which has a few bent nails sticking out of one end, but nothing that can't be salvaged. Maybe he can even use the nails themselves: pull them out, then pound them straight again.

To the west, a purpling reef of clouds is building, looking like one long dike that holds back a roiling sea. Coach waves away a fly that's come through the window. "Any time you see a bunch of flies flying around all over the place, gonna rain," he says. Then without the least bit of pause he says, "Tell me, Rick, tell me what you want."

I'm surprised. I thought we were just riding and bullshitting. I don't have time to think or be tactful. So I just straight up ask. "You started over a year ago, getting ready, training them. You started a whole year early. And yet nothing changed. They're still not coming to practice. It's the same old deal. It's like, *fuuuuck*. They might not even last the season," I say. "So what are you going to do? What *can* you do?" I look out the window. "We *suck*."

Coach drives in silence for a little while. He does not say, "Y'all don't suck." He does not say, "Don't worry." I get the sense he shuts down a little, and only half heard me. Is maybe thinking about his wife, and about Juakita. Is maybe wondering if he should gas up today, or wait on the price drop that might come Monday, a penny or two per gallon less.

"I'm gonna use that board to build a porch," he says. "Later in the year, I'm gonna have a shrimp boil for all the fellas, over at my house." Is he being gracious, politely ignoring my faux pas, my unmannered bluntness?

He appears to be trafficking totally in denial. We pass a leaning shack, the house overgrown with bushes, the yard bare and dusty, the front porch sagging and perforated with rot. A man in a white sleeveless shirt stands in the darkened doorway with a coffee cup, just about to step out into the light. The man freezes like a wild animal when he sees us looking his way. He appears ready to take a step back into the house to hide. But Coach waves, gives a shrill *Whoop!* and the man grins, a flash of teeth in the shadows, whoops back, and just like that, Coach has his Sunday morning ebullience back.

As we pass through the neighborhood of tiny houses and neat trailers with plastic pinwheel flowers lining their driveways, Coach waves at one resident after another, and they wave to him. Many of them are mowing their tiny lawns. To describe each yard as a postage stamp is generous.

It's like being in a parade—so much Sunday morning good cheer, so much waving—and we pass by one small house with an empty chair on the front porch.

"That's where I saw Ray sitting, smoking a cigarette after a workout one day. He lives with his mother. He just got out of prison," Coach says. "He's working hard. He's making a new start."

"I didn't know he'd been in prison," I say. The phantasmagoric quantity of tattoos Ray has causes me to refocus and recalibrate. "*Wow.*" And I'm more proud of Ray than ever for making all the practices, and all the games.

"Yeah, well, there's a lot of stuff other folks on the team don't know," Coach says. "They come to me with it. I just carry it. Like Wyatt," he says. "Wyatt's taking a year off, doing what's right for him. He's got a drinking problem; is trying to stop. Lost his license. He's got problems with his folks. He went to church with me last year, and he told me his dad asked him why he went to church with a bunch of n*****s."

"Damn," I say.

"Ah, they're idiots," Coach says, in a way that lets me know he's sorry for them. Sorry for Wyatt, who for a long time was the sole white guy on the team. And even though Wyatt's taking some time away from the game this year to get his head right, he still stays in touch with Coach. *So many projects.* By my estimation, it seems about half of them are going well and the other half, not so much. "And isn't that the way," as John Prine sings, "that the world goes round?"

We're headed back to McDonald's. Coach invites me in for a bite before he heads on to church. And I get on the road back to Marfa all day into the westering sun. I've given up hearing from him about what his Plan B is, with us in a world of trouble already, just one game into the season. There is much about him that is inscrutable and which, I assume, is that way by design. I've never been one to push. If someone wants to tell me something, they will. And if they don't want to, then they shouldn't. It's not like a court of law.

But he opens the tap. It took 10 minutes, but it's coming out now, as if from a deep well: a well in which the water level has been dropping steadily.

"It's this generation of kids," he says. "They don't know how to work. They're used to having everything handed to them. They just wanna sit around lookin' at their phones, eatin' Cheetos and jackin' off." He shakes his head. "This generation," he says again. We ride for a while in silence: I'm not comfortable agreeing, since he's talking about my teammates, and don't know what to say.

"I've been thinking about taking a break from football next year," he says. "We may lose all 10 of our games if we don't start getting more show up for practices." More silence. "I've been thinking about opening a gym," he says then, his voice thick with emotion.

I liked the training idea. I know Coach would miss like hell sending his men out on the field to do battle. He would miss watching the plays unfold, miss the juices flowing through the old corridors, sunlight flooding the hallways in his brain when one of his receivers catches a touchdown; or when one of his linebackers—one of his proxies, his disciples—makes a solid hit. But I can see it—the gym—working.

"There's no need to invest in a bunch of high-end equipment," I tell him. "You could just keep doing what you've been doing, old school. Flipping tractor tires, running up hills. Carrying buckets of water. I think people are hungry for that," I say. "A boot camp. Call the gym Old School."

"Me and Lou talked about it last night," Coach says. "He got fired a couple of days ago. He's looking for work anyway."

"What? *Fired?*"

"Yeah, his boss was afraid Lou was going to take his job. So he fired him for being a few minutes late twice last week."

"Shit," I say, "that's not right. Is that even legal?" Sweet Lou! One of the most conscientious, hardest-working players on the team; a man devoted to helping people, fellow athletes particularly, heal. What the fuck?

We reach the McDonald's. Coach has decided he's too late to make it to church on time, so we go inside and order more coffee, some orange juice, an egg-and-sausage sandwich.

Everyone is sitting close together, or standing in line shoulder-to-shoulder, breathing over each other as they stretch on their toes to read the overhead menu. Many people are dressed in bright new clothes, even suits, coming from or going to church, it seems. One tall thin older man, his wide smile flashing innumerable gold teeth, hails Coach with great enthusiasm, and they visit for half an hour, never once mentioning football, but instead regaling one another with near-misses of their misspent youth. How glad they are now to be churchgoers. They shake their heads as if in disbelief that they got out, or were saved, always by something larger than even their own stubborn, if formidable, will; pulled always from the grip of one disaster or another. Amazed that they are still among the living, but prospering. Laughing, having breakfast together, on a beautiful spring morning in central Texas. And I realize, with a shock, Coach's friend, the man I have been describing as old, is probably my age.

It's not so much like looking back in time, but instead, strangely, like looking forward in time: seeing a glimpse of life after football. As if there could ever be such a thing.

There is no more metaphor. This is the year when metaphor went away. Things were only what they were. Blinders were lifted and truths revealed. A lot of it wasn't pretty, to say the least. All are connected, in sickness and in health; that's why it's called *pandemic*. The wave towered over us, so close to crashing down we could feel its chill. It blocked the sun at times. I don't mean metaphorically—I mean, there were eclipses that year.

Coach worked as a dogcatcher when he wasn't working us like dogs. He caught up as many strays as he could and fed them. It's what he does in the world.

⑦

ASS-WHIPPING

THE MUSIC AT RED Raider stadium is so ominous, there's nothing to do but laugh. I'm standing on the 50-yard line—Saturday night lights, a giant stadium in Baytown, Texas—staring at a wall of 11 Red Raiders, their pants and jerseys bright red, their mirrored helmets black as bowling balls.

They are only 10 yards away: muscular, a faint sheen of perspiration on their arms and faces. They look hungry, eager, focused, lined 11 abreast. It reminds me of the way that a band of horses will line up on the Montana prairie, a single long skein of them evaluating your approach: poised, wild, powerful. Other.

Unlike the horses, these Red Raiders are not going to run away from us, but at us.

I, and three others of us, are the first line of defense against the red wave that is about to come. The Houston Red Raiders are bigger, stronger, faster, and meaner. We don't know that yet. We're hopeful, earnest; happy getting to play the game we love. The field is Astroturf, yet another of my old man nemeses. On it, players run faster, making collisions unsustainably brutal. But there is a sleek aesthetic to it that I find as alluring as it is injurious under the blast of the stadium lights, visible from outer space.

The green carpet is greener and the white hash marks are precise, making it easier to run the 5-yard outs, the 7-yard slants: identifying precisely the inflection points where one cuts back on a 12-yard curl pattern.

The yard lines themselves—40, 50, 40 again, and so forth—are identified with mathematical concision.

We're bathed in a sea of light, struggling in a snow globe of white light so ferocious it seems it will scald, sear, cauterize.

The Red Raiders' kicker is a giant of a man. He towers over the football on its tee. He looks left and right, checking on his soldiers, then takes several quick steps toward the ball, clubs it with his big foot. The ball goes sailing deep, and the horde of them rushes at us, exactly like the hounds of hell unleashed.

For the rest of the night, every time the Red Raiders score, they have to kick it off to us again. And all night, they will be kicking off, running down the field and crashing into us, crushing us as if we are toy crickets constructed of balsa wood. I'm proud of my teammates. No one has fumbled nor have we given up a single interception—but the other team is again bigger, stronger, faster. They also like to inflict pain before the night is over. Woodard, our little defensive back, will have such a bad concussion he will have to pull over driving home to Brenham, his night vision not working. He'll rest in the back seat, waiting for first light, not so much lulled by the swoosh of passing traffic as instead narcotized, suspended in some limbo-land between crushing pain and occasional relief, where one exists moment by moment, with no goal or ambition other than for the heart to beat once more, and then once more, and again. As if the heart is a crank ratcheting against the slow gears that both lower and raise the curtains of night each day. But all this will come later, in its time. First we must play the game.

Before the night is over, giant Quincy, playing on his damaged heel, will be out by halftime. Lou will damage his Achilles, on which he's already had two surgeries. I'll end up with broken ribs—I don't know this yet—as will big Chandler. I'll have my bell rung on one hit in which once again I fly a great distance, and then again with a brutal helmet-to-helmet head-on collision that snaps my head back as far as it will go, tearing neck muscles.

The bad thing about cracked or broken ribs is, if you keep playing and take another hit, they could fracture and puncture an already-bruised lung.

Why am I telling all this as backstory? I think because it is—was—too physically traumatic to inhabit in the present tense.

Ernie will twist his knee so badly he'll have to finish the game in a brace. He's our only center, who initiates each play by hiking the ball to the quarterback; without him, the game cannot go forward. All night, Kirby will be running from one end of the field to the other, tending to the fallen like a Civil War doctor wandering the battlefield.

Corey will play the entire game on a twisted ankle, unwilling to come to the sideline and cut the tape off because it would swell so much he couldn't keep playing. The evening—my 63rd birthday—is a liquidation, an annihilation.

Our numbers, which were an impressive 20, will be down to about 14.

The leading edge of coronavirus has spilled across both the Atlantic and the Pacific. Just up the road in Austin, the South by Southwest music festival has been canceled, and the world feels even more momentous, historic, challenging than it has been, which was already significant, with the quarantines, rations, and hoarding. It feels as I imagine it might have during the first and second World Wars.

Even before the bloodletting, our numbers were so reduced that I've advanced to being a starter on the kickoff team. I've become competent—learning the craft, the angles and assignations, well enough. Carter has come down from Bozeman, has curled her hair. Because it's my birthday. We're hoping to go out to dinner somewhere in Houston afterward. Get a fancy hotel room. I brought lavender Epsom salts to soak in, as I do after every game. They make the house smell nice. They make the skin smooth. Maybe Mexican food. I'm always ravenous after a game.

The stadium, the field, is bathed in light. We have 5 fans in the giant stadium and the Red Raiders have only about 10. It's like that scene in *The Matrix*, where Neo is down in the empty subway tunnel, waiting throughout eternity for the train that never comes.

We've come far. The Texas Express has to play yet again, not for any glory or adulation, but for the love of the game itself. It's a pure thing, in a world so wrought with impurity as to sometimes seem, if one glances too closely, as fragmented as a funhouse mirror.

On the field, the lines of sight are finite, clean, spare. One's self, and 21 other selves, swerving and veering in arcs and parabolas, though other times in brutal straight-line vectors.

Straight out of the gate, they hit us in the mouth. The old boxing adage, "Everybody's got a plan until they get punched in the face," is so true. I'm lined up, as always, on the front line to guard against the possible onsides kick; but if the kicks sails deep, my job is to turn and sprint back toward whichever teammate has caught the ball, to reassemble into a fluid swarm: to create a wedge, to hopefully escort our runner back up the field.

The Red Raiders line up. Twenty yards away from me is tall, rangy, muscular, with dreadlocks halfway down his back—a Richard Sherman–looking dude: number 29. He leans forward, eager with a malice I do not associate with Sherman, however. I don't really give it much thought—there'll be time for that later. And I tense as their kicker approaches the ball and sends it deep over our front line's heads. We turn as one and sprint back toward our goal line, to set up there to receive their mad rush.

I'm about halfway back to where our guy has caught the ball when Sherman overtakes me. Out of the corner of my eye I see him veer out of his way to crash into me from the side. He shoves both long arms out as hard as he can and sends me flying. I land on my chin and skid a good distance as he veers back toward the play. He doesn't make the tackle on our ballcarrier.

No penalty flag was thrown—*Home cooking*, goes the adage, where fewer penalties are thrown against the home team. And despite my shoulder feeling separated and my own elbow having driven itself into my ribs upon impact with the Astroturf, and my helmeted head bouncing off the Astroturf, and my rehabbing knee also striking the turf hard—I got up quickly to rejoin the play in case there was a fumble and a tackle to be made.

The play was already finished however, and, to show Richard Sherman he hadn't hurt me I trotted over to number 29—I think he might've believed I was going to remonstrate with him—and gave him the old Andrew Luck treatment; gave him a low five as I passed, as in, *That's your fastball?*

It's true that my affected cavalier tone was marginalized a bit by the fact that I was hopping, unable to yet put full weight on that leg—and I understood again, in a new way, why there are three units on a team: offense, defense, and special teams. I felt an overwhelming gratitude to the rest of the team as I gimped off—first play!—and gratitude, also, that I was not expected to go straight to offense; that I had some time to rest, to try to get my ringing head clear, and my shoulder feeling right again, and to assess whether I was competent.

The hit had been violent and illegal, but look, I was walking, wasn't I? Coach swatted my hand, asked if I was all right.

"He blocked me in the back!" I said—not really an answer, just indignation. Coach studied me for a minute—the quick-look concussion assessment, I guessed—then said, encouragingly, "Walk it off," and turned his attention greedily to the moment at hand, the first play by our offense.

It was an illegal block, but I felt partly responsible for it: for assuming if my back was turned, he wouldn't hit me, that he might run past me, but would not go out of his way to run over me; a penalty so egregious it is given the maximum yardage, 15 yards.

Pain is famous for its isolating qualities, as likewise are concussions. I wandered over to where Carter—one of those five fans on our side of the giant gleaming stadium—was standing on the track in the chill coastal breeze, her arms crossed, concern and unhappiness on her face.

"He went out of his way to get to you," she said, shaking her head. It seemed to me she might've been a little confused, too. "That was *mean*," she said. She might've been a little confused too, as in, *I thought you said you loved it*, and, *Exactly why did you invite me down to a game to watch this?*

"I'll be careful," I tell her, and head back to the sidelines. We've got another visitor on the sideline, an ex-player done-good, Desmond Lockett, who's gotten a contract to go play semi-pro at a higher level for a team in Virginia. With a wild clown-like frizzy Afro and delicate, even feminine features—he, like me, probably weighs all of 165 pounds—he's dyed half his hair bright yellow, the other half blue: left brain, right brain.

He's been super chill, tossing the ball back and forth with our team, catching long passes one-handed as a strip of flypaper catches a gnat or fly. And when he asks me how I'm doing—my collision did not go unnoticed—I lament again, "The son of a bitch clipped me!"

This is one of the effects of concussion—you fail to answer the questions. It's not that you necessarily get the answers wrong, though that can definitely happen. Instead, it can be like you're separated, quarantined, in your own snow globe within the larger, more global one. It's a little eerie, also a little wondrous, but you feel a slight sense of unease, sensing accurately that you're not quite as fully connected to your people, your community, as you once were.

They don't know that my ribs and shoulder are hurt. They're studying me for the bell ringing, the concussion, and my knee.

"Keep walking," Desmond says. "It'll go away. Don't stop." His voice is calm and gentle, slow and quiet amid the play-by-play announcer over the loudspeaker. His sentences are short but explanatory, direct, no matter who he is speaking to. I listen to him counsel a receiver that even though the defense is cleverly disguised, it's really nothing more than a Cover Two.

What a big old goofy, mixed-up world. Desmond's style could not be more antithetical to Coach's volcanic spewings, the gurgling fumaroles of curses, the raging apoplexy. And in my concussed state, Desmond's calm advice is almost hypnotic.

I thank him and continue striding the sideline, agitated. Out on the field, we're getting shut down. We punt, and the Red Raiders run it back down close to the end zone. They complete an easy wide-open pitch and catch, which doesn't even register to me as a touchdown, meaning I need to get back out on the field and receive another kickoff.

Instead, I wander back over to Kirby. Miraculously, the pain is leaving my knee. *Where does it go?* I wonder. Does it disappear into the atmosphere? Does it seek to gather and coalesce—recoalesce—elsewhere? Kirby gives me a couple of Motrin. He says I can take four and asks if it hurts to breathe. *Hell yes*, I tell him.

"You probably shouldn't go back in," he says. Carter is with him, and agrees.

"Ah," I say, "I can't *not*. I already feel like I'm taking from them. I have to give something."

"They understand," Carter says. "But you can give in other ways. You can find other ways to serve them."

I shake my head. "Quitting doesn't feel right," I say. But also, I just really want to keep playing.

Out on the field, the Red Raiders keep missing the extra point, but we keep jumping offsides, giving them other attempts. In my bruised brain, it seems to me they're only kicking a field goal attempt.

What an amazing thing the brain is, yet ultimately how delicate, how easily tipped off-kilter by a violent blow, certainly, but also by too little water, too little food, too much sugar, too little sleep, too much cold, too much heat. How did we ever even *get* here?

Kirby is saying something. "If you cracked a rib and get hit again, it can fracture and puncture a lung," he says. "Don't let it get hit again."

"How will I know if that happens?" I ask.

"Your pee will turn orange, red, or pink," he says. I think about Desmond's hair.

"Kickoff team!" Coach shouts. The Red Raiders have finally made their extra point.

Does respect come before love, or does love lead to respect? I'm confused. It's silly. It's just a game with fewer than 20 spectators, but I'm in. It's silly, but more than silly: dangerous. I'm "in" to my family and providing for them, too, right? And how does my getting ass-whipped serve my family?

This isn't ego, which it might have been as a young man—toxic masculinity. This is something else. Call it toxic loyalty, toxic sweetness. I don't know. It also feels a little like addiction.

These men are not my blood brothers—not B.J. or Frank, for whom I would go into war far more brutal than this—but are brothers nonetheless, if only because it is the word they use when addressing me. I am hungry to cross this bridge. I need and want to cross this bridge, and I do believe action speaks louder than words.

I run out onto the field. Sweet Lou, as always, is out there next to me. And now Desmond, as ostentatious as Odell Beckham Jr. himself, is walking out onto the field for the first time, with just a hint of urgency in his step. He's counseling me, lecturing me right out there on the 50-yard line, with God and 45 Red Raiders from hell watching, while that doom-chant *Wizard of Oz om-om* marching-to-death music is playing.

"Keep your head on a swivel," Desmond says. "Don't let him do that again. And right before he hits you, turn in square up like this"—little Desmond crouches, puts both fists up like a boxer—"and hit him, throw upward with your hips. Put your hips into it."

"Okay," I say.

Number 29, Richard Sherman, is watching us, and I have no idea what he is thinking. For all I know he thinks Desmond is coaching me up to put a shiv, or my ballpoint pen, in his spleen. For now the ball's being kicked deep again, and I fall back, then square up—there he is, suddenly in my grill again. I do as Desmond says, but it doesn't work. Again I find myself sailing through the air like a balsa wood glider tossed by children at recess, which, it occurs to me mid-flight, most of these men were a scant 10 or so years ago. And once more I bounce when I hit. Number 29 has moved on to other prey—is pursuing the ballcarrier, my teammate, little Melvin.

I jump up and pursue the play. *Play all the way through the whistle* is another of football's life lessons. And here, as is often the case, it pays dividends, for little Melvin is keeping the play alive; is breaking back to the empty side of the field, the passed-by side, where—*trundling*, essentially—I'm the only player.

Richard Sherman is hot on Melvin's tail, having over-pursued, and now has to cut back. He is closing in on Melvin like a barracuda.

All I have eyes for is Sherman. He can't see me coming; he thinks I'm dead and gone.

The shortest distance between two points is a straight line, and it is a thing of geometric beauty and elegance, of mathematical bliss, to simply draw a bead on Sherman and sledge my shoulder into his chest fair and square, rattling his teeth, I hope, and halting his pursuit of Melvin, who rounds the post of my pick and goes up the sideline unmolested for another 60 yards—not to the end zone, but almost. It's the biggest gain we will have all night.

When I hit Sherman in the chest, it was like running into an anvil. I bounced off him. I did not level him, did not clean his clock. I stood him up straight, but he did not buckle or wobble. He certainly did not go flying backwards. He did not cease to exist. He was simply negated. Stopped.

And in the bathtub, for days afterward, soaking in those lavender Epsom salts, I would play it over and over: the annoyed and surprised—tricked—look on his face; the irritation at being taken out of the play, but also by me, whom I imagine he regretted not having neutralized again.

And what I thought about there in the tub, in the pleasure of slow relaxation and rehabilitation, was the conscious decision I had made to not hurt him—devastate him—when I realized I had him.

I could have taken his head off. I could have put my helmet into his chest and separated his soul from his body.

But I bore him no ill will. There was no violence in my soul. Desire to protect Melvin, yes—but I did not seek to harm Sherman; only take him out of the play.

Another long touchdown for the Red Raiders; 14–0. Another kickoff.

This one's a squib, an onside kick to the right. I'm lined up left. Corey covers it, curls up fetal, as per the drill. The smart money would have been to kick it hard at me, but again, because I'm small, it's possible they thought I was a hands guy. Once again, Sherman lined up across from me, able to cross that 10-yard distance to the bouncing ball in approximately 1.1 seconds, while the ball itself would not travel much faster, meaning they could have kicked at me and Sherman could have hit me the instant the ball touched my hands. I've been mentally preparing for this for weeks, but it did not come my way. I was glad for that.

We stall on offense: three plays, then punt the ball back to the Red Raiders. The Red Raiders execute another successful long pass play. It's been this way for years. We can't make our corners grow any taller. I don't know if other teams are watching our game films, scouting us. I imagine that they are. When they have 8 or 10 coaches, why not?

There's no way Coach can prepare that way with all his jobs. There's no way any of us can. I wonder if after Desmond's pro or semi-pro career is over, he will become a coach, or a coach and a teacher. Kirby and Jean Ann have known him since he was five; used to drive him to school in carpools. He went to school with their son Mason; played ball with Mason, who said Desmond's always been smart. When Kirby and Jean Ann's boys were in high school, I vaguely remember a small band of boys coming through their house at all hours. They were good kids. They liked being over at Kirby and Jean Ann's. That curious willingness of teens to sometimes mingle with older folks.

A fourth kickoff, this one deep. Eager to try out my new Desmond-coached technique, I turn and run back toward the wedge, twist to set up. Here comes Richard the Lionhearted, arms and fists bowed up high, like the blade lifted on a bulldozer, intense malice in his nearing eyes—malice, and a thing almost like terror—the terror that he might fail, might somehow lose.

I throw my arms up likewise, square my hips and lift up; and still, I am uprooted by him, find myself flying through the sky, still in that same silly position, but blocking no one and no thing now, only God, or, I suppose, any passing seagull.

And as I soar through the air I remember a large flock of killdeer, fleeting, feeding, and skittering at the far end of The Rock last week as we practiced; the birds keening and wheeling into a swarming flight when a red-tailed hawk cruised over.

I bounce, landing on my padded tailbone, but it doesn't hurt much at all. It's awesome that my helmeted head didn't strike the Astroturf this time. This collision was at least as hard a hit as the first one had been, and it occurred to me that Sherman might have been razzed for getting blocked out of the play by me a couple of kickoffs earlier. That if he had already been gunning for me, he really was now. That from an evolutionary perspective, it could be said that my best choice, if not of the highest ethics, would have been to try to take him out—to damage him; to fuck him up in the legs, when I'd had my chance. To hit him in his thighs rather than his chest; to hobble him, so that he would either not have been able to come back on the field, or would have had to do so in some compromised fashion. So that therefore—fast-forward back into the future, to the moment when I'm flying through the air, my arms still crossed and locked as if seated in an imaginary chair—none of this might have happened.

Some years ago, the New Orleans Saints' head coach, Sean Payton, famous for having inherited the future Hall of Fame quarterback, Drew Brees, was also famous for having had the gall to open the second half of the Super Bowl with an onside kick. There was only a 1-in-10 chance of recovering it; but if the receiving team recovered it, there at midfield, they would have a three-in-four chance of moving the ball into field goal range. Bad odds. But Payton and the Saints won the bet: recovered the kick, went on to score, won the Super Bowl, and gave pride to a city that was grieving after the governmental clusterfuck of Hurricane Katrina.

Payton was, and is, famous, or infamous, for a third thing: "Bountygate." He and his coaching staff were accused of paying cash bonuses, ridiculously small amounts—essentially Monopoly chits, compared to the players' multimillion-dollar contracts—not for making stellar plays, but for damaging or injuring opposing players to the point where they had to be taken out of the game.

The coaches paid their players to target the other team's best players, shelling out cash afterward in the locker room. The league investigated. Payton and his assistant coaches were found guilty. The team was fined, docked future draft choices, and Payton was suspended from the team for a year.

That which weakens one, weakens all. There is a dark vault inside the heart of football, the heart of America, in which violence is marginalized, sanctioned, and, from that, normalized.

What happens to the players, and to the people in their lives—the concentric circles of their social networks—is happening to all of us. Little wonder that now and again a wisp of smoke arises from the burning, smoldering mass: Colin Kaepernick and Ed Reed of the San Francisco 49ers, kneeling during the national anthem, protesting the ridiculously outdated and never fully accurate lyrics, "Home of the free and the brave."

We score a touchdown! Shane, the new quarterback, completes a pass to Shaun, the former quarterback, now positioned at wide receiver, on a deep slant. Shaun's already behind eight defenders when he catches the ball. He just has to outrace and outmaneuver the other three, which he does with ease, and now we're only down 20–6. Despite the Red Raiders' homefield advantage, and greater size and speed and numbers, this is not insurmountable. They're a better team, but sometimes lesser teams win. A wobble is introduced into the system. The superior team makes a mistake, which leads to another mistake. The ball is tipped, or bounces crazily, to the lesser team's advantage. A player muffs a punt. Fourteen-point swings are not uncommon; can happen within the span of a single minute.

Coach is psyched. He seems like a man 20, even 30 years younger, leaning forward as he runs down the sideline to congratulate the offense as they come off the field.

How many games has Coach won in his life, I wonder? Surely the vast majority. How keenly he bears the weight of losing: this seemingly sudden affliction that has begun to plague him, here in middle age. As if it is not only a thing to which he is pretty much completely unaccustomed, but more. As if he is finally seeing—being forced to look at—a thing he has been trying *not* to look at. A thing he has been trying to scheme and game plan to get around, or away from, to contain and confine, much, if not all, of his life.

It feels big, and now, on the fancy Astroturf of the sidelines, dressed in his Express purple long-sleeve silk jersey and his navy sweat pants, Coach's exuberance is fierce and big. He is as direct and brutal in his praise as he is in his criticism.

Over on the other sideline—how far away they seem, as if on a farther shore, and there are so many of them—the Red Raiders begin to boo loudly. It sounds like booing from a stadium filled with 60,000 fans. The Red Raiders are so talented that they excel even at booing. For all I know, their coaches are booing our good play.

We try an onside kick of our own, after our score. Desmond, whom Coach has tasked mid-game with being the unofficial special teams coach, gathers us into a calm sideline huddle before we kick off, and in his near-whisper announces to us he wants us to kick to the right side.

The ball just has to travel 10 yards. After that, if we can fall on it before they do, it's ours. The onside kickoff, as well as the regular deep kickoff, can be two of the most violent plays in football. Already, the NFL is changing its rules to discourage kickoff returns, and colleges are experimenting with alternatives as well. It's strange to realize that out here on the coastal prairie and rolling hills of Texas, we're playing by dying-out rules, a football way of life that is fast on its way to extinction. That already, we are like ghosts—playing games seen by no one, clanking and clanging against one another with our cries and exhortations drifting some short distance beyond the stadium before the slow roll of sound waves unravels, and is absorbed by the night.

I keep thinking about how calm Desmond is: how his voice is like a balm, as reassuring as Coach's is tension-making.

With many of Coach's entreaties, we want to go out onto the field and succeed, whatever that looks like, for Coach's sake: to make him less angry, or to receive—earn—his respect; to make him proud. He is a figure of great authority.

With Desmond, however, we're inspired to do our best and to succeed for ourselves; to earn our own self-respect. As if he believes we are so close to it that he doesn't even need to raise his voice.

Our kick by Isaiah is a little too hard. It skips and hops ahead of us like a rabbit, but skitters past the requisite 10 yards, and then farther into the interior. I'm chasing it, but the ball is already veering toward two enormous Red Raiders.

For a moment—whatever unit of time exists that's smaller than the melt of a single second—I'm running after the ball. The stadium lights shining down on it are catching the smooth mahogany sheen of the ball, and as it skips and hops—four, three, two more steps, and I'll be close enough to dive on it—a memory shutters through my muscles.

I had spent time as a child in the Texas Hill country, where I delighted in chasing armadillos, which, it occurred to me as I ran after the glistening football at the Red Raiders' stadium, resembled a football. It was so strange to see the football advancing along the ground like that; the ball's rolling course was not unlike the movements of the armadillos I pursued as they sought to dive into their holes before I could grab one of the prehistoric-looking creatures by its long scaled armor-clad tail.

The gleaming brown ball made a funny skip toward the first of the two immense Red Raiders' middlemen, and he fell upon it so suddenly it seemed he'd injured himself. He curled up then like a child settling in for a nap; unwilling to give the ball up to anyone but the referee. Red Raiders' ball again.

I'm the first one to the big fella. He lies on the ball like a little boy, a 275-pound little boy. I tap him lightly on his padded shoulder. If statistics are being logged in Texas United Football Association, I will be credited with my first solo tackle. What a big old mixed-up world. What percentage of it always is but smoke and mirrors, desire and dreams?

The Red Raiders score again right before the half on another long pass play. Are they better than us individually? I don't think by much. I think our hearts—Neil's, Lou's, Ernie's, Chandler's—are as courageous and determined as those of anyone on the field. But we're on the field a lot, while the Red Raiders are substituting, so they're always frisky. On our sidelines, our players sit in a gradual silencing.

We get the ball back on kickoff—the ball is kicked so deep there's no return, and with my aching ribs, I'm glad for that—but we cannot advance the ball. Instead, we're being pushed backward. Shane's sacked twice.

On third down, with Shane running around deep in our end zone, looking for an open receiver, there are none; they are still running deep routes, their backs turned to the peril in which Shane finds himself, and Shane is pulled down for the ignominy of a safety.

It's just two points for the Red Raiders, but the real bummer is that now by rule we must punt the ball to them from our 20-yard line, meaning that even if our special teams make a good stop, the Red Raiders are going to have the ball somewhere around midfield.

It's only 28–6. Of course, there's another half to play. At this rate it could end up 56–16, or 28–28, or anything: 70–6, 80–6, 100–6. It all depends on how we respond, one play at a time. It's a cliché, but for a good reason.

We've never practiced a safety kick. Some of our offense has trotted off the field and some of our kickoff team and punt team have gone out onto the field. A great surf of players coming and going, and the clock is starting again. We have only 30 seconds to get it right. And the mayhem is felt powerfully by Desmond as he tries to count the players coming off the field and those trickling out onto it.

It's the first time I've seen Desmond look urgent. He's like a mother waving children in ahead of a storm, while simultaneously hurrying others out to catch a waiting school bus. He's gesturing to *go, come, stay, go*—assigning players into slotted positions on the fly. He comes halfway out onto the field; says he needs two more. He waves to me and Lou on the sidelines, and we dash out there and line up in yet another new position.

It's exhilarating, inhabiting a self beyond the old and familiar. When I woke up this morning—entering my 63rd year at some point shortly after kickoff—indeed, possibly entering it as I was mid-air, flying west, bouncing hard then on the bright green turf—the thought that I might be lining up on a punt was not in my mind.

This moment, and the *next*: all new, all surreal, and yet not surreal. As real as anything, and more real than most things. The tips of cell receptors tingle and spark with adrenaline, anticipation, even fear.

We line up at staggered depths. I have no idea if we can take a running start from, say, five yards behind the punter, but I back up and time my advance with his own. I'm directly beside him in the center lane; I'll be going right into the teeth of their blockers.

It hurts my ribs to even breathe. And while I want to execute well and keep the punt returner from making a big gain, I'm equally vested in avoiding a direct hit, particularly a helmet larger than any cannonball, to my already fractured ribs.

Stay in your lane is the mantra when covering a kickoff or punt. Just do your job and trust the other 10 men to do theirs. Converge only at the latest possible moment, as if cinching a knot. The gunners—the fastest players—get down the field first and quickest, staying along their respective sidelines, trying to keep the return pinched in toward the middle, toward the great scrum.

The night before my birthday, down at my father's farm in south Texas, where Carter and I had gone to grill some steaks with Dad and his wife, Maryanne, my dad had warned me there might be some teams out there that could possibly be targeting me, given the novelty of my age and profession. I reassured him I had already wondered about that, but that in all the games I'd played, I'd never seen or experienced that—maybe just a whiff of it, on that 22 blast, two years earlier; not necessarily the hit, but that they hadn't offered a hand to help me up, instead dancing around whooping and cheering. But that's the game, right?

I'll be careful, I told him as we were leaving Saturday morning, *don't worry*. And now with the beating I've been taking, I'm glad he's not here. I'm sorry for Carter having to watch. It's harder for her because now I'm doubly motivated. I'm able to try to evade the blocks rather than seeking them out. But all Carter can do is watch. I tell myself I will stay low, if I get close enough to make the tackle. I will lower my head and drive my shoulders at his ankles.

The temptation is to hit a runner up high, but because their power is in their legs, a strong runner can pretty much run through an arm tackle. It's hard to wrap your arms around someone's chest—easier to wrap around their legs down below the knees; wrap and squeeze, vise-grip tight. Tackling a runner up high is one reason so many defenders have their seasons end with torn biceps, triceps, and pectoral muscles. It can be like getting your arm caught and being dragged along by a locomotive. This is what was driving Coach apeshit a couple of weeks ago: our missed arm tackles.

I'll have to get low. The punt is in the air now. White is running at Red; our numbers are mixing and matching, merging in a great zippered chain of muscle and passion, a clot that seeks to congeal around the dashing, darting ballcarrier.

As I veer left and right, pretending to drift away from the play, running around the Red Raiders who set up to block me rather than running into them, I find, after passing through a couple of such players, that I am center lane again, with the runner, a chunky powerful man, also in the center lane, about 10 yards out and coming strong.

I'm dimly aware of some other Red Raiders on either side of me, and some of my own teammates also flanking me left and right. And I can feel in that instant not only the setup, but the way it has to play out; the runner is hemmed in. He has to keep on coming at me; he has no place left to veer.

I'm just about to get low and ready to take him on. I'm still running straight at him when an enormous Red Raider fills my vision, having sprinted from that lateral area I've kind of noticed and disregarded. I never dreamed he, or any of them, could get to me before I got to the runner. My head was not on a swivel.

The hit was so sudden I barely had time to register it: his face, round and sweating, dark as a purple grape; his black helmet; the width of his shoulder pads far wider than my own; and the savagery—him dropping his head to butt mine with his helmeted forehead, heavy as that of a ram's, as he plowed over me.

The sound of our helmets was like that of a bowling ball colliding with the lone pin. My head snapped back on my neck farther than I would have thought it could go—all the way back, as if I'd been decapitated—and I heard and felt crackings in my neck vertebrae, felt neck muscles rip—and I was blown backwards by a force so explosive I still marvel. The back of my head touched my spine.

I never saw his number. Rolling over onto my side, I saw that other of my teammates had gone in through the gap vacated by the big guy and had the runner down on the ground, like a lion, or lions, with a gazelle: and dazed, operating only by routine, I stood. Strangely, though I'd felt a great flash of pain in my ribs upon contact, that was secondary now. But I could not trot off the field; nothing was working right, and now everything hurt—and though there was soft tissue muscle trauma, pretty much head to feet, it felt more that I'd been electrocuted than blocked.

I tried to trot, just to show it was nothing, but all I could do was walk, and slowly. Crookedly. The sideline seemed an impossibly farther shore.

"You okay?" Coach asked.

I shook my head no. "Helmet-to-helmet," I said, and Coach winced, then turned his attention back to the game—a play was unfolding. Fifty-one seconds left in the half. Desmond was watching—cool Desmond—but he looked rattled, as if looking at a ghost. I went straight to Kirby. He, too, appeared to be looking at me as if one of us was from outer space.

I could hear how loopy I was. With that initial hit, I'd been fixating on how he, the guy who looked like Richard Sherman, had hit me from behind. I'd kept repeating some variation of that news to Carter, Kirby, Coach, and my teammates.

On this hit—a quantum or two harder than lil' ol' Richard Sherman's hits—there was no doubt in my mind what had happened. "I got hit. I got hit hard. His helmet hit my helmet," I heard myself saying. "Did you see that?" I asked Kirby. He hadn't.

"How are your ribs?" he asked.

"My ribs are great," I said. "My head hurts bad." I turned, looked back to the game, where our defense had dug in and was making a stand: shutting down the run, harassing the passer, and staying tight on coverage in the secondary. "He hit me in the head with his helmet," I heard myself saying again. "He head-butted me."

The clock appears stuck, stranded in molasses. Even as I write these words a week later, I have to check myself to keep from writing the word *morasses*. But that, too: stuck in morasses. Other words I will mispronounce in conversation at the rate of about two per day are *dissociated* rather than *disassociated*. *Residents* instead of *representative*, while on hold to the villainous Wells Fargo. I said *skillet* instead of *skit*, go figure—*bruthed* instead of *bruised*, and, less disturbing, *cognizant* instead of *cognitive*. This laxity with individual letters—my bread and butter—will last for nearly two years.

The surprising thing is not that players like Andrew Luck retire early. The surprising thing is that hundreds, thousands of others, don't.

Forty-nine seconds are left in the half, then 42, then 38. It seems the half will never end. It seems that I alone exist in a state, a seam, in which I can see and perceive the slow crawl of time beneath me, and its fleeter passage ahead—look at how quickly the thin-stretched gilded tatters of sunset cirrus stretch laterally along the curve of the earth.

I head over to where Carter is standing, looking more concerned than ever. She didn't see the hit either, though she saw me being slow to get up, saw me struggling to walk off the field. "You should stop," she says again. I try to tell her what a bad message that would send to these men I'm becoming friends with. How it feels to me I'm using them. Writing books is what I do, just as playing football or scooping Blue Bell ice cream or catching dogs is what they do. But my ability to endure physical discomfort, even pain, and not give up, just as they are not giving up, is a bridge where I can meet them.

I definitely feel I'm on the midpoint of that high arched bridge. In for a dime, in for a dollar, is how I try to live.

I am not considering my career at this point. I'm just trying to finish the game. To play within my rapidly diminishing limitations. I am—no doubt, much to Coach's chagrin—not trying to damage anyone. I'm not trying to put my foot in anyone's ass. And to be fair, there is no prayer that he does not begin, every game and every practice, with the entreaty to keep us all safe, and concludes each practice and each game with thanksgiving that all have been spared, that all are mortal and live until they are chosen by the Lord to live no longer. This is the part where he reminds us that the few make many and the dead make none. And he asks for, or gives, thanksgiving for the relative absence of injuries. It's his first action item. And he thanks the Lord that all have arrived to the practice or the game safely, and asks for their safe passage home to their loved ones.

No work is ever wasted. You get out of a thing whatever you put into it. It's not so much give-and-take as instead, I think, something akin to prayer: the work, or faith, goes in, and goes in, and goes in—the belief—and then one day, or in one moment, there is a shift. Maybe not a momentous or geological shift—but other times, yes.

I didn't come down here to take without giving. As long as it's just a pain management issue, I'll go out onto the field. It's not like my skill level is going to be the determining factor in a 35–6 blowout, but neither am I thinking clearly. This is the mind of the concussed. This is why trainers, coaches, and even players take a teammate's helmet away.

Are there any healthy addictions? I can't think of any. Are there any addictions where one walks away, but then eases back into the addiction at a more reduced, more manageable level? Again, I cannot think of any examples. Perhaps football will be the only exception. Though I cannot imagine any pleasure or joy—coaching, for instance—bringing anywhere near the specificity of pleasure that's involved not just in the game, with its finite, allocated minutes and moments, but even in the daily and meaningful preparation for the game itself.

I think this is the limbo-land Coach himself inhabits between joy and rage, and in which—it seems to me—the latter is tapping him on the shoulder and pulling him down, bit by bit. I can hear Evan yet again, the last time I saw him: *Nah, Coach, that was the old Evan last week. I'm done with all that bullshit. This is the new Evan.*

I knew that Kirby and Coach were going to ask me who the president is. I was thinking about these things even as I was limping off the field and prepping my answer (I was also so much wishing I could trot, in the time-honored tradition of the hard-knocked, who through sheer will, are somehow—miraculously, it seems—impervious to the hard knock.)

George Bush, I thought craftily—it's a trick question, but that's the fitted key to the intricate lock that will let me get back onto the field with my team; these men who have come to trust me, despite having no reason to, and who have come to respect me based not on words, but instead, only deeds.

I was cognizant enough to know there had been two George Bushes. In those last steps to the sideline, I played out how the conversation would go, when my friends and loved ones tried to trick me by asking *which* George Bush. Trying to take away my joy. *The older one*, of course, I'd reply. On this matter I was crystal clear.

For a long time, the headaches would return. The date was March 7, my birthday. I had been running strong and healthy at the end of my 62nd year, and yet in the first hours of my 63rd, I was gimping, hurting in a hundred places. In the coming hours, the stock market—that ridiculous pseudo-barometer of the economy—would go off a cliff, dropping the dreaded 20 percent into "bear" territory.

In those same hours, the number of COVID-19 cases in Italy and the rest of Europe would skyrocket exponentially, while in our own country we had no idea how many had been exposed to it. How many had contracted it, nor even how many had died from it, with the exception of the seemingly singular case of the nursing home in Seattle. Within those same hours, the NCAA, Major League Baseball, National Basketball Association, and NFL would suspend operations, as would the Metropolitan Museum in New York, the Smithsonian, the Mormon Church, and all public and private schools in four states, while that reckless orange fool in the White House, the

Narcissist in Chief, sat up late at night tweeting about Joe Biden. What a big old goofy world, where the clown who once profited from telling folks they were fired, publicly shaming and humiliating them—was forced now to experience the slow-motion of his own firing, come November.

By the same week's end, only 5 of the 50 states would not yet have any recorded cases—Alaska, West Virginia, Maine, Idaho, and Montana: anomalies in testing, I felt sure, rather than any remnant purity. Though still, it was a strange feeling, knowing I lived in what, for the time being, could be said to be one of the safest places in the world yet was, for purposes of work but also joy, placing myself in harm's way.

We are always in harm's way.

"Head on a swivel," Desmond counsels me again. "You've got to keep your head on a swivel." What he does not say is *You've got to do a* better *job of keeping your head on a swivel.*

Our defense holds. It's halftime. I don't remember anything. I remember Carter looking concerned and saying I should come out. I don't remember what Coach said, or any of the players. As when one tries, upon awakening, to remember the tatters of a dream, I recall noticing the different colors of the scoreboard, and the various numbers making no sense to me.

At some point, it ceased being a football game and became a thing to endure. More and more I went out to the warning track to check in with Carter, who sometimes was visiting with the other two women, Michelle and Jamie, but who at other times was just standing out there by herself, wearing my fleece pullover, her down jacket, and then my down jacket, but was still cold: as was I.

I was shivering. I remember that.

I remember Lou walking from player to player, bent forward, leaning into their faces, saying things like "Let's go; whole new game! Second half, second half!" I remember looking around with the somewhat disassociated observation of a journalist, curious as to whether I could gauge who truly believed him, who did not, and who was somewhere in the middle.

I remember Coach, who had calmed down somewhat, saying to no one in particular, "Okay, we're in a dogfight. This is a dogfight, is what this is"—repeating it as if he too had been concussed, was being concussed, despite not being out on the field.

Whatever he said was, it must be assumed, important. But I have no memory of it. There were steady headaches, and then headaches that came and went. Once they had ceased to be steady, I was cautious and relieved; but there would still be mornings where they still came back.

My loved ones were sympathetic that I had been blown up, but also cautiously relieved. *You're not going back out there, are you?* they'd ask. And my answers vacillated with the days. *No. Not for a long time. I don't think so.*

Certainly I was nowhere near ready, and some days couldn't imagine being ready ever again. There was the obvious rib and head pain—my shoulder blade had stopped hurting, but there was a new pain all throughout the rest of my upper body. My upper back felt as swollen as a turtle's, so that I was taking Aleve frequently. I had to lie down on my back often to still the stabbing. (In writing the phrase *lie down* I just spelled *lie* as *le*.)

My intent is not to garner sympathy; to say that I asked for it is an understatement. But I have to consider: would the Texas Express players' lives be safer, better, stronger, without the sport, or lesser, weaker, less interesting? *Yes.*

It's semi-pro—beyond college ball, but less than the NFL. It's not a business for them, but it's not a game either.

On the field, a voltage of fury, rage, and hope passes through them, out in that compressed space around which we gather as if at a feast. The voltages bounce and skitter, flowing through each of the 22 conduits as they scramble, veer, and ricochet out on the field, the energies charging and discharging from one conduit to the next. There is such beauty, such creativity and power, to the players' high-speed adjustments.

We see the powerful men deliver and absorb the extreme physical manifestations of desire, fury, hope: not the furthest extensions of these emotions capable within us all, but the furthest we as a culture are willing to let them go.

There are rules; there are boundaries and borders. But for 60 minutes—sometimes graceful, sometimes ironic and sophisticated, other times simple, but always violent—those extreme forces flow through the bodies of whichever 22 are out on the field.

Little wonder that despite the meticulous ankle- and elbow-taping, the snug fit of the helmets, and the tight lacings of the shoulder pads, the body cannot withstand it. Future Hall of Fame cornerback Richard Sherman—the real Richard Sherman, formerly of the world champion Seattle Seahawks' Legion of Boom—tells each new incoming crop of rookies (that word, *crop!*), particularly the running backs, that they should "cherish every carry, because they play in a sport with a 100 percent injury rate."

•

I'VE BEEN THINKING about courage. I won't be disingenuous or falsely modest—to be out on the field, looking into their eyes at 10 yards, at 5, and then point blank, requires a deeper level of courage or bravery. Not the deepest, by a long shot. But deeper. A friend of mine's wife of 60 years is in the last stages of pancreatic cancer: two or three weeks to go. I don't presume to say that football even touches the limits of courage that's demanded of him, of them, in this passage. All I'm saying is, playing football at an elevated level takes one step, however small, beyond one's comfort zone—or beyond mine.

Bravery is when you know no fear. Courage is when you know fear but go ahead with it anyway.

And when you are, *ahem*, less competitive, it takes even a tad more.

Again, I consider the voltages that flow, howl, through them, through us.

In no way do the games build bodies stronger. The games wreck precious objects. We, the theatergoers, throw money in the tip jars. We applaud it as an ancient and even honorable transaction. It is just *so* out at the edges. And these men—the shadow league—are out at the edge of edges. And Coach is their Fisher King, their dark one and only.

They await his satisfaction. They await their own.

•

ANOTHER THING I'M learning from Coach and the Express is this: I am now better able to understand that which was always curious, even incomprehensible before. How could a player at any level, who once loved the game with such joy and intensity, ever move away from that condition, even as the object of the obsession, *football*, did not change?

It always puzzled me, the way a thing, once pure, could become a tangle of complications.

It happens to some sooner than others. But the diminishment, to some extent, happens to all. It may ultimately not be debilitating to all, but almost all. I keep thinking about those 107 brains in Boston, where even the field goal kicker displayed dementia. I keep wondering, whose was the one brain that did not? How old was he, and is there game film from his life? What if plain old human error was at play, and that 107th brain was a mix-up—was not the brain of a player at all? A nun, a priest, a truck driver?

To say that we need more research—and that with the sport being a $100-billion-plus industry (approximately our entire military budget) we can't afford it—is facile.

•

THE BODY, IT occurs to me—able to go where it pleases, across any given terrain—is perhaps the second greatest freedom. On weekends, driving the Prius back to Marfa, I'd stop in the Hill Country, on a ragged patch of land; all that's left from a once-upon-a-time much larger piece of land leased and then owned by my family for nearly 100 years now. I'd go for walks, on those early spring mornings, on that little scrap of land we've been able to hold onto for nearly a century now. Ghosts everywhere, and stories. Doves calling, dry oak leaves falling on the tin roof of the bunkhouse, bare branches scraping against the roof. The mild spring wind off the Gulf Coast, 200 miles to the southeast, with the desert of West Texas still the better part of a day's drive ahead of me.

On those walks in this place known so intimately to my grandfather before me, and to my father, myself, my daughters, nephews and nieces, through the ancient act of hunting, I'd look out at rolling blue ridges and stony hills to the horizon that once were ours. I'd remember countless hikes, countless hunts conducted with the intensity of youth, searching for our quarry: whitetail bucks or wild turkeys or wild pigs.

The incredible intensity of those beat-by-beat moments, the five senses of the hunter—a trillion images of the physical world filtering through the body: a wood duck drake surprised from the trickling creek beneath the canopy of live oaks, flame-lit water rolling off its wings, the feathered head cobalt and emerald, the eyes fierce and focused on life. The arch of a yellow scorpion tail.

Walking the increasingly diminished land that is still ours—new taut-strung barbed wire fences running in all directions—it would occur to me that the body itself is the greatest freedom. Or the body, in the condition of health, at any age.

●

THE REASON THEY quit—*retire* is the more common word—is that they just can't go any longer. One in 1,000, perhaps, goes out on top. Maybe one in 100,000: John Elway after "The Drive." Who else? No other. Barry Sanders, Walter Payton ("Sweetness"), Calvin Johnson ("Megatron"), going out just before the top. Andrew Luck, way before the top. It is impossible to know where the top is. This is of course a blessing. It is not impossible to know when one is on the downhill side; but it is almost impossible, I think, to guess where the bottom actually is. For that is the place one is resisting. And having been trained to be a warrior, it is no longer in one's skill set to possess the ability to identify the bottom, much less even acknowledge that is where one finds one's self.

I knew all this intellectually. I'd heard older players refer to "the grind." But to fully know it, I wanted to experience it. Wanted to know it with the body, even in this late year.

And could not, cannot, help but wonder at the shadows cast ahead in these young—in Kojo, and, farther out, in Dooney, Melvin, and Quincy—in Coach, which I imagine as a scatter of dry leaves, each hit to their body separating from the body a single dead leaf, and with those accumulating leaves swirling ahead of the players toward their final resting place, toward which the minds and bodies of the players are also moving.

I suppose the going away, the diminishment, comes the way a single simple letter, dropping from a word, falling away, fluttering like a glint of mica tumbling in a trickling current, causes the entire word to be repurposed. Or perhaps the newer altered word carries forward a similar, but also different, meaning, and whether more nuanced or now awkward, it might not always matter: the word still might retain sufficient rootstock to be functional, if no longer as graceful and precise.

My headaches and confusion, after the Houston Red Raiders game, weren't the seeming randomness of dementia, where a person might, in the middle of a sentence, refer to a tuba as a toaster, or a bird as a door. This was instead by comparison neat and precise—a "t" replacing a "y"; a "V" falling through the cracks. As if the individual letters themselves, accustomed to running down the field and staying in their lanes, had received a hard block and been knocked out of position, punched away from all the others and falling, as if through a sieve, downward into some limbo, a repository of no-words, just random letters. Or like talus rolling down a mountainside before coming to rest in each individual stone's angle of repose, letter of repose.

By noticing which letters were most vulnerable to these crackback blocks—T's, F's, S's, R's, what have you—might we plumb farther the mysteries of the human brain?

How to quit a thing you love? Almost always, the decision has to be made for you. Almost always it is the influence of others, as well as that of the bad-ass negotiator, time. One is never in control; and, one day, a traveler realizes it.

That night in Baytown, I possess the strange and not altogether unalluring fantasia of the deeply concussed: I'm on the sideline, wandering like a ghost, as our team fights valiantly. The defense is beginning to make stops, learning the Red Raiders' favorite and most effective plays and making adjustments, like the body attacking a virus with T-cell antibodies, and with our offense putting together some longer ground-eating drives, for which I'm grateful. I do not want to go back out there any more than is necessary. I have had almost enough of a good thing.

My head does not hurt yet. That will come later, I suppose, when the internal bleeding congeals, and the bruise hardens to, what, dead cells? Scar tissue?

But about the fantasia, the phantasmagoric: the game in Houston. At one point during the Red Raider game I look behind me to the running track that separates the field from the unoccupied stands and see that Kirby and Carter are jogging after a giant moth lured here from the nearby marshlands by the brilliance of the stadium lights.

They run behind it like children, Kirby lifting his hands up toward its careening flight as if in prayer. The moth veers clumsily away from each of them as they seek to converge on it to capture it so they might carry it back out to the fields to safety, as if not understanding or accepting the moth will simply return to that which it cannot resist.

Still, it's fun, beautiful even, to watch the lilting flight of the moth. Even from a distance I can tell it's one of the large owl-eyed *Cecropia* genus, the size of a hummingbird, or sparrow—and for a while, I forget about the game, and am spellbound.

In the future, as I continue to notice my steady, unrelenting new manifestation of simple misspellings, and await a correction or recovery, I can't help but wonder, *What if it doesn't get better? What if this is, forever and ever, the new normal? The new normal?*

No addiction can exist without the flashlight's guiding beam of denial. No true recovery can be built without the eradication of denial, and instead acceptance of what is real. In the meantime, all I can do is drink lots of water, get lots of sleep, take my vitamins, and be grateful that at least I can recognize the misspellings as such, and be alarmed at their sudden prevalence. At least I know what I'm doing, as I step into the future, leaning forward into each next day.

●

ONCE YOU'RE INJURED—whether ribs or hamstring, groin or knee—a merciful kickoff is one in which there is no real contact. Sometimes it's like that: you see a guy coming; you pick up his number, and begin tacking toward him. But he's looking past you, tacking toward your runner, who you, of course, can't see. You can only guess and extrapolate by the focused gaze of the approaching tackler.

Trotting off the field after one such skirmish—there was some light contact, but not so severe I was knocked to the ground, nor, rest assured, did I knock my opponent to the ground—I found myself panting: hyperventilating in a mechanical, metronomic fashion. There wasn't any reason for me to be so out of breath; after but a single play, I was panting as if I'd just sprinted a mile, and again, with a bizarre regularity, an automated central nervous system kind of pace. I wondered if a rib had broken and pierced a lung. Was there a way to find out sooner than having to wait to see if one's pee turned orange?

It wasn't so much the rapidity that freaked me out as the unalterable quickened rhythm of it, a *rat-tat-tat-tat* that was not abating, even as I stood there on the sideline talking to Kirby and Carter.

My heart didn't feel like it was racing at all. Just my lungs, my breathing.

It also felt like I wasn't getting any air in, and that the air I was getting was somehow strangely dry, even for the humid marshlands of southeast Texas, so close to the Louisiana border.

"Isn't this kind of abnormal?" I asked Kirby. "I've never felt like this in my life." My head was still ringing from that first hit—the ground having risen up so quickly to slam into my pretty navy blue helmet.

I couldn't make my sentences match the thoughts in my head.

"I don't know," Kirby said.

My breathing was still skipping fast, like a boxer jumping rope or working the speed bag, and I could tell Kirby and Carter thought maybe I was just winded. I resolved to stay close and check in with them often. There was very much the feeling that something ominous was near: that I was in some in-between place, terribly mechanical, terribly dispassionate. That it was an electrical fast twitching of tissue and ligature, of veined membrane and fascia. It seemed possible it would outrun itself, so that the breathing would have to stop, the way that an engine without gas or air falters, then stops.

I waited for what came next—cardiac arrest?—but after a few minutes, the old rhythms returned to me, and I was allowed to keep going forward, farther into the living, and farther into the light.

•

IN THE MIDDLE of the third quarter, the Red Raiders are suddenly and somehow down near our end zone. I recall a series of quick passes over the middle: their big fresh receivers, their bright red uniforms unsullied, catching passes over the middle and then turning upfield. They've previously made a long touchdown drive—passing, passing, passing—and this one is replicating it, which is heartbreaking, both for the running up of the score, but also for the eminence of, in the parlance of radio broadcasters since football time immemorial, their *ensuing kickoff*, after each score. Meaning: more ass-whipping up for me.

The next score comes against Lou, though it's not really fair to write it that way. As linebacker, he was in a zone scheme covering the middle, but the tight end and double-set wide receivers ran a pick, releasing one of the receivers to the back corner of the end zone, raw-ass alone.

Lou left his own coverage and dashed over to defend that corner, but didn't quite get there in time. He was still an arm's length away as the pass arced up into the halogen lights and then came spinning down into the receiver's belly, cradled, touchdown.

In Lou's last lunging leap to try to get there in time, his outstretched hand was a split-second behind, and just inches away from the ball, and the receiver caught the ball, *received* it, as cleanly as if no one was within a thousand miles.

It's March 7th. The phrase *social distancing* has not yet been born, but will in the coming days. On this particular play to the end zone, I can see everything so cleanly, so clearly. There's something wonderful about a night game. The players are suspended in light, an illumination so intense it seems it might scald or purify them—they are composed of living flame, and the darkness beyond the lights is absolute now, blacker than any night.

Lou lands crookedly after missing the pass. To a casual observer, it might have seemed he'd twisted an ankle or even a knee upon landing. But I'd already seen the awkwardness coming off his initial leap. Even in the air, flying, he was lame; and even more when he landed, so that it would have looked like that was where the injury occurred.

Lou came gimping off the field, unable to put any weight on his foot; and whether plantar fasciitis or Achilles tear, it wasn't good. He hobbled to the bench, banged his helmet down, and began unwrapping the ankle—his right—which earlier in the evening, Kirby had taped so assiduously. Lou's already had two Achilles tears, each requiring almost a full year of recovery, and the idea of a third one felling this young man, still in his mid-twenties, was too cruel to consider. I pushed it to the back of my mind: *Wait and see.*

My second thought was—selfish—that I was going to miss him out there on kickoffs.

I catch a break, though. The next kickoff to us is an onside pooch kick—kicked a little deeper and harder, skittering quickly through the gap presented by the five of us on the front line and into the middle ground. It's still a live ball, and the Red Raiders almost get to it first, but one of our players bobbles it—the Red Raiders are almost upon him—then secures it, falls to the ground in a tuck, and I get to run off the field without even being touched.

My head doesn't hurt. If anything, there is a buzz going on up there that is almost nice—from the neck up. My brain is having a little party while the rest of me is under mortar attack. Mortal attack.

I am not ashamed to say it is around this point that I began to look at the game clock after almost every play. Praying for every precious second not to be extended, but removed. The melting of the clock is a miracle. I watch each pass spiral through the air, knowing each rotation of the ball buys perhaps another hundredth of a second. The running plays are the best, for the clock doesn't stop—each run can take up to 30 seconds off the clock—but it is not cowardice, for when it is my time to go back out on the field, I will. The game is out of hand—41–6—and more and more of our thin supply is being diminished.

In my brain fog, I do not see the play in which Quincy breaks his tibia—I only notice him, later, standing next to me on the sideline, blocking out the three-quarter moon. He's no longer wearing his helmet, jersey or shoulder pads, and his skin glistens with sweat, his face limned with pain. It is a dogfight.

I do not consider the possibility of getting a third concussion. I've gotten religion and will have my head on such a swivel. If I have to go back out there it will be rotating like an owl's. I know how idiotic this sounds to even be considering going back out, but it's a Bermuda Triangle of addiction, denial, and commitment.

Clearly I'm not capable of thinking right; even if my ribs are broken, they will heal. Even if my shoulder's dislocated, it will heal. My head? I simply can't think about it. If I keep my eyes open, I'll see the next one coming.

I realize now how ridiculous this is.

Muhammad Ali was never the same after the beating he took from Joe Frazier in 1971. Frazier was cruel, it was alleged, trying to prolong the fight so he could do damage to Ali, who Frazier felt had mocked and disrespected him in the weeks preceding the fight. Many people believe Ali's early onset of Parkinson's was related to that single event.

I'm not thinking about this, though. I'm thinking about these young and some not-so-young men who welcomed me into their community and supported me in this goofball project. They are as earnest as I am. How could I betray them, pulling back at the first sign of hardship to say, *Ah, I was only funnin'?* There's also something else—I really love this, really don't want to leave. Can selflessness and selfishness exist at the same moment, in the same desire? No one ever said the world, or life, was simple.

I'm all but staring transfixed, slack-jawed, at the clock. Now Kirby and Carter are, too. Coach is by himself at the end of the field, watching our spirited defense chase the quarterback. Watching them, I find myself wondering, how can we be down 41–6? It's only later in the week, watching the game film, that I'll understand the Red Raiders were starting to substitute freely, sending out their second, third, fourth, and fifth stringers to get game experience.

The quarter ends. This is the point—the end of each quarter—where the two teams switch ends of the field with the formality of square dance partners in order to keep any one team from having a disadvantageous benefit of the wind or the sun in their receiver's eyes. The concept of democracy: a level playing field is as difficult to achieve in football as in life.

●

HERE IS HOW addled I am. I've been watching the golden glowing numbers of the electronic scoreboard. When I look out to the field I see both teams merging, giving each other bedraggled low fives. I see our bench going out onto the field and do not understand it is just the offense, carrying water bottles out to the beleaguered defense during a time-out. I see what I want to see, the end of the game, and I run out onto the field to congratulate the other team as well as my teammates.

I'm all the way into the midst of them before I realize there are still another 15 minutes to play.

The players are spraying Gatorade bottles of water into their mouths, aiming the streams of water through their face masks, and when they're done, tossing the bottles to other teammates, who reach for them like lost souls in purgatory. Rainbow arcs of spray are created when the streams of water hit one of the face masks' crossbars, creating a cool mist that lands on all of us. Steam is rising off the players' arms and heads.

The referees are looking for the ball, trying to get the Red Raiders to their new end of the field, and the Texas Express to ours, and I realize at some groggy level that it's only the end of the third quarter, but I'm seized with hope, remembering that in Texas, there is a so-called "Mercy Rule" (also known as the "Slaughter Rule") that ends the game when one team gets too far ahead, to show mercy not just on the young men's self-esteem—why end up with a score, say, of 100–0?—but also on their bodies.

It was a bit of a bad dream to be out there, secretly celebrating the end of the game, when there was still some hard shit ahead.

Again, I'm amazed by all the things we cannot see when in the throne room of the concussed, to which all warriors have been exiled, across the ages. George Plimpton, in his wonderful book, *Shadow Box*, described how Ali spoke of the concussed state as being down in a basement: what Ali called "the Near Room," where alligators played trombones. *Exactly.* Fantastic, ominous, alluring.

What I did not see or know was that Kirby and Carter were intervening on my behalf: speaking to Coach, and to the team, telling them to not let me go back out on kickoffs, should the opportunity—the necessity—arise again.

Again, I set up my clock watch. The Red Raiders made a long drive before our defense stiffened and held them near the goal line, but finally, on fourth down, the Red Raiders scored again.

I buckled on my helmet for what I hoped would be the last time that night. I was running a little unevenly, to guard the pain in my ribs. I was already on the field when another Express player—Isaiah—came running alongside me, tapped me on the shoulder and said he had it.

I didn't feel demoted. In my memory, his jersey was as brilliant a white as if it had just been laundered, which confused me, for we were in a dogfight. It's only now that I realized what should've been obvious: Astroturf doesn't leave any stains. But in my rattled brain, I thought he was going in because he was fresher and stronger, and because I had been taking a beating.

I felt such sweet relief. Hands down, the best relief is that which comes when you're not expecting it. Humbled, I turned and headed back to the sideline. No one said anything, which I thought was a little odd, but in the Near Room, what isn't? Time was so cattywampus.

Later: five minutes, or a century? I couldn't have told you. Coach is self-isolating down at the far end of the field. I walk down there with my notepad in hand to ask how he's feeling. WTF? But I do.

The caul of gloom that surrounds him is like an electromagnetic force field. He winces over each missed tackle, each jump offsides, as if it is he who is out there being battered. Standing next to him, I can feel his concussive, galvanic shudders.

"Captain Rick," he says softly, "I haven't told anyone, but this is my last game. I'm going to hang it up after this one." His voice is barely louder than the sound of quiet breathing. I don't know what to say to this. I feel a sadness, but I do not try to talk him out of it. *Kirby*, I think. I wonder if Kirby could take it over.

I do not say anything. Coach is bent over as if in pain, both hands resting on his knees, his back bowed. The Red Raiders are inside our 10-yard line again. Coach straightens up. His face is hard. "Neil!" Coach shouts, seeing something in the Red Raiders' offense that electrifies him. "Line up over center, and the second he snaps the ball, you unload on him! Hit him like a ton of bricks! Punish his ass!"

Neil, who's playing off the line, moves in a little closer to the center.

"No!" howls Coach, pumping his fist. "Line up right over his motherfucking ass!"

Is their huge center the player who head-butted me on the free punt? Possibly. I'm on another planet.

It's one of those quiet stretches in the game where neither side is calling out encouragement; no trash-talking, no nothing—there's just clock melt. And now the Red Raider center, perhaps wondering what he has done to deserve being the target of Coach's wrath, is cutting Coach a bewildered side-eye, though he remains down in his three-point stance, the most vulnerable player on the field. If Neil does as Coach has instructed, Neil can crush him the instant the center moves to hike the ball.

"No, *Goddammit!*" Coach shrieks again, waving his arms for Neil to get even closer. "Get! Right! Over! His! Motherfucking! Ass!" Coach screams, and Neil scooches even closer, and finally with a bit more resolve. "Put him on his motherfucking *ass*!" Coach repeats, and now both sidelines are tense. And all the players on the field are tense. When the center finally snaps the ball, Neil does indeed lunge right over the top of him, driving him back into the quarterback, who, in turning away to avoid Neil's bull rush, runs into the arms of Chandler, coming in from his defensive end position.

And as if crushing an empty beer can, Chandler collapses the quarterback, killing their drive.

Now it's our ball, and we should be able to run out the clock, but this little victory comes with still more cost, for Chandler is limping off the field, holding his ribs, which he says are cracked as well. It's the second time in as many years I've seen him get injured—he plays with what analysts are fond of describing as a "high motor"—and it doesn't matter if you're puny or a giant like Chandler, bones are only so strong. They snap like dry branches when force strikes them calamitously. With their slatted bars of calcium, they do their job of encasing the delicate internal organs, including the lungs. What a marvel the body is! But ribs, being the first line of defense, can be extremely vulnerable in a game like football.

And then the clock is all zeroes.

"Let's go," is all Coach says, already gathering up gear and bags. The rest of us stream, single file, onto the field to do the hand-slap congratulations, and I'm glad to be wearing my yellow and black receiver's gloves, though if there are COVID germs in the Astroturf or on our cleats or on our gloves, it seems they will be spread even in the simple act of pulling our gloves off. But look—other than our broken bones and bruised brains and pulled and torn muscles—look how healthy we all are, running out to midfield shuttle and the gauntlet of opposing players with our murmuring hand-slapping chorus of *Good game, good game.*

I look for Number 29, but he is already gone—like an assassin, I think; his work complete.

"Come on, come on," one of the Red Raiders says. "The sooner we can get this done, the quicker we can be out of here." Just because we were beaten 41–6 does not mean both sides aren't hurting. A dogfight.

We gather for prayer, mixing it up as we always do after a game. I slide in behind a couple of giants, one in a red jersey, the other in white.

The home team coach always speaks first. He congratulates our valor as they always do after one of our losses—but this one seems to really mean it. The Red Raiders murmur ascent. Already, the hostility is fading.

It's cold. I'm shivering suddenly. I simply can't get warm. It's trauma. With one gloved hand on the back of one 300-pounder and my other hand resting on the back of another, I know I'm communicating my shudders into the entire huddle of perhaps 60 of us. And at one point, the giant Red Raider with his hand on my trembling back pats me. *There, there.*

Afterward, back on our sideline, Coach gathers us for the debrief. "I'll see y'all Thursday. We'll see who shows up. We'll see what happens," he says quietly. He does not speak of quitting. He talks about finding courage within ourselves. He talks about the need to look in the mirror.

It's not the first time he's addressed the need to look within ourselves, and not just as football players, but as men. As a linebacker, a former linebacker, he's furious that their shifty little running back did so well against us on the occasions he was able to break containment and cut back up into our thin secondary.

In a few days, none of it will matter. Or will seem not to matter.

There are those who say there is a grand design, a deep order to everything, seen from a distance of time and space, that's impossible for us down at ground level to comprehend. But that night, it mattered. "If y'all don't want to play football, just tell me so, right now," Coach says. "By God, y'all need to decide if you want to be men or pussies," he says, and I flinch. *Oh, Anthony.* "Don't be whining to me about the refs, or about being manhandled. Somebody holds you, slap him in the head.

"Isaiah," he says, "come over here." I think there is not one of us who does not believe Coach is going to slap Isaiah—easily one of the biggest men on the team—upside the head.

Isaiah approaches. "Come closer," Coach demands.

Isaiah edges in another step.

"Closer," Coach insists, patting the side of his leg as if summoning a dog. Isaiah steps all the way in, so that they're chest-to-chest. For some reason, I have never thought of Coach as a big or even very formidable man, due perhaps to his advancing age, and, at times, easy manner. But standing there thrust up against Isaiah, Coach seems to be inflating, swelling with muscle, crackling with hostility. "Go ahead and hold me," Coach says. "Make like you're holding me."

Coach's timing seems impulsive, reckless, fascinating: why coach them now, after such a beat down?

Isaiah places his hands tentatively, gently, on Coach's shoulders—a teenager at prom: first date, first dance.

"No!" Coach says. "Grab me by the chest, by the jersey. *Here.*" He tugs at his own jersey and illustrates being held, and Isaiah lowers his hands, scolded, and grips Coach's shirt, though again, carefully.

"*Grab it*, goddammit! If you're going to do it, *do it*," Coach hisses. "Act like you're holdin' me!" And finally, chastened, Isaiah grabs a double handful of Coach's shirt.

Quick as karate, Coach lifts both his fists high in the air, then slams his elbows down on Isaiah's vulnerable forearms: leverage, speed, power. It's a wonder he didn't snap them like branches. Isaiah's hands release their grip reflexively; his arms drop and swing away crookedly.

But Coach isn't through. Now he raises a right hand to cuff Isaiah's ear, stopping his open palm suddenly just at the interface of skin and pain.

"That's how you do it," Coach says. He nods to Isaiah that he can back away. "Don't be coming to me complaining about the refs not calling holding. Take matters into your own hands."

The technique was impressive. Later I will wonder why he's never thought to share it with his linemen. Maybe there's never been a need to. Maybe they've never been manhandled.

Attentive to his instruction, what I noticed more than the effectiveness of the maneuver was Coach's facial expressions during the attempted hold, then the uplift of the arms, and the violent, downward separation. His face was a flashcard montage of concern, a micro-wisp of fear. Look again, and it would have vanished like a ghost behind cascading masks of agitation, then determination, followed by a few frames of rage.

●

SO VERY MANY of Coach's prayers invoke armies—referencing the struggle of our few, our band, and how in God our might could be as great as or superior to that of armies of "10,000" and "20,000." Or, on really troubling days, "40,000."

I wasn't judging—judge not lest ye be judged—but his religiosity seemed to have a fluidity to it, a come-and-go aspect, which seemed to potentially undercut any of the rock-ribbed foundational qualities one might expect from a more zealous warrior.

What I realize now—that night with his threats to quit—is that he is a man struggling. That he cannot quit. That the games and practices are the thinnest laminae that separates him from an abyss that lies beyond even more despair. And that these losses—which he views as humiliations—are like the debilitating rays of light, disintegrating that thin shield and leaving him vulnerable. Leaving him fragile, shivering.

"Y'all were *valorous*, and all that," he says. "I commend you for that.

But God damn it, you have to decide if you want to win or not. They're not better than you." And again, the beseeching: "You got to come to practice." His voice has dropped back down into its quiet register. But as is so often the case, that merely precedes the rising again. "Y'all got to come to practice," he says. "We can't win if you don't come to practice. You got to get up off the couch and stop layin' around smoking cigarettes, eating Cheetos," he says. He does not add his usual, ". . . and jacking off," perhaps because Carter and Michelle are standing nearby on the track now, watching and listening as he lays the whip across all of us like, well, what can I say, like Jesus accosting the money changers in the temple.

And just like that, with a swerve, he's back up into the lofty chambers of fury and maybe rage again. "Y'all are on track to lose all 10 of your games," he says, his voice thick with disgust. "The choice is yours. Only y'all can decide. I can't go out there and play the game for you. I wish I could, because I *am* a football player." He thumps his chest for emphasis, pacing before us now. "By God, I *am* a football player."

Anger is fear, I tell myself for maybe the hundredth time, watching him, trying to peer down into the darkness to glimpse or even guess at the nature of the wound that's still evidently so raw, so unhealable. Or which perhaps heals, though thinly, so that it is easily disturbed, and with the pain somehow worse, not better, with each resurrection.

It's like a fever. It washes over him. I think it must feel to him as if he can't breathe. As if his lungs are filling with soil. As if iron bars are closing in all around him, his ribs squeezing ever tighter against his lungs until he can no longer breathe.

He's done with us for the night. With a full third of our team crippled, we limp and hobble off into the night. The Red Raiders' side of the field is completely vacated, as if they were never here.

Carter comes to join me and offers to carry my duffel, but I tell her it's important to me that I carry it—not just for my pride, but so that my teammates will not be demoralized, seeing me so beaten—but I ask her to walk extra slowly, so that it looks as if we're merely sauntering. And she does, her arm in mine: for sweetness, not aid.

It's a long walk to where we parked. It seems like half a day ago. The parking lot is dense with the scent of weed. I find I'm craving a cold beer. The pain, as they say, is racking. I'm moving slowly in the darkness. Carter helps me lift my duffel into the car and as I struggle to come out of my cleats without bending over I realize I've left my tennis shoes on the field.

I couldn't any more make that walk back there than I could run up Kilimanjaro. Carter hurries back to find them—it turns out Dooney picked them up for me—and I climb up into the car, lean the seat back, take a couple more Aleve, and we head back west into the night, away from Baytown, limping forward into what we know not.

8

PRACTICE

MARCH, 2020: THE DIFFERENCE in the world between last Saturday's game and Thursday's practice is as profound as any I have experienced. The Kennedy assassination and 9/11 are the only similar timeline markers that come to mind, capable of shaking the ground we stand on and the nature of all of our assumptions or denials about the world we enter into each morning.

The globalization of the pandemic, and the speed of its transmission, coupled with its invisibility, is unparalleled in my lifetime. John M. Barry's terrifying book, *The Great Influenza*, about the 1918 flu, should be required reading. My own feeling is, there isn't enough respect for the virus out there. That there is a sense of entitlement or, just as bad, taking-for-grantedness, which is a close cousin to arrogance.

It's hard to witness. I feel like we're just standing here flat-footed, waiting for it to wash over us: the kickoff team's gunners coming at us from all directions. And in our midst, the holy lands of the United States have only just now recorded their first case. Soon enough there will be 10 million of them, then 20 million. But for now, today, just one.

Science has gone into hiding. We are led by an ex-reality show host and broke-ass real estate developer. We have put ourselves in an untenable, unwinnable, situation. Things now can only play themselves out—what physicists sometimes call "a forced move in a designed space"—wherein the outcome of a thing simply cannot be otherwise.

Our relationship with time will soon change. In the coming isolation, the days will paradoxically pass faster—so fast we will lose track of them. Sports leagues around the country will cancel their seasons.

The actor Tom Hanks and his partner, Rita Wilson, will be among the first celebrities to contract the virus, helping us all along the hurried on-ramp toward the realization that this is not a drill. The chief executive of the United States—I prefer not to utter his name—will, upon hearing a couple of weeks later that Hanks was discharged from the hospital, fail to comprehend the meaning of the word *discharge* and will rush to tweet, before being corrected, that Hanks died.

The executive did not win as many votes as his opponent in the 2016 election, but it was enough to change much in our country. And the stain of his presence may, through his political appointees, be injected into the judicial system and linger for another generation.

Football. Everybody plays it, everybody watches it. In theory, football—like hunting, perhaps—is one of the increasingly rare social activities which in the past has, for the most part, sought to transcend politics. Notable of course is Colin Kaepernick's elegant, silent protest toward the epidemic of racial profiling and violence by police in this country—a free speech gesture that instantly polarized fans egged on by the same chief executive who called the players "sons of bitches" and said they should be fired.

Kaepernick sacrificed his career—he'd come within one throw of winning the Super Bowl while playing for the San Francisco 49ers—but who knows, perhaps his loss was also his gain, in that he might've avoided the onset of CTE.

I had hopes that we, the Texas Express, might be able to have Kaepernick come out for a game, either to throw some drills to our players, or even to draw attention to the struggle of young Black men and the disparity of socioeconomic strata, while highlighting also how ridiculous is the monopoly of NFL owners, 31 of whom are white and 31 of whom are male, with the median age of ownership being 74.

Kaepernick, one of the most qualified quarterbacks on the planet, could not find work, even as one starting quarterback after another was removed from the pool. Drew Brees, a torn thumb; Ben Roethlisberger, a broken elbow; Alex Smith, a gruesome compound leg fracture. The year previous: Teddy Bridgewater, the same injury. Even Tim Tebow's flagrant celebration of Christianity, a few years before, failed to divide the league and fans; as long as he could play, they let him play, no matter his personal beliefs. But Kaepernick—a Black man—had made the time-dishonored mistake of rising above his station. Of crossing boundaries.

●

I DRIVE NONSTOP from Marfa again with my bruised lung and broken ribs, to arrive just as the team, or some fractional representation thereof—the same old regulars, plus a few more new guys—is gathering beneath the lights of the park.

I'm at the wrong end of Jackson Park, next to tennis courts where, illuminated in a pool of hot white light amid the darkness, an army of old fit silver-haired white ladies in shorts and T-shirts are playing tennis with wooden paddles. *Pickleball.* I've heard of it.

The sound of so many of them whaling the tar out of so many pickleballs is disconcerting—the wooden paddles so much more violent than that of the buoyantly-strung tennis rackets—and I walk quickly away from the scene, which looks to me like a tableau of being a little too close to madness.

With the world poised at the edge of a cliff, what else to do for some, the forgotten and the marginalized—the elderly—but slam and slam again those wooden rackets, wielded like clubs?

I hurry across the dark soccer field to the other side where I can see the small clot of young men, my team, gathered under a single overhead lamp, their plastic shoulder pads glinting like river rocks, and their navy blue helmets like polished gemstones.

Kirby is there, though only for a while; he has to go to a Mason's meeting. Our old standbys are there—Neil, Ernie, Kojo, Big Ray. So too are some of our heroes from Houston—our two quarterbacks, Shaun and Shane, and Dooney and Corey, father of Little Man. Coach is in an easy, almost ebullient mood, which puzzles me. He's *merry*; loose in a way I've never quite seen him. The man of a thousand faces.

He shoots the shit for a while, making no reference to the Red Raider game. He tells us he has to run Neil and Neil's girl, as she's referred to—her name is Jamie—back to Neil and Jamie's apartment with their groceries. Then he'll be right back. I ask if I can ride with them. I don't really want to be in such non-distancing proximity—the news is only just now starting up, no panic has occurred yet—but, though cautious, I also am hungry to hang out.

It's a tight squeeze into the back cab of Coach's big fancy Ford Lariat. There is an upended laundry basket's worth of sweet soap-smelling tangled clothes, as well as various bags of groceries, shoulder pads, helmets, and whatnot. Coach kind of claws everything into a larger pile in the center so I can fit my narrow self in the back. Up front, Neil looms, and in the back seat behind him, next to me, Jamie.

Coach fields some phone calls on the ride back to Neil and Jamie's. All of a sudden, other, lesser leagues have taken note of our situation, and are extending offers—essentially encouraging us to jump ship, to step down a level or two in competition and join their league.

Coach waves the proof around on his phone—the illuminated texts and e-mails—and scoffs. His phone begins to ring. He looks down at caller ID; sees it's yet another team that's heard about our ass-kicking and wants us to take a step down and join them.

"Texas Roadrunners," he says, looking at the phone. "No way I'm gonna answer. I don't even know 'em. *Roadrunners*," he says.

As if on cue, another call rolls in. "Port Arthur *Bumblebees*?" Coach slaps his knee, the epitome of jest. It's just a typical Coach moment, but I feel the first subtle cleaving hair's-breadth variance between his plan, and, for lack of better phrasing, mine. All along, given Coach's incredible and ceaseless devotion to the mission—caring for, and leading, these hungry young men—it has seemed to me that, given the scatter of their lives and their sometimes limited resources, any attention and commitment paid to them whatsoever was a plus. That even tilted attention was better than none at all.

In no way did or do I hold Coach responsible for the serial battery and other mayhem that has begun to move with the team like a trailing shadow. It's a terrible thought to consider, but I wonder if it would be even worse if Coach were not present in their lives, giving them hope, demanding discipline and accountability. Providing sideboards, and creating a vessel with the potential for unity.

In the 1963 memoir *Run to Daylight!*, Green Bay Packers' coach Vince Lombardi compares two of his finest defensive players, Ray Nitschke and Dan Curry, both linebackers and pretty much identically shaped—six feet, three inches, 235 to 240 pounds. (Linebackers today—playing the middle and most violent part of the field—have changed little; they might on average be an inch shorter, but no lighter. This is, I think, further evidence that, on defense, linebackers are the immutable heart, the gearworks of the sport itself.)

"Nitschke," wrote Lombardi, differentiating him favorably from Curry, "[has] said that he has enjoyed belting."

I see the same dynamic in sweet Neil, who has been tasked with replacing Jamaar, who clearly loved plugging holes violently and directing the rest of his defense to do so; but who is now off the team, having been charged with domestic abuse before he played even a single game.

I do not see in Coach, however, anything resembling the nuance Lombardi ascribed to himself in treating players of different temperaments with individual adjustments. Perhaps it's simply a matter of capacity. Without any assistants to help him, any flexibility with player protocols could end up relegating Coach to babysitting 15 to 20 young men in any given week. Easier for him and his faith, I think, to have isolated, unmalleable rules. *My way or the highway.*

But there in the truck, something feels off. At first blush, the recruitment to a lesser league, or the merging of two teams, sounded interesting to me. We've been outscored 90–12 in two games. We're being crippled, young and old alike—cut down as if with a scythe. Some will heal; others will suffer injuries that will affect them for the rest of their lives.

What would be wrong in realizing we're in over our head, and stepping down a level? It's just a game, right? Does he really think we can win against the big city teams, with only a dozen players going up against such greater numbers, and with only eight or so of us even practicing once a week?

We reach Neil and Jamie's apartment. They climb out, gather their bags of groceries, and take them inside. Without a car, they try to get a week's worth, whenever they can get a ride. (Back before Neil's knee surgery, Kirby and I would see him limping down the road with a double handful of groceries, the bags twisting in his hands and bumping his legs as he trudged. And always, Kirby would stop and pick him up and say, *Neil, why didn't you call me?* And Neil would shrug and smile and look away and down, an unvoiced answer of *I didn't want to*, and *I didn't need to*, and *Thank you, I appreciate it.*

Neil has no real business playing middle linebacker. He has the heart of a lion, and can and will play any position on the field, but the killer instinct, the desire to do damage—the wrecking ball frenzy required of the middle linebacker—is not compatible with his loving spirit. And the fact that he has been forced into this critical position by Jamaar's expulsion is only further evidence to me that we are in over our head. And while adversity can be a forge for the smithy of character, I feel as a team we might be skating past adversity and closer instead into the territory of calamity.

Neil gives Jamie a chaste kiss, then climbs back up into the tall truck, and we head back toward the practice field where the rest of the team is waiting. The talk turns to the virus. The consensus from the front seat is that it's nothing to worry about. Neil surprises me by bringing up the HIV epidemic; that it was created to harm Black people. He shoots me a gentle look to let me know he does not hold me accountable. And Coach nods vigorously, saying, "This coronavirus, or whatever it is, is something created by a bunch of old white men who can't be trusted." He glances in the rearview mirror to catch my eye. "No offense to present company, Cap'n Rick."

I feel unmoored—as if suddenly on a raft of ice, spinning fast away from the mainland. I struggle to find a common ground.

I scramble. I have no real idea of what they think of the chief executive, but back before he turned orange, with those ridiculous white bags around his puffy-fat eyes from where he has lain beneath a sunlamp with his eyes closed for long periods, baking, while wearing blinders, goggles (there is no metaphor)—surely this is an old white man we can all agree is dangerous.

"That man would sell us all down the river," I say, unconsciously or subconsciously using an old slave aphorism.

"Amen," Coach agrees, and I feel a quick hit of relief—attachment, reconnection. *We're all in this together.*

There are still zero cases in Texas; it's just isolated in a rest home in Seattle—but in no way do I believe we, America, are protected by an invisible translucent shield, a meniscus of grace, from that which seeks to harm only the innocent in China. I do not believe that by virtue of geography or any other kind of superiority we will be spared the coming wave. It would be nice to think so, but I do not believe it.

We know that hand sanitizer kills the virus, and that this evening I have been shaking hands with and hugging players, a couple of whom—Coach, and the super-healthy Kojo—have a severe cough. I have a little travel tube of sanitizer in my pocket, and there in the darkness of the back seat I open it and apply it to my hands. It's been five days since the ass-whipping. Maybe the virus is already in all of us. Maybe it's in the wind or the soil, the cold late winter/early spring sky, the grass across which we run. Maybe it's on the door handles of Coach's truck and in the tight enclosed cab. Maybe . . .

"Whoooo, boy!" Neil exclaims, jerking in his seat as if someone's just ripped a foul and enormous fart.

"It's my sanitizer," I explain. "Did you think it was my deodorant?"

They both laugh, a little, yet I feel, in my ridiculously white liberal way, another degree of separation—not an estrangement, but a distancing. I know how it must look—that I'm timid, weak, frightened—and I wish they would choose to see it a different way. That if I were any of those things, I would not be out on the field with them. I just feel I have a responsibility: to myself, but to others as well.

Still riding there in the dark, all of us jammed into the cab of the truck, there is that distance stretching, expanding, as the cab fills with the scent of green apple sanitizer.

●

WHEN WE GET back to Jackson Park, Ernie is leading the men in stretches. "All right, jumping jacks on me, jumping jacks on two, jumping jacks on *what*?"

"*Two!*" shout the players. And I get that feeling I always get when the practice is first beginning, and we are in unison, perfect and unmarred: the sensation of pushing the dory out into the waves—feeling the sand or smooth stones underfoot, and then lifting one's self up into the boat, and into a new medium that is neither land nor sea, nor sky and gliding, and pulling into it. The unification more powerful than shared prayer or song, for it is not merely hopeful, nor passive; it is *active*. We are embarking on a journey, and trying to control what we can control, and we are doing so together. There is a sweetness in the blood that is the childhood cadence of counting, *One! Two! Three! Four!*

Coach is so chill. Neil walks out onto the lawn to join them—*Saigon Squat*, the crouched groin stretch, then crossed-ankle toe touches—and it pains me to not be there with them. One can feel loved or trusted or supported, but the body knows, or believes it knows: street clothes are the uniform of a pariah, of one who is weak or unlucky, or the body politic must consider this—both.

They've all been where I am, with my cracked ribs and concussion; they know it sucks. They do not mean to distance, but there must be one. It is biological. They are each supreme captains of their bodies, and therefore of their destinies; and during practice, and during the games, and during the season, the body is its fullest and best self.

The body does not exclude the mind—they remain connected—but the body is the captain, and it is a magnificent thing, a remembrance. An old memory from a time when we were more physically engaged with our existence.

There in the warm-ups, with everyone clapping their hands on *one* or *two*, it is a milder, less carbonated version of the way it is in a game, with so much more at stake, when the quarterback, the captain, has told us the snap count, with the ball to be hiked on *one* or *two* or even, dramatically, the first *sound*.

I think about the great Peyton Manning, and other crafty veterans like Tom Brady, Aaron Rodgers, and Drew Brees, who could manipulate defenses with their voices and the cadences of their snap counts, pulling over-eager defensive lineman across the line of scrimmage just before the play began, offsides: a five-yard penalty. I think about the coveted blessing of a free play, wherein the quarterback could heave the ball down the field, going for it all, knowing there was nothing to lose, that they were playing with house money, for even if the ball was intercepted in the secondary, the play would be coming back for a do-over, repeat the down. But with a five-yard gift tacked on, moving the ball ever farther down the field.

In the game, waiting on that snap count, you're lined up in your position, poised, and whether in the backfield or up on the line, no matter. You're listening so intently, waiting for that crystalline moment when the one word at just the one right time is uttered, releasing you, telling you to *go*, to enter fully, as passionately as you can, the world of the physical.

Tensed there, waiting for that command to explode—to surge with all the power and speed you possess, all the yearning and all the will—your first responsibility is to yourself; to not flinch, to not leap until the call comes: *leap*. Control what you can control: your own response.

But there is simultaneously a connection and a trust to and of each and all the other 10 of you who are similarly paused and poised, waiting to surge together. The success of the 11 depends upon the coordination, the synchrony, of each individual. You are isolated, but in your isolation—in the myth of your isolation—you are connected.

It's ridiculous. I'm a grown man and then some. But I love it. I love the clap of hands when we break the huddle and deploy to our positions. I love the perfect waiting—the perfect stillness, concentrated almost to an unbearable, quivering tension—and then: life, and light.

There at the park, Coach weaves and sways in his relaxed cobra-swagger as he shares the gospel according to Coach. He'll do anything to motivate us. Tonight, he's like the well-meaning but flawed, imperfect patriarch of a big old fucked-up complicated family. If we won't win for Jesus, or even for Coach or for each other, the way he wants, then maybe we'll at least do it out of self-interest.

Before practice starts, Coach, who has had the opportunity to look at the game film from the Red Raiders game, motions for me to come to the front of the circle. He puts his big arm around me and pulls me in closer, his ungloved hand gripping my shoulder and neck as I imagine he might grasp a runaway dog by its collar. I wiggle and writhe like a child receiving unwelcome affection from an elderly uncle.

"Y'all men should be ashamed of yourselves after that game," he says. "This old man is older than y'all's *grandfathers* and y'all were making him get out there and take a beating for you. This man has the heart of a lion. I need y'all to man up," Coach pleads. "Why'd y'all tuck your tail in that game? You all played with heart," he says. "I admire that. You're learning to laugh in the face of adversity, but I can't have you all laughing at the end of a game after you've lost. Laugh later on," he says, "but not there on the sideline, right after a game."

As he discusses the logistics of losing, I feel his grip loosen a bit, and I use the opportunity to wiggle away. I know what he's doing, trying to fire the players up with what often seems to be the only tool in his psychological playbook—shame, or sometimes, shame with a twist of anger or rage—but I couldn't be more mortified. I fear my singling-out risks having the effect of creating more distance.

Who would want to be the Goody-Two-Shoes the teacher uses to punish the others? I've been working hard to earn the trust of my teammates, and this threatens to turn my efforts totally bass-ackwards. I slip away, back into the throng, an unwilling participant in praise. I take my place quickly at the back again, and glancing around, I want to believe the players understand what Coach was doing. That they understand I in no way share Coach's sentiments.

"My arm is long," Coach tells us, extending one arm toward one side, then the other in the opposite direction. "It reaches from Texas to California, from Texas to Arizona. It reaches from Texas to Florida," he says, naming some of the places where he has placed players previously in his career: Arizona State, various junior colleges in California, Texas Tech, Minnesota, North Dakota. The football universe is vast, the constellations myriad. There are so many rooms in the father's mansion.

One of our star linebackers, Gabriel, has been courted after the Red Raider game by another big team in Houston, the Panthers. Gabriel has posted on social media that he's tempted, and is asking what we would do. Some of the players are excited for him, while others are grumbling, feeling abandoned. Used and discarded. Coach certainly is among the latter, while Kojo, one of Gabriel's closest friends, is supportive and understanding—a prelude, it occurs to me, to the perhaps inevitable time when Kojo, too, is tapped.

Only for a moment, however, does Coach fuss about Gabriel. His feelings are hurt, sure, but he's pleased to have 14 of us tonight.

It's really kind of a dream practice: *playful*. It sucks, my being in street clothes. The team breaks up into clumps; the backs and receivers run various pass routes. There are no yard markers with which to calibrate any precision for the route trees, and it's really just street ball, with receivers wiggling and waggling, breaking off their routes unpredictably sometimes in order to get free of the defender. The passes from Shane are not always accurate, though he does have a cannon for an arm, able to power the ball downfield no matter his footwork and the inattentiveness to form.

The receivers, as well, are off. Watching them, it's hard to imagine they're semi-pro: easier in their loose, wandering routes, their exclamations when the ball bounces off their hands, or they fumble the sure and easy interception (still brain-battered, I just wrote *imagination* instead of *interception*) that they have become anew the children they once were, when the game was new to them and they were first coming to the sport, their fast-growing and absorbent minds soaking in greedily the complicated rules and elegant logic. Understanding, quickly, its organic power and effective system of checks and balances; as if the game, so brilliantly conceived and at times executed, was a thing imbued almost with life itself, and which would remain vital and immortal, even as the children were carried on past childhood into whatever future awaited, beyond the boundaries of the game.

Later, Coach—still merry, like a patriarch who has all of his large and loving family gathered around him—divides us, *them*, into two teams: Bigs versus Littles. "Rick is the out-of-bounds," he calls. Coach is quarterback for the Bigs—it's touch, not tackle, of course—and it simulates the hurry-up offense. All six players become receivers, allowing only one rusher to pressure and pursue the quarterback.

It's easy pickings; both teams move up and down the field on the other. It's simple pitch-and-catch, sandlot ball. The joy, the glory of play, burns hot in their hearts. They are *competing*, though it means nothing. The perfect shape of the football is spiraling, arching through the night sky, a great and primal beauty, like the arc described by the heave of a long javelin throw.

The receivers catch the ball every time with both hands, then tuck it quickly and safely away into the cradle formed between ribs and bent elbow. The ball is protected by bicep and forearm, with the player's heart beating against the taut drum of the football—the same amount of air contained within it as there had once been in a lobe of lung of the child the player had been a few short years ago.

Mercurial doesn't begin to describe Coach. It is not until all of the players are covered with a sheen of sweat that Coach finally winds the practice down. It's almost 10:00 p.m., and some of them have to drive to small towns half an hour away or farther.

Coach calls us in, gathers us in—he's breathing heavy, still coughing a bit, as is the otherwise exquisitely healthy Kojo—and, as ever, we draw in shoulder-to-shoulder, holding hands, to pray. Coach surprises us all by asking Kojo to give the prayer—I am holding Kojo's right hand with my left one—and after a moment's pause, Kojo lowers his head, as do we all, and Coach begins to speak to the Lord, thanking him for our health.

"Kojo," Coach interrupts, still in his merry phase, but with some small, almost indescribable edge in his voice, some jocularity that feels in some way slightly conscious that the mood is jocular.

"Kojo, what do you think you're doin' with your eyes right now? You got to close your eyes when you pray," Coach says. "You can't be lookin' all around while you're talkin' to *God*."

Which is exactly what I've been doing, too—watching Kojo watch all the downturned faces as he speaks. And anyway, how does Coach know Kojo's got his eyes open?

Kojo, for all of his naïveté and innocence, is cunning in other ways—always looking around and thinking. I like how he asks so many questions. *Obey little, resist much*—Whitman—and, of course, *Question authority*.

After Kojo and Coach get done with their back-and-forth joshing over the eyes-closed/eyes-open thing, Kojo falls back into prayer, head down, but his eyes are still alternately opening and closing, side-eyeing around while all the other players close their eyes. Yes, I'm still watching.

Kojo follows Coach's template for a while—thanking the Lord that all of us arrived at practice safely, and for our health (Coach has been coughing big spraying coughs that discharge more aerosols even than usual, via his shouts), but with a mischievousness I didn't know he had in him. Kojo goes on to praise his friend Gabriel—Gabriel the Deserter—at great length, talking about how happy we all are for Gabriel's good fortune, and ask that he be kept safe, too.

Practice 165

Amen, we say, and practice is over. We're free to drift. And a few, like Ray, just out of prison, still have far to go. (I picture his mother in Hempstead waiting up for him, asking how practice went. Asking if he likes the folks he's hanging out with now.) It's the same band, only 8 or 10 of us, at practices. It's tight. We can't win this way. But it's tight.

It's clear to me now, and I think increasingly to Coach, that there are some who show up for practice as well as game day—a small core. There is another subset of those who show up for game day only. There are still others who show up for neither, and there are some who, almost inexplicably, show up for practice, but are absent on game day.

In all, there are as many permutations as can be mathematically created, and Coach must deal with the seemingly infinite variations, a different arrangement each week. *Why?*

For a man to whom utter control is often paramount, this must claw horribly at whatever howling wound still resides within him.

For a man with such a wound, the solace and promise afforded by the opportunity to give his earthly troubles up to a celestial being far greater than any man must seem like a sanctuary indeed. I say this not to belittle or marginalize his faith. Indeed, what courage it must take—the courage of hope—to step from a mindset of complete control to one of complete surrender.

With practice and prayer over, we remain in a loose cluster—bullshitting, as we transition out of our fully football selves and into our other selves. We remove ourselves once more, grudgingly, from the snow globe of the park's lights and disperse back into the shadows.

From time to time, I surreptitiously reach into my pocket and flip open the lid of a travel-size sanitizer Carter gave me. I give it a squeeze, feel the wet pulse of it, rub it between my hands. I'm not quite old enough to remember the segregated water fountains in either Texas or Mississippi, but I know they were still around when I was a youngster. I'm old enough to carry that natural shame, that dismay—the inability to change the past. I'm concerned that my mania for hygiene might widen the gulf farther, just as we were closing it. My fear in this regard is electric; my heart is racing as if I'm doing something incredibly wrong, and I feel a million miles away from my team.

Kojo's asking Coach about Evan, which is interesting, given that Kojo never knew him. Evan the Legend: the arbiter of and cautionary tale for youth gone wrong. Kojo's fascinated and is trying to figure out where Evan went off the path; how a player under Coach's umbrella, Coach's shadow, could stray.

It touches a nerve in Coach. There seem to be so many nerves. Or maybe there is just one huge nerve, hidden deep, surrounded by a core of muscle—the protective fibers spiraling like the stripes on a barber's pole: day, night, day, night.

"You want to know what got Evan in trouble? He didn't listen," Coach says. "He didn't listen to me. I went to court for him. He wouldn't *listen*."

"But what did he do?" Kojo asks, fascinated by the depth of Evan's fall from grace.

"Ah," Coach says, "He fired his gun up in the air three times." (Later, when I tell Kirby this, he will raise his eyebrows. Evan fired through the wall of an apartment where his ex-girlfriend was living.) Coach pivots to address Shane.

"*You*," he says, in the harsh voice he saves for shaming—the voice laced with despair, which, to my sensitive ear, sounds like disgust—"You should be playing at A&M right now."

Shane ducks his head in acknowledgment, the very picture of regret and shame. I don't know what trouble Shane got into, had no idea he was yet another of Coach's reclamation projects. "You should be starting at A&M," Coach says, digging his spurs in, and big Shane droops his head even lower; says nothing.

"You got to do what I tell you," Coach says.

Shane's hawking phlegm. Kojo is still coughing his dry cough. Not for the first time will I wonder if some of them, some of us, have not already been afflicted with the coronavirus, but have kept muscling on, motoring on, and are fast healers, already coming through the other side of it, fit as they are, and have now developed some immunity.

Practice 167

And there is a part of me that hopes this is the case, even as there is, of course, another part of me that hopes no such thing. I still have so much work to do.

I remember the Bible story about Passover: how the righteous, if I recall correctly, would place the blood of a lamb on the door so that the Angel of Death would pass over them—would keep on traveling, searching, I suppose, for the wicked, or at least the unrighteous.

I find myself remembering how in the autumn, up in Montana, when my daughters were young and I would be out in the mountains, chasing for days and weeks on end the elk we so loved to eat when I was fortunate enough to find and catch up with an animal, I would come in from the garage at night after long hours of butchering.

Invariably there would be a smear of blood on my cheek, on my jacket and my pants, on my hands, on my knife's sheath, on my arms. And I'd leave a brush of blood on the door or the doorknob in my coming and going, my back-and-forth transport of the bounty. I'd wash it off eventually, but it pleased me to see it there, the signature of the hunt, and a seasonal ritual marker. A pagan, I supposed, taking note of such spiritual doings in the fall rather than the spring; but it felt good to me—respectful and even worshipful—in synchrony with the north country. It did not make me feel righteous, but it made me feel connected to something ancient, and powerful—as does Coach, I realize, feel connected to his religion, and feels the duty to share it. Feels that it is what the lost sheep need. Feels, perhaps, it is an act of generosity to share it, promote it.

I am trying to understand him. I'm intent upon not judging any of them. They are my friends; we are a band. Are not all men brothers?

Is it really so ridiculous, in such an increasingly confused world, to consider that in some strange way, there is a purity retained in the spirit or essence of football, and a terrible beauty? That it is a place, controlled if not necessarily safe, where great and concentrated emotion can prevail, can rise from within us and flow out of us?

Is this not what art does? And, sometimes, religion?

For all of the tawdry commercialism in the pro game (and to a lesser extent, in the college game, where universities and other businesses profit grossly from the labor of and violent damage to student athletes), I do think there is a purity of logic, an intellectual, primal elegance, like that of chess, in the sport itself, if not always in the men who play it.

And there is a hunger, a craving, in the boys and men who flock and throng to it: a desire for connection, communion, and a simplicity of meaning at the surface, overlying a vast network of complicated and often opposing forces.

How can a person *not* be drawn to it—a world out on a field where every complicated thing is so clarified? And how can we, as spectators, not watch?

Would I ever let a child of mine, beloved above all else, play the sport? *Hell no.* Are you crazy?

●

ALONG WITH SHANE'S imperfect past, his unidentified misstep named but not identified, only lumped in with Evan's grand felony, Coach keeps searching for trouble, for opposition: a roving middle linebacker, searching the gaps one by one, trying to determine what danger—what *threat*—might be coming through the hole.

Coach is definitely back on the other side, unfrivolous now. As if realizing and remembering, perhaps, that he is not here to be soft on any of them. That the best he can give them are the rigid iron sideboards of discipline.

"This damn *virus*, or whatever they call it," he says, his voice thick with scorn. "God is going to take you when he's ready, and not one minute before," he says. He is using his Coach voice, his linebacker voice; and while it has heretofore been sweet and somewhat charming, in a roguish way—his gathering together of this band of misfits that we are—there is a new depth of anger to him.

And if all anger is fear, what is his?

"God decides, not man, when we die," he warns again. It's the same voice he uses when he's telling Neil to line up directly on top of the

Practice 169

center and thump the motherfucking hell out of him. The same voice when he's screaming at Kojo to catch the goddamn ball.

"God is in control of everything," he says. "I've faced death before," he says, and there's an irritated part of me that wants to say *No shit, Sherlock, who hasn't?* But then I look at the faces of the mostly young men who are still gathered around him in a loose circle and see they are spellbound, as rapt as I've ever seen them. Attentive to the complicated and mysterious rivers of blood and fate and future and destiny that run just beneath the feet of all of us.

"The first time, I was 19," he says. "I was fooling around, seeing this married woman. She was 23." He nods toward one of the players. "You know her son," he says, and identifies the man, who I realize must be full-grown, in his thirties. "I was in *shape*," Coach says. "I was the baddest dude in the county. I told her to come with me, to leave her husband. I went to meet her in a parking lot. When I did, this dude, her husband, was in the car with her. I went over there and told her again to leave him, to come with me."

No one's breathing. Why is he telling us this stuff? When he never has before? Coach's voice is steady, strong. "This dude got out of his car and walked over to where I was standing and put a pistol to my head. This cat said, 'If you ever fuck with my wife again, I'll kill you.'" He lets that sink in. "Praise God, praise Jesus, God decided to spare me," he says. "I give thanks," he whispers, then swoops back up to the evangelical surge: "I give *thanks*!"

This isn't what I wanted, I think. *This isn't what I signed on for. This doesn't feel good*, I think. But just as in a game, when you're on the front line to receive a kickoff, and the other 11 are lined up right across from you, waiting for the next moment, the next instant, when they can be released upon you like wild dogs—there is no choice but to put your ears back and go right at them.

The integrity of the game depends upon it. This is one of its many lessons. If you're going to do a thing, you have to be all in. "Fill your hands, you sons of bitches," cries Jeff Bridges, playing the part of Rooster Cogburn in the Coen brothers' remake of *True Grit*.

On the railroad tracks on the hill, just above the park, a night train passes, freight cars heading south—no lights, no horn, no wail, just the relentless, rhythmic clacking that is the sound of the tracks' unfolding. The thing that can only end one way.

"Story time's over," Coach says, as he comes back up out of his intense-place. He looks over at the shirtless Kojo, his washboard abs and tiny waist. Kojo has his arms crossed, has been listening as rapt as any of the others. "Kojo, stop playing with your titties," Coach says, and everyone laughs, and we start to drift back to our cars.

And again I feel the rift, the widening, not just that I couldn't practice, especially in the two-minute touch drill, but also at the inexplicable widening wrought between my fret over the towering wave of the pandemic, and I'm chagrined at my coach's and teammates' absence of fret. This combines with the slow but steady creep of awareness that I will never play again—that a thing I love is being taken away from me by a thing I can no longer control: time. And there's a feeling also that I've stayed around a little too long—that I'm somehow to blame for my own loss. Three broken ribs? Four? Did they break off at my spine? It hurts to even breathe. But no way am I going into a hospital right now. Suddenly, I find myself stranded. As if afloat on an ice floe. Each unto our own.

"Kojo," Coach says when we get to the cars. "You got to stop worrying about Evan and about Gabriel. Your heart is too big," he says, with a surprising gentleness. "There's some things you just can't change." And with that, he gets in his big truck and drives off.

●

KIRBY DOESN'T SLEEP well. Jean Ann has retired from teaching elementary school kids. She remembers some of the players who were her students, like Desmond, who was "so sweet and so smart." She has taken a job working for a concert ticketing agency in Houston, so she's down there five days a week, living with her sister and brother-in-law. Bad timing, that, as it will turn out. But for now, it's just Kirby and their three dogs—Sasha, the old French bulldog, and Peekaboo and Scout, the aging Yorkshire terriers, who scamper along the spine of the leather couch.

The desk in the kitchen is piled high with papers, correspondence Kirby undertakes in his duties as secretary for the local Masons' organization. His and Jean Ann's two sons, Mason and Cade, 25 and 22, are living on their own now: Mason works construction and takes engineering classes at Blinn Junior College in Brenham, and Cade is finishing up his degree at Texas A&M, a couple of hours east, in Huntsville, over toward the Louisiana state line. Without Jean Ann, the house has a stillness to it that I remember in my own home, in the days, weeks, months, then years after everyone had first left.

The leaving occurs in stages, transgressing and regressing like tides.

In the living room is the largest television screen I've ever seen. The people on it are so large as to be frightening, particularly when it is just their faces talking. I don't have a television at home. None of it much interests me, but there's almost always something on. I like the TV show *Better Call Saul* because of the trouble Saul always gets into. Like stuff Kirby and I might've stumbled into in high school, had we not always been so incredibly lucky.

In Kirby's backyard, there's a swimming pool. He hasn't cleaned it since Payton died. The grass in the yard is tall—waist-high in places, emerald green, lush, hypnotic when a breeze blows—and the water is the color of a lake far back in the cypress swamps of Louisiana. Topwater minnows, *Gambusia*, stipple the calm surface. For a while Kirby had a giant bass living in its depths. Maybe it's still down there; he doesn't know. At night, bullfrogs groan and drum, a deep wild reassuring sound, though Kirby says sometimes the neighbors complain.

Payton's room is closed, unchanged. Many of her things are in the garage, which has never been opened, has not been sorted. The boys' rooms, where the boys still stay sometimes in their comings and goings, are still decorated as they were when they were in high school—when they lived here last. Posters of NFL stars of five, six, seven years ago, not even recognizable to anyone now. Stuffed deer heads, sporting event trophies. Various prize ribbons hang from the deer's antlers.

I sleep in Cade's room. Both young men are immense now—giants, really. Kirby and Jean Ann are glad they don't play football anymore. They played in high school. It's too violent, the boys say; everyone gets hurt. They don't want to.

Kirby has trouble sleeping. He awakens when he hears me come in the front door after practice; greets me, asks if I'd like anything. A frozen sausage and biscuit, microwaved? Blue Bell ice cream? *Anything*.

"A glass of wine," I tell him. He's moving with the same daze I'd see as a child when I went to the zoo and the nocturnal creatures—fennec foxes, kit foxes, lemurs—shambled forth in their day blindness. He asks me questions twice sometimes, so that I think he must be sleepwalking. It's hard for him to get to sleep, and he usually has to take some kind of medicine.

We sit at the breakfast room table. He has a little glass of red himself. It's about 10:30 p.m.

He had a health scare earlier this winter, just before I arrived. He'd had shortness of breath and had gotten a chest X-ray, which revealed a large mass on his right lung.

Blood tests didn't show any abnormalities, but the CT scan and MRI were inconclusive. For more than a week doctors puzzled over the shadow. It was about the size of a sparrow. We hoped it was just a fibrous mass, scar tissue from his decades spent as a volunteer firefighter—though I didn't like clutching at that straw, for his other lung revealed no such mass.

Good news, bad news: it turned out to be pneumonia. Only now do I wonder, could it have been COVID, before we knew COVID was afoot? Too late to go back and figure it out now.

He was given antibiotics and told to rest, and has been on the mend. But now his head, too, is on a swivel. He tenses, as do I with my bruised lung and the cracks in my ribs, at the sound of another's cough.

I am not afraid of dying. I am afraid of leaving my family and friends with days, years, decades still left on the field.

Kirby's irritated to hear of Coach's utter nonchalance regarding the coronavirus. More than nonchalance: his, Coach's, challenging of it.

I don't think of myself as a timid sort. I've gotten lost in the mountains hundreds of times; have bushwhacked through the forest between grizzlies, lions, and wolves, often carrying a full backpack of fresh elk meat with no flashlight, just following the terrain of the mountain down, farther down, into even more darkness. I've been stalked by mountain lions, charged by rhinos in Africa and bears in Montana. I try desperately to imagine it from Coach's and the younger players' perspective. Is it machismo—were they so wounded in youth that they feel they must prove their masculinity by some replacement condition, such as stupidity—that they must exercise it in this one splendid opportunity, or be lost, damned forever?

The COVID-taunting doesn't make sense to me. Really, it just seems stupid, callous, selfish, cruel.

I wonder if, at depth, it comes from a place of anger or even rage. I wonder if it—the refusal to consider the lives of others—comes from a rage so deep they do not even see it.

That is the most generous perspective I can deduce.

Kirby continues to ask me the same questions twice. *Who was at practice? Would you like something to eat?* He grows sleepier and sleepier. In the morning he'll barely remember that I made it in. The land of sleep is such interesting and amazing territory. But it's pretty damn amazing up top, too.

Mason comes in not long after Kirby goes back to bed. He's got that young person's late night settled-in wakefulness, not an adolescent's bouncing-off-the-wall mania; he's a grown man. Instead, his is just that excess brim of energy, some unutilized vitality that the day, despite its length, wasn't able to use up.

I can tell he just wants to visit—he's just driven in from Houston—and so although I'm at the opposite end of the energy meter, I sit down at the other end of the big L-shaped wraparound and couch. We visit, even though what I want more than almost anything is to crawl into bed and sleep; to let the body and the mind begin again that remarkable, miraculous process whereby over the span of only hours, one is made young again, even if only for a short time, once more. And to awaken, then—reawaken—to the first dove's slow calling at dawn. The first cracks of light around the edges of the shut door.

Tomorrow—it's almost midnight—is the 13th anniversary of Payton's death. She is for all of us forever suspended at the age she was, just turned 13, though it is not impossible to think of the young woman she'd be now, with the same joyous and spunky attributes—stubborn!—carried forward to 26.

Her birthday fell on the precise day between mine and Kirby's: mine, March 7th; hers the 8th; Kirby's the 9th. Like the hammer strike of one select but random key, punching out a space in what was otherwise a long and uninterrupted sequence of joy.

Mason would like to be a contractor and own his own business someday. He's a charismatic young man, with his dad's sense of humor, both his folks' sweetness, and his mother's practicality. He'll be good at it. I can see his name, *Simmons*, on the side of any number of trucks. I can see his workers on the sides of roads, rebuilding ravaged thoroughfares, wearing yellow protection vests; pink construction ribbons on stakes flapping in the summer wind, with no end to the large contracts, given his firm's reputation for integrity and honesty.

As I visit with him, what becomes apparent to me is that it is not just the science and knowledge of engineering that Mason loves—*how to make a thing work*. Just as much and perhaps even more, he loves the mystery of it: the things not known; techniques not yet discovered, much less mastered. The whole world in front of him.

"I think I'd like to work someplace out West," he says. I love how sometimes there's a thing in the voice that tells you a little more than just the words themselves. And there's something about the practiced casualness with which Mason tells me this that makes it seem to me he has not yet shared this dream with his parents. A trace of guilt and hope, concern and euphoria—relief, rapture, anticipation, relentlessness, forethought, consideration, whimsy.

"Wyoming, maybe," he says, "or Colorado."

"Ah," I say, hoping I'm not betraying Kirby or Jean Ann—and I don't think I am—"the West is best. It's so amazing."

Mason nods. "I've been to New Mexico once," he says. "When I was manager for the girls' volleyball team. We went up there for a tournament. The year we were champions. There was a blizzard," he says, "and it took the big bus we'd chartered like 17 hours to go about 100 miles. We got as far as a place called Trinidad before we had to stop for the night. We stayed in this nasty little hotel right on the interstate."

"The Motel Six," I say. "I've stayed there a couple of times. Loud and *cold*. The heaters don't work and the wind gusts in through the cracks in the doors. About 6,000 feet," I say. It pleases us both that we know the same hotel, so far from home for each of us.

"In the morning, it was the bluest sky I've ever seen," he says. "I had to go out and put chains on the bus tires. I'd never done that before."

"Damn," I tell him, "I've been jacking with snow chains all my adult life and I don't think I could put them on a *bus*."

"It took a while," Mason says, flexing his fingers. "But I read the directions. They went on okay.

"Most of the girls had never seen snow before," he says. "It was knee-deep. I was the only guy on the trip. So they kept asking me to go out to the bus and get their bags and stuff." He laughs. "I was going back and forth all morning." Being of service. Doing good. His name, mason. His father's son.

"It was the first time I ever saw anyone smoking weed in the middle of the day," he says, "acting like it was no big deal."

"There are a lot of places like that now. Shit, I hate the smell of it," I say. "They've stunk up a lot of nice big cities with it now. Seattle," I say. "Denver. I don't see why it has to smell so bad. They don't call it skunk for nothing."

"I'll smoke a little bit now and again," Mason says, neither agreeing nor disagreeing. Just two men, an old one and a young one, shooting the shit at the end of a long day. Telling stories.

"Man, " I say, "I've got to get to bed. I've got to get up early and get some pages made. I'm about to black out," I say, rising. And it's true:

sometimes now sleep comes over me so quickly it feels I can take only one more step, max, before kneeling, then curling up on the ground wherever I am, and descending, blissfully.

As sweet as the day is long, Mason rises to give me an embrace before I careen toward Cade's bedroom. He towers over me, and for just a moment, I feel frail. What must he think? One of his best friends from his high school team here in Brenham, Courtland Sutton, is a star for the Denver Broncos. For both Mason and Cade football must by now just seem like a job to them, like any other—something people do, like engineering. For them, there is a clean and finite timeline— high school graduation—demarcating for them the time between when a thing was done for play, and then for work. Cam Newton played here in Brenham, at Blinn Junior College, before going on to Auburn and the Carolina Panthers, and the Super Bowl.

Work and play. It must seem to Mason that for Coach, and most of the rest of the Express, they are trapped in some gray land between the two, where the game is both these things, and also neither. And in the darkened house, with my best friend sleeping hard finally, and his older son wide awake, I take shelter for the night in his younger son's bedroom, while Jean Ann works in Houston; and the presence of the one who has, inexplicably, gone on some distance ahead of all of us, is so strong, that eve before, that it feels she might still speak to us, and we to her, if only in our choices, actions, and, always, our memories.

●

KIRBY AND JEAN ANN took her and the boys to Hawaii the summer she was 12. She swam with the dolphins and it changed her life. Already an animal lover—with rabbits, dogs, Guinea pigs, and her own horse— she experienced a new level of communication with the dolphins: their quicksilver brilliance, joyful streaks of sublime intelligence, and muscularity exceeding even that of her other favorite animal, horses.

I can't even remember her horse's name now.

I remember her. Even before she was gone, she was such a force as to be unforgettable. Each day she imagined how she wanted her world to be and then acted upon it. She was going to be a veterinarian; was going to save lots of animals' lives. She commanded that Kirby and her little brothers be kind to all animals.

Whenever there is a spider or ant in the house, he picks it up and carries it gently, reverently, outside. Aware in the act of his every breath, and of the veil, the faint breeze that ripples the curtains now and again.

After the accident—he was the first responder, he received a call from someone who'd seen it happen—he rode on the Life Flight with her to Houston, but she was gone. They resuscitated her mechanically, but her brain wasn't giving a signal and wasn't going to.

She was gone, but not gone. She is gone, but not gone.

I went down to Texas immediately. Kirby and Jean Ann's church was a large one for such a small town, and because Jean Ann was a teacher, she knew every family in town, every child. They got a lot of support, a lot of love. It could never be enough, but it helped. They were picked up and carried for a while. At some point they were set down, where they lay curled up as if turned to stone, or as if buried beneath the ice, or whatever other story we use as an abstraction to convey an unbearable grief, an unacceptable ending.

I've brought some stones for her, gemstones from the West Texas desert: agates and crystals, the color of a dolphin's blue skin, the color of her eyes.

Kirby and Jean Ann and Payton and the boys were living on the farm, Kirby's grandparents' farm, when it happened. By the time I arrived, the horse had already been taken away by Kirby's cousin, Stormy, who was a bull rider. In the first days, Kirby felt anger toward the horse—couldn't bear to look at it, wished it harm—but that rage faded; he could never hate a thing Payton had loved. It is also true, however, that he and his family would never look at the horse again. And 13 years later, Stormy himself would die relatively young; another candle gone, to speak of it in a way we generally speak of such things.

We were all in a fog, alternately grieving and benumbed. The scent of her molecules, the singular chemistry of her, was still on her beagle as I petted him. Her rabbits were still in their hutch. Everything was still the same, except it wasn't. I was a young man, and a writer, and everything I saw, I noted with a hyper-acute clarity of the senses incandescent with pain. I wanted to make notes of what I was feeling, but to do so, knowing I might then convert it to art, was too distressing to consider. I let it all go past; did what little I could to give some small comfort to Kirby and Jean Ann simply by being.

She had a parakeet in a gold cage. I thought how fast birds' tiny hearts beat—a couple of hundred times per minute. But the only thing I even remotely remember now from those days after—other than remembering Payton herself: her strong tomboy grin, her voice, her sass, her confidence and imagination—is the little trail that led into the woods at the edge of their yard: a narrow footpath, really just a game trail, worn by nothing more than the daily comings and goings of her and her dog on their way down to the barn and back each day.

I stood one morning at the edge of those woods, in the bright spring sunlight as the funeral plans were being prepared—the hearse, the church, the county cemetery, where people would stay, what the words would say on the program—and I stared down at the little trail, seeing it as the signature of childhood, and the signature of joy.

Out in the yard, redbirds and blue jays were fussing at the feeder and splashing in the birdbath. I felt these sounds bathing my brain, falling upon the heated mind like a soothing rain, faint stipples of relief upon inescapable pain.

I looked down at the trail through blurring vision and imagined how quickly, day by day, that tenuous path would become grown over, barely visible in weeks, and, not much longer, indistinguishable from the woods through which it had passed—one path, and only one path, made by the traveler. I studied the trail: took it into my mind and into my body; knew I would carry the thread of it—the representation and memory and essence of it—within me, for as long as I lived and, I suppose, longer.

I sewed it up into me so that the coming weeks did not matter, nor its quick invisibility. *It was here.* That was the one thing for which I needed no notes.

TWO STORIES FROM Kirby's and my youth: the joy that precedes and, I want to believe, follows grief. The joy that is part of grief, I suppose, and vice versa.

He and I used to play a game on his grandfather's farm. One of us would drive the big tractor while pulling the other behind in a red wagon, holding onto a rope like bull riders. A cheap carnival ride. Long summer days of adolescent boredom alternating with unquenchable play and joy. I pulled Kirby through the stock tank, once. He, in turn, pulled me through a patch of poison ivy, knowing of my terrible allergy. The days fluttered past, delightfully unaccounted for. A calendar was merely an abstraction, a blank book with no writing on any pages beyond the moment.

A second story: Kirby's first year in college at Texas A&M. On one of our night rambles, we went out to the equestrian center where some of the finest horses in Texas were corralled. I don't know why. Maybe they were gathered there for some kind of upcoming inoculations. A dozen or more horses in that big corral. Sleek racehorses: muscular, with perfect conformations. Sweet-smelling. *Spirited.* Young.

These were different times. There were far fewer people in the world. A lifetime ago, a generation before. Two generations.

You could park in the parking lot at the veterinary science building. You could walk across the parking lot, slip through a fence, and walk out to the corral. There were lights around the Vet Science building and parking lot, but not in the corral.

The horses could see you coming. They would be eager for the company. We were, what, 18? We only did this once, but I remember it.

We climbed up onto the steel tubing that formed the corral and petted the horses, surrounded by a sea of the sound of their nickering; the sharp scent of the dust plumes stirred by their well-shod hoofs shuffling—some edging nearer to us, others, sidling away. A herd, like a school of fish, swarming—coalescing, unraveling, gathering together into a knot of unified muscle, unbraiding.

We each slipped onto the back of the horse nearest to us. At this, the herd became, in every sense of the word, electrified. We had crossed over the boundary between horse and man, and were now a part of the herd—no saddle, no reins or halter: only mane. The herd took off as one, galloping around the corral—a stampede, with us in its midst.

Our selves were immediately lost. We simply hung on, trying to survive. We became horses. The ribs of other horses jammed tight against our legs, our knees, on either side, as we leaned forward and clutched our horse's mane.

There was a strand of electrified wire just inside the railing, strung at the level of the horses' shoulders to keep them safe from trying to lean over the railing, and, I suppose, to keep people out. But now we were in.

Around and around the corral we galloped, a night stampede. In just that single act—crossing over a nearly invisible boundary—it felt as if now we *were* horses. And as if despite the specificity of each, there was no one horse, only the herd. And that we were in its center.

Kirby and I had found our rhythm, but were terrified of falling off and beneath all the hoofs. We were shouting, I don't recall what; only that it was a mixture of fear and exaltation. But at the beginning of the third lap, there was a shift—center stream, we felt it communicated through our ankles, up our thighs, into our chests and arms—and the herd began to seek actively to discard or otherwise expel us.

Kirby's and my horse ran tighter to the rails now, purposely scraping us against the electric wire. The voltage was substantial—enough to cause a 750-pound thin-skinned animal to step back—and now our yells had no exaltation in them whatsoever.

For me, the charge went straight up into my molars. I felt I was gnashing blue sparks: that as I shouted, my words were at risk of bursting into flames, igniting with oxygen, then burning to cinders and ash and falling away, useless. The herd was intent on melting us against that fence, but the electricity that passed through us passed into and through them as well. This had the effect of scattering the herd now; and the relief we felt when our horses shied away from the electric wire

Practice 181

was so profound, so sweet, that in a strange way it almost made the long electrocution worth it.

Still our horses ran, following the railing, though others bucked and pitched out in the center of the corral. As if communicating in a way Kirby and I could no longer discern, our horses brushed up against the hot wire once more, rubbing us against it in the manner of a welder making one delicate finishing adjustment with the torch.

We'd had more than enough. We leapt from our horses—*ours*, I think now, marveling at how quickly the human mind can take ownership or possession of all things—and sprawled in the loose dirt of the arena, clumsy and earthbound once more, with the impact juggling our minds, our bodies. It felt so sudden: as if we had stopped cold, even as time had continued on, rushing ahead. Galloping.

We stood up in the soft sand of the arena, like aliens ejected from space. Nothing was broken. We had some grit in our teeth. Our thoughts—the still-roomy vacuous newness of our minds' mansions—were a little upended. A mild concussion, I'm sure. Cups and saucers rattling within—that jiggling sound—but nothing else.

There was little in our brains to be scorched clean by the great equine voltage. I'd probably only had a couple of concussions up to that point. Two that I can remember. When I think of it now—the horses rubbing us for a long time against the electric fence, and the phantasmagoria of blue shuddering sparks in my teeth—I like to imagine that it burned out, *fried*, the myelin sheaths of scar tissue that had begun to build up over those sites of earlier trauma, earlier bleeding and damage. That the slate of the brain, and of life, was laid bare and clean again, ready for the world, and the communities we would go on to inhabit would begin filling the mind and our lives once again.

I do think now and again about Neil Young's lyrics in "Hank to Hendrix"—*The same thing that makes you live / can kill you in the end.* We were 18. Payton was—where? Not here yet. Jean Ann was where?

All the days, all the hours, a kaleidoscope of puzzle pieces. There are borders, boundaries, to all lives, to all days. When we get out to the farthest edges, it is referred to as madness, or depression, or rapture. A little farther still, and all words fall away.

●

NOW WE ARE old men. The trail of joy that Payton blazed through the woods on the way to the barn and back each day is a tangled forest once more, a map with all trails and waypoints erased and dust-blown. But the filaments in our minds glow golden, incandescent, igniting within. We see an image of a dolphin; we hear a child singing to herself; we see a girl with a dog; we carry a spider outside and release it back into the vast world. With every breath in, and every breath out, that trail remains, pulsing. He keeps it. Jean Ann keeps it. Mason and Cade keep it. I keep it. Boundaries and borders no longer matter. The little path remains well lit, even in a darkening world.

●

KIRBY AND I ride out to the little country cemetery, out toward the higher hills, out past the tiny town of Independence, population 140, and Washington-on-the Brazos, population 265. Roughly a couple of centuries ago, Texas was struggling to become a state, a territory, a new nation: reimagining new borders, wresting control from Indigenous people through long decades of life-and-death battles for a thing ultimately as permeable and abstract as a line sketched on a paper map, able to be erased with but a single gesture.

All borders exist in order to be dissolved.

Kirby examines the stones I've brought. One has tiny cathedral spires of calcite crystals that will refract sunlight and miniature, sparkling glints as the sun rises and sets each day—innumerable such ignitions, extinguishments, ignitions, extinguishments—and that smooth, polished geode interior, with the beguiling deep-sea blue.

"It's the color of the water in Hawaii, in that picture," I say—the picture that still hangs in their living room. The picture of the perfect day. Payton in the water with the dolphins, themselves the same color.

Kirby runs a finger along the edge of the stone, carefully. "It's shaped a little bit like a dolphin," he says. "Here, see the head?"

I see.

•

I DRIVE THE little borrowed Prius, with Kirby giving directions. We've got the windows down, our arms out the window. The hills are green; bluebonnets line the roadways; there's no traffic. The oak trees glow with that pale green quality their leaves make for the first few days after emerging, early in the spring like that, the leaves almost translucent in the midmorning sun. It's easily the most beautiful day of the year thus far, and I drive slowly, and we visit leisurely, as if we are not on our way to the place where we're going, and yet also, as if we know full well, we are—which we do. It is a fixed point, while we draw closer, as if tethered to that fixed point. Being drawn.

We pass the place where we found the giant snapping turtle crossing the road in a rainstorm. Past the place that Kirby's grandfather, Ben, always claimed mistakenly was the highest point in Washington County. There's no arguing with old people.

When Payton's class graduated from high school—five years after she passed—they had a banner with her name on it at the graduation ceremony, and her name on the program. It was a source of pleasure and pain both: the sad sweetness that rises and falls each day. There was one boy, Kirby says, one of her classmates, who couldn't get over it. He stayed in touch all the time. "At first it was nice, but then it got to be too much," Kirby says. "Once he took dozens of silver helium balloons out to her grave site and tied them there. We finally had to ask him to stop," says Kirby.

We're getting closer. I can see the big trees on the high point of the hill, with the commanding view beyond. Tendrils of Spanish moss droop from the limbs of old oaks; the immense juniper trees possess dusky blue berries like little Christmas lights. I remember the funeral service. Same time of year, same weather. Nothing's changed; everything's changed. The sweetness is all that was; the tragedy is what was not. At the funeral, three young cows—winter calves, on their way to becoming stocky yearlings, the new grass high upon their thick ankles—walked slowly closer, three-abreast, made curious by our own gathering, our own herd's weeping.

Today there are three full-grown cows, also in tall grass, watching us from an adjacent pasture, but they are older—less interested in anything. There's no way it's the same animals: it's just the same time of year, same view.

There are some new gravestones. The living keep coming to this place, with no attention paid to the cattle. The comings and goings must seem to the cattle as uninteresting as the passage of ants into and out of tunnels or the winged paths of herons that roost along the river, far in the distance, flying in at dusk, and departing with each dawn.

We go to see her first. Our hearts are pounding hard. The breeze ruffles the lush grass on the other side of the fence. Someone—not Darion—has mown the grass so recently that while there is not the same-day wonderful scent of the fresh-cut blades, cloying and rich, neither have the new-cropped blades begun to put forth growth; their tops are still sheared off clean.

It's pleasing, calming, to behold the order, and again, in the way that a passing bird's shadow in bright light can make you spin around looking for the bird—but too late—you can't figure out in which direction the bird was flying; it's gone.

I have the flash of thought that this is what old people do: that I, and my best friend from high school and best friend in the world, are walking in a cemetery, admiring the job the groundskeepers have done.

A dove is calling—the old bird of my childhood, a mourning dove; not the beefier European collared dove that sounds almost the same, but also not. How to describe the difference? The mourning dove has more soul, and is a bit calmer, a bit softer. We have all lost much and, this being life, will lose more. We are, of course, given much. It's dizzying sometimes knowing where to look and where not to look.

We crouch beside her headstone, which is pink granite from the Hill Country:

Payton Simmons
March 8, 2000–March 17, 2013
Daughter, Sister, Friend.

There are already little things, graveside—small stones, dried flowers. Carefully, as if patting the hair of a sleeping child, we pull and gently pluck the individual strands of grass the trimmer has missed. We brush away whatever few clippings of grass are drying in the sun and breeze on the concrete. I wait for Kirby to place his little blue stone at one end of the small array, as if it's a toy on a child's bookshelf, and then I nestle my little crystal shell at the other end. As if it's something she'll see in the morning when she wakes up.

Our eyes blur again, but we hold our position—we hold steady in the terror that is no longer a terror, but a thing. We allow the pain, the grief, to pour down over our hearts as if our blood has been injected with a dye that will ultimately cast everything as if in bronze, and then, more painful yet, we stand, finally, to look out at the rolling hills, and behold again a world without her.

I do feel her here, with us, two old friends—her father, and his old friend—walking in the place where part of her is, part of her was. It does feel peaceful—not good, but calm, as pain continues its circuit through us and, here in a small country cemetery of such grief, back, I suppose, out of our bodies and down into the ground.

"This is the first time I've ever been able to feel all right, while I'm out here," Kirby says. "Thank you for coming out here with me." His voice is thick.

We leave her, then—there is no other way to say it—and walk slowly through the graveyard, stopping to investigate the scripts of other lives. There's an entire other cemetery for the yellow fever epidemic of 1839. We're nervous about the pandemic that has not yet been named a pandemic. Part of us feels we're worrying excessively, but a larger part feels others are not worried enough. Some of the headstones are for soldiers who served in, and even survived, the Civil War. There's one fellow who was born in the late 1700s. Another headstone, for a man gone 150 years now, describes earnestly how "Though the beloved is departed, that spirit shall shine bright in the memories of all who knew him." *Wow*, a part of me wonders, with a surprising spark of something that feels surprisingly close to anger, *How's that working out?*

There's some flowery language on many of the stones. I find myself remembering a phrase from Amy Hempel's short story, "In the Cemetery Where Al Jolson is Buried," about becoming "fluent, now, in the language of grief."

●

AFTER A LONG time—a period, it seems to me, in which time refuses to move—we wander back to the car and drive slowly away, with the windows still down, our arms perched out the open windows, as we did when we drove places together almost 50 years ago. "Do you have time to go get a beer?" Kirby asks. "There's a little country store in Independence. You'd like it."

I look at my watch as if that might have any bearing on my answer. How can it be noon already? "Sure," I say.

We take back roads. We pass families participating in the time-honored Texas tradition of photographing their toddlers out in the carpets and fields of bluebonnets, which are just now beginning to peak. Dressed up as if for Easter.

We talk a little about Coach's insistence on ignoring the virus. He does not deny it exists, but asserts there is only one way to be safe from it. This irritates Kirby more than it does me. It's an old argument— that government is created to conspire actively against "the little man"—big business, big data, big everything, profiting so much off the lower tiers of socioeconomic bracketing as to track their every movement. Does "the government" *really* make its every decision based upon the little man's whereabouts, like a hunter relentlessly following its prey? It seems laughable. What passes for deep state conspiracy is surely instead but mayhem and idiocy.

I tell Kirby I think two factors might be at play. It's a way for the beaten-down and the voiceless to build a myth—perhaps necessary to the preservation of identity; a way for "the little man" to believe he is in fact relevant, even critical, to the great world's turning, to be so selected, so targeted.

And that it's a way, as well, of building walls, within which one might be able to still cultivate the myth of community—one which, persecuted, finds its identity in what it is against, rather than for.

It seems ridiculous. It seems but mere fodder for the no-man-on-the-moon theorists. But I think it's just a way for them to have a voice, to not feel or be invisible.

Coach is a different matter, I think. His rejection of the virus comes not from feeling invisible or unimportant, it seems to me, but instead straight from the wound of his religiosity. I remember, again, his disdain for any authority other than his own. I remember how, when he and Kirby went to see Evan off, and the judge told Coach to stop talking on his phone or he'd be held in contempt, Coach replied that such laws didn't matter; that God's law was the only one he listened to.

"I remember how embarrassed I'd get in the grocery store," Kirby says, "when I'd take my grandmother grocery shopping. She'd be pulling stuff down off the shelf, reading the text out loud at the top of her lungs. Then she'd see I was embarrassed, and would say in an even louder voice, 'Oh, nobody's lookin' at you!'"

"Exactly," I say. A lot of the conspiracy therapy theorists are so marginalized by one form of inequity or another that it's almost a survival skill to believe they're still relevant enough for The Man to be listening in on their conversations. Beaming cathode rays at their brainpans, trying to exercise thought control—often, even as they sit, betranced in front of the blue glow of a television they consider to be but mere entertainment.

We talk about Ben some more—Kirby's dapper old grandfather, a feisty bantam of a man whose every eccentricity mortified and delighted us—never dreaming we would one day and soon enough accumulate our own.

We were fascinated by his delight in collecting knives, and by the way he would call out, when we were riding with him somewhere, the names of streets as he approached them, particularly the numbered ones. "Forty-second . . . Forty-third . . ." We'd cringe in anticipatory tension as we drew closer to the next intersection—would he say it? Was he finally sated? Might he finally pass by one unnoticed, unannounced?

A mania would grip us, our hearts beating faster as we waited, wondering, hoping but also not hoping he would not announce it, this one time—and then, at just the last second, with us already sailing halfway through the intersection—the zesty pronouncement, the cheery salutation, "Forty-*fourth*!" And we would collapse into paroxysms of laughter.

We're almost at the store. The bluebonnet photography fields are behind us. Kirby's torn about whether to go to the Austin Bison game tomorrow. He wants to support the team but knows with his damaged lungs he shouldn't take the risk. I tell him I don't want to go, but feel I have to. That I'll wear gloves and try to maintain a safe distance. It's going to feel enough already to not suit up; to be wearing blue surgeon's gloves will feel even stranger.

"I don't know how to communicate to the team that I think Coach is wrong," I tell him. "This is about the best way, the most respectful way I know how. I don't care if it pisses him off. It's the right thing to do. Lives are at risk," I say. "The best I can do is show I don't agree with him on this. Not by words, but by action."

Kirby agrees. "It's such a sore point with him. Like, his God gave him, us, brains to *use*," he says. "Are you supposed to walk out into the middle of traffic and expect cars to stop?" His voice is calm but incredulous. "When Kaepernick was taking a knee for the national anthem," he says, "my father supported it. He said that was why he fought in World War II, so Kaepernick could do what he was doing."

"That's so awesome," I say. "I didn't know that."

"Yeah," Kirby says. "I thought so too."

The things people see, in a lifetime. The things people do. Nazi concentration camps. Charging a hill in the Pacific with a bayonet on the rifle. Surviving. Some people do survive.

The parking lot, nearly empty despite the noon hour, is crushed shell. There's an ancient gas pump, an ice house that contains hay now, not ice. There's a rusted screen door. The white paint on the boards is weathered and flaking. Inside, broad pine plank floors, stained dark. Wooden shelves are swag-bellied from decades of holding Vienna sausages, deviled ham, whatever. On the back wall, there are some fishing lures and various hardware among the toiletries, some latex gloves and spray cleaner, but no hand sanitizer. The woman behind the counter knows Kirby, but hasn't seen him in years. They visit for a while. She seems a little harried; the world has only just this week entered the leading edge of hoarding as the first fires begin to flicker.

All the ancient phobias and fears that identify us as a species: fear of being abandoned, fear of paucity, fear that the world may not be large enough or wonderful enough . . .

We order a beer and go sit on the back porch. We're the only ones out there. There's a sign that says *Please Don't Feed the Goat*. There's a barbecue pit and, far beyond its native habitat, a palm tree. There's a belly-swollen black goat and a slender, more effeminate white goat. I suppose I can see how someone might think it's fun to toss a french fry to the goats, a slice of pickle, a slice of tomato. Kirby has a palm tree in his backyard as well, which, like this one, is a giant, perhaps from the same era. Were they a fad back in the 1940s and 1950s? Did returning veterans plant them in their backyards, remembering fondly their brief days of R & R on tropical beaches, between all the fighting and all the killing—all the dying?

Kirby says his tree is starting to lean dangerously over the house and that he needs to saw it down before it falls. He called a landscaping company in town, who told him they could do it for $1,000. When he mentioned the tree to Coach, Coach said he could do it for $400.

"Shee-yit," I say, "I'll cut that thing down for free." It's no different at all from the way we got into so much trouble in high school. And yet look, here we are. We always got out, didn't we?

"Had you told Coach about the $1,000 estimate," I ask, "before he told you $400?"

"Why yes," Kirby says, "I think I did."

We sit there sipping our beers, watching the goats, watching the palm tree, and the pale cirrus wisps scattered across the blue skies of spring. Something is coming—we know it—yet what can we do about it? Little to nothing. Perhaps that is all Coach means. Still, I intend to wear gloves. Still, I intend to keep my distance. To pull away from the herd. To lead by example, even if ridiculed.

My ribs still hurt badly, as does my back, my shoulder. But these are nothing compared to the other injuries and ailments. Why does the world look so serene in our almost every glance, when—look more closely—it is a hurricane?

9

BISON

I SHELTER AT MY family's hunting camp up in the hardscrabble Hill Country north and west of Austin, a place we've been coming to for nearly 100 years. None of us any longer has any interest in hunting; instead, it is the shape of the land that soothes us and the depths of history within. The passion I had for hunting as a young man no longer exists but it certainly helped me learn the land more intimately. No. What I miss is how much it meant to me when I was younger to be so on fire for something.

I lie in my top bunk, my face close to the tin roof, and remember my grandfather as a young or youngish man, my father as a young man. I listen to the lulling sound of the branches scraping the roof in the night wind, as they have in hard times as well as good. Later in the night, the sound of rain speckling the roof reminds me of the pebbling clatter of acorns in the fall. The hunting camp is one of the rare places in the world where time behaves differently—where, if it is not perfectly suspended, it at least slows down enough to be barely noticed by us. A tonic, in these hard times, and the times I believe are coming.

●

A LEISURELY BREAKFAST—cold coffee from the night before—and a leftover burrito from the Stripes gas station in Marfa. It's March 14th. I've contacted the league to see what their plans are. They have not returned my inquiry. The ache in my ribs is sharp, reaching around to my back. It's hard to breathe deeply.

I have not felt old, out on the field, playing catch with "the fellas," nor, certainly, in the games—particularly in the anonymity of the uniform, the helmet, the protective face mask, the receiver's gloves—but this morning, the distance between me and them—40 years or more of other experiences, extra experiences—feels substantial.

It's been fun and games, up to now. Well, mostly fun. The memory of how just last week I was *worshipping* the melting, golden drip of the scoreboard clock has receded already. What I am remembering—already—is the fun and games.

It is such an ancient lesson. *The right thing is the hard thing.* I guess that's what makes life interesting. How boring would it be, if the right thing was always and only the easiest thing? There's no sugarcoating it: my wearing gloves—not playing it safe with my fancy receiver's gloves, but wearing the blue plastic tight-fitting medical supply gloves I bought this week at the Dollar General—will create a distance between me and my team. It risks undoing maybe even all the work I have done to earn their trust.

I hope the respect holds. I believe it will. But I have to be willing to risk it for what I believe in. I have the sinking feeling that the party is over and that as the elder, it is my duty to speak my truth. My fear. The blue surgeon's gloves will be essentially a sign of protest. Coach isn't going to like it. It definitely doesn't fit with his theology or messaging.

Another old lesson: *nothing stays the same.* Make all the plans you want, the world may not seek to destroy them, but will definitely be drawn to them, will incorporate itself into them, causing them to alter, like the lipid sheet of a protein slipping through a cell membrane and causing a cellular response, a counter-response. It's as when a defensive end lines up on the edge, waiting for the play to begin. Will he stunt or twist or bull-rush? The very act of the offense taking the field summons him to his stance and attracts his gaze.

Despite my fears and suspicions, I still, like all the rest of us, in varying degrees, exist on the other side of innocence. This is only the beginning.

The innocence of the cruise ship, the innocence of one elderly person in one rest home in Washington State. And never mind, really, what has happened, is happening, in China. Pay no mind to that. We're safe over here. It's a hoax. It's just like the flu. We've got it under control. The economy is all that matters.

I leave deer camp in the early afternoon, driving with my little vial of sanitizer beside me.

Two weeks from now, nearly a quarter-million Americans will have come down with COVID, with maybe 10 times that many carrying it, but with no testing available, no ICU beds left. But of course we do not know that yet.

The package of blue gloves sits on the seat beside me. My heart is heavy, my spirit is low. I do not feel I'm going into a game, but the leading edge of a slaughter.

The game is held at one of those giant high school sports complexes that are larger and in far better condition than the professional stadium I recall from my youth: the Houston Oilers' Buffalo Stadium. It's Astroturf, of course. It seems that our ragged field in Brenham, The Rock, represents the end of an era: one of the last places in the state where the game is still played on real soil, the earth cushioning our bouncing and bruisings, absorbing our blood and sweat, while just below, the tiny microbial things that are the underpinnings of all life take temporary shelter from the brief and hurried clashings of the titans above.

Wrote Charles Darwin in 1839, "It is difficult to believe in the dreadful but quiet war of organic beings, going on in the peaceful woods and smiling fields."

On turf, the game is so fast. It's a thrill, making one's cuts to change direction—like skiing, or, I suppose, playing on roller skates. I've read estimates that the game is 10–15 percent faster on an artificial surface. That might not seem like much, but when you're talking about supremely conditioned athletes who are already moving up and down the field at the outer limits of human abilities, well, they don't call them *limits* for nothing.

The peak athletes are already adapted to do all they can. Tendons, ligaments, muscles, bones: to add 10 percent or 15 percent stress to the human frame that is already under maximum duress is an interesting and rarely discussed or acknowledged decision. I'm thinking of the great Joyce Carol Oates book, *On Boxing*, in which she criticizes New Yorker writer A. J. Liebling for appearing blind to this moral paradox. "The problem . . . must have been how to sell a blood sport like boxing to a genteel, affluent readership to whom the idea of men fighting for their lives would have been deeply offensive; how to suggest boxing's drama while skirting boxing's tragedy."

With artificial turf, the game looks prettier, with vibrant colors and line markers that never blur. And visual beauty can be as much of an aesthetic for some as functionality. But with each passing week, I am less enthralled by the novelty. I miss the feel of the earth beneath me. The thought begins to creep into my mind—just a tendril at first, a shadow—that there is a lack of soul to the geometric precision of the artificial turf. That the fake grass, never wavering and never changing, avoids looking at the one tiny truth within the grand fable that is football, which is this: that time, even when we exist within a 60-minute bubble, is moving on, flowing over and all around and across us, whether we call *time out* or not.

The slow and incremental deterioration of even the greatest players' abilities is never invisible, but rather, seen by all but the player. He is the last to see it. Running backs are over the hill at 27, ancient by 28. Safeties and cornerbacks, 29, *maybe* 30. A few quarterbacks are now famously playing into their late 30s and early 40s, but only one quarterback, the New Orleans Saints' Drew Brees, has ever had his best year at the age of 39 or older, which he did in 2018 when he set the league record for season-long percentage completion, 74.4 percent, including an insane Monday night performance in which he was 24 for 25. Brees lamented the lone incompletion, saying he "should have done better." (The next year, Tom Brady, at the age of 44, will have *his* best year.)

But as the weeks pass now, with each fancy stadium's turf seeming identical to the previous, I realize something else is missing: the signature, as each game progresses, of war. On sod fields of real earth, there were fewer injuries, which was a good thing. But there was also, over the course of the game, an accumulation of divots and skid marks, clumps of black soil and tufts of shredded grass thrown up by the players' cleats.

The center of the field, in particular, metamorphosed dramatically over the four quarters of the game, as did the players' uniforms with the degree of blood-and-grass and dirt-stain serving as a real-time barometer, like the digital clock at the far end of the field. Despite the snow globe quality of time, the 100-yard hourglass, there was a different scale of mortality going on down at ground level, in every grunt-and-grapple play, with all 22 combatants fighting to draw breath, and to advance the ball deeper into the future.

On the artificial turf one can forget the real nature of football, if one is not careful, and can begin to look at the sport instead as simply a track meet conducted at ever-greater speeds.

I arrive at five o'clock for a seven o'clock game. The ticket takers are already set up—a young woman with long braids and eyelashes, a pink T-shirt and stonewashed jeans, and a girl who I think must be her younger sister, as well as a little girl of perhaps five or six seated behind a folding table that pretty much blocks access to the giant field in the giant stadium, which is ringed by chain-link fence.

The enormous stands are empty, which doesn't bother me. It's the only way we know how to play—though I have to wonder how the pro game would adapt to such insularity, come September: if the teams, the league, the industry, would survive were their games, like ours, to be played largely in an isolated vacuum. To be played in a kind of silence. (The pros would, that COVID year, amazingly, continue playing without fans—not unlike the Express—and would be little deterred.)

I feel I'm entering a tunnel—a tunnel of life and light—even though there are no physical walls or boundaries, no scaffolding or girders for such a tunnel's framework.

I feel that we all are entering such a tunnel. We're near it but cannot see it yet, though I think some of us can hear it. Some of us know of its coming already.

I pull my blue surgeon's gloves on and heft my duffel bag full of gear, nod to the ticket lady, and skinny through the narrow gap between the table and the gate. I don't even have the $10 in my billfold. Is the doubt I see flicker in her eyes simply that of wondering if I'm a coach, or a player's grandfather who's trying to avoid the fee? Is she trying to decide if, with my duffel, I'm a player? She says nothing, and I'm through, into the lion's den.

Out on the field, some Bison—large men in dark jerseys, and again, clumped in orderly groupings by position—are playing catch and running little routes. A punter, alone, booms one high kick after another to his bevy of punt returners.

I don't see any of my team.

On the near sideline, a few players—elephantine, yet not unfriendly—sit in various stages of preparation, lacing up cleats, adjusting taped ankles, or just sitting, visiting, watching all the other players warming up on the field. Although I do not recognize them, I wander over to say hello, hoping somehow that they might be attached to the Express as part of the mysterious cloud of come-and-go players who trail Coach across the years, showing up for one or two practices per year, or for one or two of the games.

They're not, of course; as I approach the Bison squad, their faces exhibit some magnificently calibrated communication that shimmers between mild gentility, eager hostility, crackling aggression, stunned confusion, and mild disbelief. As if, *Why is the enemy walking right into our camp—is he trying to make trouble already? Can't he wait another 30 minutes to get his ass whipped?*

They are guarded, cautious. The pregame headspace of all players is a carefully cultivated garden of approaching fury. Sometimes even rage, but almost always—ideally—an incandescent purity which in some players approaches rapture: burning so hot it can transcend negativity or the desire to harm others, and becomes instead almost impassive, untouchable, in its immensity, its drive.

I walk right on up as if I intend to sit down with them: as egregious a breach of personal space as were I to approach a stranger's bench in Central Park.

"Is this the Express's side?" I ask. Me with my street clothes and physician's blue gloves.

They shake their heads now as if in pity. "Nah, man, y'all are over there," the nearest player says, pointing across the field to the one solitary bench, the farther shore, where no human habitation is visible. Again it looks like the subway bench in the movie, *The Matrix*, where Neo gets caught in limbo for all time, or so it seems.

For a moment, I imagine myself saying *Fuck, am I going to have to kick all of y'all's asses by myself?* But so finely tuned is the ongoing pregame calibration, resonating with volatility—*waiting* on the violence, but keeping it at bay, for now—that it's possible the mountain of a man who has kindly directed me to keep on traveling might not see any humor in such a pronouncement.

So instead I thank them and strike out across the prairie, the last passenger pigeon, the last panda, trundling with my broken ribs and COVID phobia, 1,500 miles from home, and isolated, as well, by the cruelest of boundaries, the quarantine of time: 40 years too late to be the match of any of the opposing players, as we continue to play out this ceremonial, ritualized addiction, this engagement, with hypermanipulated time.

Here, if nowhere else, our efforts can still sometimes control the outcome of things.

My heart's fluttering. In my post-concussive state, I forget for a moment how many we need to field the team. For some reason— the extreme greenness of the field, and the time of year, birdsong, spring in Texas—the number *nine* comes to mind: as in, *If we can just get eight more . . .* Who knows what I'm thinking, for the neural wires are crossing to clutch at baseball—a non-contact sport. Survival, maybe.

I often wonder about the value of art—the evolutionary value—and wonder if art helps accomplish this same need: stretching, expanding, making more supple, more capacious, the mind and even the spirit; making us, as I believe art does, better humans.

To put the physical body through such despairs and euphorias as are accomplished in the realm of art, and to do so with cunning, rapture, fear, exaltation—all the passions—is this not a service to the brief snapshot of our existence?

Nobody gets out alive. Smoke 'em if you got 'em. Be smart, but push the edges, if only to keep the edges from closing in.

Mary Oliver asks in a poem, *What is a prayer?*

I stand beside my empty bench, chagrined yet again by the authority of the clock. Even if a sufficient number of my teammates do appear, there will barely be time to stretch, much less run our drills. Again, it's surreal; in the depth and breadth of my addiction, my resolve to remain in retirement begins to waver.

I definitely can't take any hits—not even a bump, not even a *tap*—but I think I could pull my pads on, if someone could help me pull the jersey on. I could line up out wide, just to draw an extra defender away from the main play. I couldn't tackle anyone or be tackled, but I could catch a quick pass to the sideline, then step out of bounds.

I have not tried to jog yet, much less run. A few days ago, when I was crossing the street in Marfa, a car approached, and I sought to quicken my steps, which immediately made my ribs stab. But that was two or three days ago.

This hunger to put on the helmet, to suit up, is a fever, if not an illness; I see that now. But knowing intellectually as well as physically the folly of desire does nothing to dull its edge or its call.

And while I know it is not my yearning, my prayer, which summons my teammates, as their bodies begin to drift toward me, coming from beyond the horizon, that is how it seems, when I first see them in the distance; and my heart leaps, as if it believes, against all evidence, that it is going to get to play—that I'm going to play.

It is the old practice stalwarts Neil and Dooney, and just-out-of-prison Ray, and Coach. (Kojo is not here yet—perhaps he's still in a bathroom, coiffing, or polishing an earring, or adjusting his socks.)

They walk slowly, looking fatigued already. Watching them, it is as if the ground beneath them is hollow, as if there is no hope or faith or belief or confidence—no strength other than a will to endure. And more than ever, now, I want to play. I want to help rally them—to block and cut, to twist and run; to get low on the tackles, and to weave between danger, ever-present danger, to the best of my ability.

The few make many, says Coach, *but the dead make none*. And as if receiving a religious epiphany, I get it now. I know it not just with the grappling of intellect or philosophy, but with all of my body. And if Coach tells me he thinks he is going to need me to suit up, I believe that I would not be able to say *No*. That I would say *Yes*, with the leap of life.

●

COACH SPIES MY blue gloves immediately and says nothing directly—bristles, if I read his body language correctly—nor does he ask where Kirby is. Kirby has sent me with a box of trainer's tape and scissors. Despite the pain in my ribs I help Coach carry his enormous duffel loaded with helmets, pads, jerseys. With Jamie (Neil's girlfriend) and Michelle (Quincy's girlfriend), I help by laying out the jerseys in a long row so each player can find his.

Spread neatly as they are, with short-sleeved arms outstretched, the empty jerseys look like religious artifacts, tunics of the saints, and the fact that there are so few of our players left intensifies the impression that those who are still upright, searching among the long line of jerseys for their particular uniform, are about to go out into what will surely be the last battle.

Luke, a scrawny, scrappy young white kid with black circles beneath his eyes—as if he's already been in a fistfight—and with no small number of teeth missing, moves down the line. It'll be his first game of the season; he's attended no practices, and I've never seen him before. He stops and chooses my jersey, number 27.

Coach pauses in his haste long enough to inspect the jersey critically, a horse trader examining flesh. But it's too late, the jersey's already been claimed by Luke, who adjusts the ragged sleeves and announces himself ready to deliver an ass-whipping to the Bison that they won't soon forget.

Already flimsy to begin the season, the jersey is now substantially more abraded and tattered from my many skids across the Brillo pad of Astroturf in the Red Raider game. From behind, the 27 looks like a 21.

Coach takes the cardboard box Kirby has sent me with and begins taping ankles. I tell him I wish I knew how, that I'd be happy to help, but I'm worried I'll tape it too loose or too tight. Coach doesn't respond—only says something about trusting in the Lord, not man. He can only be referring to my surgeon's gloves.

"I'm using the mind I've been given," I say. "And I'm thinking of others, not just myself. Like, I'm not going to walk right out in front of a car and then count on the Lord to bail me out of that, either," I tell him—the first and easiest example of harm I can come up with.

But it's a huge tactical mistake. "I have!" he cries, facing me directly, his eyes wild, and I can see how easy it would be, how easy it is, for some of his players to get into a jawing match with him.

We have about 15 minutes until kickoff. Now is no time to get into a theological argument with him. Like a child, I find myself starting to wish I'd picked another example: bonking a Namibian black rhino on the snout, or twisting a grizzly bear's nose.

It's ridiculous. I shake my head and take my leave. There are always gulfs and isolations between all beings, and this is, I understand, as it should be; it is who and what we are.

In the act of first standing—*Homo erectus*—we forged our developing identity as the solitary, the upright and the isolated, and carried into the future our fevered twin-lobed brains, with one hemisphere advising us one thing while the other advises the opposite.

Little wonder we're drawn to images of physical grace—the swan-leap of a wide receiver, and the incredible balletic catch—as visual proof that a refutation, an opposite, exists to the condition of our eternal clumsiness, our existential strife.

Hit, hit, hit! advises the epigraph to James Whitehead's 1971 novel, *Joiner*, about a college lineman. (A generation later, Elwood Reid would write a similar novel, set in Michigan, *If I Don't Six*.) There are 10, 11, now 12 of us—enough to populate the field, if but briefly.

League rules call for a minimum of 14 players, so that injury reserves are available, to keep the refs and other teams from not wasting their time should a player or two go down with a twisted ankle at the beginning of the fourth quarter. And for a long time, our number is only 13, so I believe I am indeed going to have to—am going to *get* to—squeeze into my pads after all, to provide that requisite bench "depth." And there is no part of me that is made unhappy by this realization—as if such a gesture could erase the distancing I've summoned by wearing glowing blue gloves in the midst of so intimate a team sport; choosing, selfishly, I know it must seem to them, to fracture that bond and its requisite: trust.

Our absence of trainers seems exacerbated when a couple of the new players, spying my blue gloves, assume I'm a medical trainer, and ask me for help taping. There's not even any time for warm-ups and stretches; no time for the stirring ritualistic pageantry of the pregame. Only the game itself, as relentless and self-governing in its own approach now as war.

Me? No, I'm not a trainer, I'm just lodging a silent protest against the league. Oh, and, yeah, so it seems, against our coach.

Again and again I tell them I'm happy to try, but I don't want it too tight or too loose. They decline, and choose instead to wait.

Do they think *I'm* infected, I wonder, and trying not to expose them? Only Neil and Coach know my ribs are broken. There is deep within football the warrior's ethos of playing hurt, as a test of and testament to one's commitment to family, the team. And so, inexplicably in my street clothes, it must seem to them now I'm in double protest.

Why do we assign such power to another, as we do to a coach: one whom, like a pastor or priest, we entrust with helping make us better? Coach's displeasure with me, which I knew would be coming, doesn't bother me much; it's only in rare moments like these that I tend to remember, and remind myself, that not only am I a grown man, I'm far and away the oldest on the field.

As an environmentalist in Montana, fighting on the front lines of the timber wars for parts of five decades and having navigated scapegoating and death threats, I don't care that Coach is bothered. I'm annoyed instead that *I'm* bothered; that it even matters to me.

I remember a piece of advice I give to beginning writers who, when called upon to read their work aloud to an audience, grow nervous. You *should* be nervous, I tell them; all that means is, it matters.

Still, I don't like how deeply Coach's judgment invades the walls of my emotional defense, which I'd assumed, this late into the journey, were pretty impenetrable.

More players are joining us, running toward us from across the far side of the field, not in their hip-hop cool saunter with headphones attached, but hurrying, moving faster than a jog—not sprinting, but almost. Shane, our tall, strong quarterback and Shaun, our short, fast quarterback—without either of them, I don't see how we could play—and still others come trotting. Kojo and Woodard join us—a slow and paltry trickle of reinforcements, so puny and forlorn that I cannot help but think of the Texas childhood myth of the Alamo, where, outnumbered 10,000 to 186, the defenders nonetheless refused to cross a line in the sand that would have allowed each to ride away to safety under cover of night. They all (but one) chose instead to remain for certain death by the sword, even as General Santa Anna's Mexican army was playing the eerie *Degüello*, the bugle call of *No Quarter*.

Ernie—who looks less like a football player and more like a junior high math teacher who just happens to have thick calves—takes those players who are taped down to the far end of the field to lead them in jumping jacks. But there are only a dozen, and their counted cadences are all muted and their movements lethargic, as if in a contagion.

Coach is still wrapping ankles; he looks like the steer wrestler who, having roped a steer, hurries down the line to bulldog it and then tie its legs quickly with a length of rope. He glances at the lackadaisical jumping jacks going on down near the goal line, curses, finishes his tape job, then straightens up to go intervene on even that, the simplest of tasks that's not being done correctly.

I hurry along with him and ask him, "With so few players, how will it affect your game plan?" I sound like a damned TV commentator rather than a player. *Never question Coach's authority*—unspoken Rule Number One on any team, not just Coach Barnes's teams.

He's so furious he won't even look at me. Instead, he snaps, "Not a goddamn *bit*. They're football players. We're going to play *football*." And once again the spit flies from his mouth, as if the rage is sublimating from the gaseous state straight to a solid one.

Would I be experiencing, witnessing, all of these vibes of religiosity and Biblical myth were I to be with another team, another coach? Yet the question is irrelevant—I did not choose another team or another coach. This is where I want to be. This is where we have all chosen to be. We have sought him out.

"Come on, *now*," he shouts at the haphazard, tiny assemblage of the dozen or so players who are lollygagging through the last of their jumping jacks. "You got to be *ready*!" He points across the field to the legion amassing. "They're damn sure ready, and if you don't hurry up and get right, this *instant*, they're going to kick y'all's asses up and down the field all night long. It's up to *you*, men. Come on now, let's show some *spirit*!" he shouts, his voice breaking from its rough bark at the end into the higher register of plea.

Shaun tries to rally them. His voice, thin amid the lethargy, rises like that of an adolescent's, neither man nor boy: *insisting*, talking the talk, exhorting the team to get right, to get right *now*. And like water ripples stirred by the wind, a few semi-fervent replies echo. Coach is clapping his hands, urging them to jump faster. Like a ragged old engine that won't start on a cold day, the team's spirit is sagging again, silence is returning; and when some of the players glance over at the bench where another four or five of our team are still fooling with self-taping their ankles, or struggling to get dressed, Coach snaps, "Don't be looking over there. They'll get here when they get here. What we've got right here is what we're goin' with."

The bridegroom approaches, yet again: the referees, in their striped shirts, adjudicating a game we love, but with the authority of wardens. It's two minutes till seven; there's no way we'll kick off at the top of the hour, but the home team, aware of our predicament, is being generous and giving us—loaning us—a few extra minutes.

The entire 60 minutes will still be played. We—they—will still all have to pay.

•

COACH WAVES OFF the approaching referees with the precise gesture of a man on an important phone call. The referees stop and stand at some distance—curiously, the tiny clot of us has self-isolated ourselves way down at the farthest end of the field, in the most distant corner—and now Coach gathers us in for prayer.

I join the warmth of the forming circle, the humidity of their calisthenics-warmed bodies radiating. There aren't even enough of us to make a circle. I know intellectually it makes no sense, but what I feel emotionally again is that I have double-quit: first with my ribs, and then with my gloves. And though I know it's ridiculous, it feels that my own physical distancing from those in whom I was previously so interested, and with whom I was so engaged, is casting a pall on their spirits, just as my own are low. That we are all connected, and that the ache of one spreads quickly into and through all the others.

Whether seeking to make amends for his earlier churlishness and perhaps remembering belatedly that I am in the age class most vulnerable to COVID, or possibly only grasping at straws in an effort to jumpstart this strange plague of lethargy, and as if handling a window-front mannequin, Coach grabs me by the arm and tugs me to his side, leans in on me again, his arm around me, pulling me in like a boxer in a clinch, and breathes down onto me. I can feel the bristle of his gray two-day-old stubble pressing against the side of my head; the timbre of his words is so deep they resonate through my skin and into my bones.

"It's a privilege to play this game," he tells us. "This man is 62 years old and is out there playing better than you all are. What is wrong with y'all, letting this old man show y'all up? He plays better than you all are—is working harder. Why aren't you all trying harder? Do you not want to play football? Do you just want to quit and go on home?"

This is the part where I almost wonder if, and wish for, someone to say *Yes, we want to go home*, or *Coach, it's no fun anymore*. It's the exact point where Kirby and I would interrupt and ask if we could take Waldo coon hunting, and I miss Kirby terribly at this game—possibly our last, with the end so sudden, so premature.

It's too over-the-top, and while I'm willing to do almost anything to help the team, supporting Coach's odd claims is not among that list. "No, sir," I correct him. "These men are the warriors; they're teaching me. It's an honor just to be on the field with—"

"Nah, nah," Coach interrupts, releasing me then to fall back into the fold. "I see what you're trying to do," he says to me, and quickly declares that gambit a nonstarter; and curiously, I don't blame him. He's just throwing shit at the wall, desperate for something to stick. Now he turns to his go-to, God: puts both arms around the nearest players, bows his head, and dives again into a variation of his now ancient themes. How the hearts of champions can overwhelm and vanquish foes a thousand times greater than those we will meet on the field tonight. And in a subtle twist, the acknowledgment that there is something larger and more important than football, which is the path of light and service to the Lord that is the way of the righteous.

I've heard this deference to the Lord—this humbling, in post-game prayers—after we've gotten our butts whipped, but do not recall ever hearing Coach speaking of such larger concerns *before* a game.

There is no talk tonight of "putting our foot up their asses." Instead, Coach dials himself up into an incantatory frenzy, leaping into the air every time he says the word *Jesus*, every time he shrieks the name *Jesus!*—thanking him for all blessings, and recommitting to do his bidding and his service. And while there are heartfelt *Amens* from within our infinitesimal gathering, none have the electric quality of Coach's shouts and screeches. In no way do I mean to diminish or marginalize the description of the place to which Coach travels, in this one prayer. I mean only to say that it seems to me that the rest of us do not follow him all the way there, but instead remain behind, mere observers.

And as the fever finally breaks over Coach, and age and mortality return him to who he is—a middle-aged man with hypertension, and a little out of shape—he releases us, them, with a drained whisper: "All right, *kickoff team*."

And as every one of them, save for big Ray and little Shaun, go out toward midfield to receive, I have the most terrible feeling that I'm turning them out to a battle from which they will not return: out toward an irreversible fate—one that depends not at all on work or on faith, but on the far more terrifying vagaries of luck and grace.

The game begins the way they all begin: with hope, if not confidence. Gone immediately is the luxury of indolence that had cast such a strange spell over our small number in the pregame warm-ups. Instead, in the manner of sink or swim, we're tackling and running hard. The game looks at first like any other, when examining the man-to-man battles, the intricate whirring of each cog as the gears of the sport advance upon one another and mesh: the pass rush, the offensive line, the receivers. The quarterback seeking to heave the ball down the field like a javelin, cleaving the crystalline shell of time in which all play. And always, on defense, the middle linebacker, a roving rogue of passion who exists for only one thing: calling out orders and deployments to his teammates, then leading the attack against the rogue invaders who seek to swarm into the holy land that is the territory of the defense.

If the play is a run, the linebacker plugs the gap; lowers the hammer on the runner. If it's a pass, he falls back or slides sideways and swats the ball away. He rejects all efforts by the offense to colonize his kingdom. The linebacker, always, is Coach's living, breathing arbiter.

●

NEAR THE END of the first half the Bison, in a trend that is familiar to us now, are beginning to pass at will, with big ripping runs after the catch. *Shredding the defense*, it's called. Our players are exhausted, as if they've already played a full game—which, by having to play special teams, offense, and defense, they have. The Bison are running through our arm tackles. When we're on offense, their pass rush breaks easily through the faltering wall of our line, angry sea-storm surges of Bison parting our wall of mortal flesh. Our quarterbacks' desperate heaves, thrown high and long, hang in the night sky like ducks seeking a pond upon which to land, and the Bison secondary wait for them, gather them in, then sprint for the end zone.

And once more, our special teams are called out, to receive yet another damned kickoff.

Shane and Shaun, our two quarterbacks, are both getting rocked. They take turns spelling one another. Big Shane's ribs hurt from where he took a helmet under his arm, and Shaun is limping badly with an injured knee.

Coach has tasked me with being special teams coach—responsible, among other things, for being certain we've got 11 men on the field; and as the casualties mount and the fatigue roars rampant through the collective body of the team, there is less passion, less interest, less motivation to get out there on the field and face the savage charge of the ever-fresh and ever-powerful Bison.

Trying to shepherd 11 of them out onto the field to receive the kickoffs is like counting fish in an aquarium—always, there's a slender player blocked from view by a larger one. The surge of panic when one thinks there are only 10 players on the field, rather than the requisite 11, or 12—a penalty—is worse than the dreams of walking into the classroom of a course you registered for, but never attended. I still have those dreams, 40-plus years later; how to shed myself of them? How to rid one's self of the thread of a fear, once it gets down into the canyons and furrows of the mind?

Complicating my task tonight is the devastation of the game. While all were willing at the onset, the rivets are popping out now, so that big men like Ray are gasping as if in search of an oxygen machine. His skin glistens silver under the high floodlights; and the skin of the Black players is like rivers seen at night, dark waters reflecting the stadium lights like stars, or candles.

The big men sit on the bench and look for a volunteer to take their place while the smallest and most fragile players wander the sidelines, similarly hoping for a miracle, just a breath: one tiny respite in what should be a seam of time between the grind of offense and the pounding of defense.

It gets harder and harder to round up 11. On one kickoff there are but 10 volunteers, then 8, then, spectacularly, only 6 out on the field to receive a kickoff. It's a bad look: as if we're quitting. *Please*, I ask the players, and when, after a desperate scan of the field, they see what I am seeing, they finally lean forward, hands on knees to push off and give them the momentum they need to stand and then lumber out onto the field, where they and their teammates' bodies are being broken down and betraying them.

Kojo, among them, is as evasive as a zebra fish in the pet store aquarium as the swoop of the long-handled dip net searches, pushing aside the seaweed, seeking him, only him, the brightest. I stalk him, waving him out there—he is not injured, but he keeps turning away, gesturing to Coach. Only if Coach insists will Kojo go out into the scrum.

Each time, with seconds melting and the referees just about to reach into their pockets for the yellow penalty flag—only then must Coach, with his boiling mind on so many other matters, turn and screech at, and select, the two, three, four players nearest to him, no matter what size, and order them out onto the field.

And we call this a game? And we call this fun? Tonight we are but cannon fodder for the *idea* of sport; and my bright blue nitrile gloves of protest seem to me at least a horrible mockery of the idea of team, where, or so it is taught, we live and breathe as one, succeed or fail as but one organism.

Big Shane, nursing bruised ribs and possibly a separated shoulder—no longer able to throw—is putting himself out there on the kickoff team: our starting quarterback. And Shaun, the shifty little runner, seems near the point of delaminating. He's cramping. He comes off the field at one point and lies on his back, has another player stretch his hamstring, pushing on the extended heel like a man endeavoring to shove against a pry bar, trying to force the taut and swollen muscle fibers back into an elongated, if no longer elastic, attenuation. We have no ice, nor even any water with which to hydrate—time just ran up onto us; we were caught unprepared—and I hurry across the field to the concession stand.

What was I thinking, playing again? It is a sickness. It is a fever as dangerous as it is lovely; it is a flaw in the fabric of life. Why do we always want more? How wonderful it is that we burn brightly. Is it preferable to want more rather than to want less? To be so dimmed and diminished as to one day want no more spark, no more strange and dangerous fire.

Limping across the field on a simple errand, agonizing with the thump of each step and clutching one arm tight against my ribs as if to form a kind of cast, I am keenly aware that I have overreached.

The young woman at the concession stand does not hide her mild puzzlement at the ancient man with the blue gloves who comes to the counter asking for ice, only ice, in a Ziploc bag, if they have one.

I love that she does not shut down and say that they have no Ziplocs. She does not ask if I am a medical trainer or COVID protester.

Her coworker, who has remained seated, looks skeptical, but the young woman sets to searching her province as if on a scavenger hunt. There aren't even any plastic bags, but then, inspired, she opens an entire new box of paper popcorn holders, the supply of which is housed in a plastic sleeve. She places the popcorn holders back in their box, then carries the precious plastic bag over to the Dr Pepper fountain. She holds the bag beneath the high spout as if in a milking operation and dispenses a slurry of ice into it.

"It's his hamstring," I say. "We don't have any ice. We don't have anything. Thank you."

I turn and gesture back to the far side of the field, to the tiny band of five or six people who are not out on the field. Coach is the only one standing among them; the others are kneeling or lying on their backs, their legs folded and beneath them at odd angles as they seek to work out the terrible cramps. Others stare skyward as if with the unseeing eyes of a battlefield combatant in one of the grand murals by Titian or Bruegel or Raphael.

Surely, up in the shimmering halos of the high intensity halogen lights, angels hover, waiting to descend, kept at bay perhaps only by Coach's continued howls and his haranguing of the referees, and of opposing players, and of his own team, and of—well, maybe there is no need to search for new words when the old ones appear to be perfect: his rage against the dying of the light.

The half ends while I'm waiting. The kind woman finishes milking the ice machine down to its last few sputtering, clinking rasps of ice, ties the bag off, and hands it across the counter to me like something I've won at a state fair. I thank her again and, embracing the tubular bag like a dance partner, hurry, though still unable to jog across the field, back to the scatter of our small band.

The ice feels good against my ribs as I walk. And I'm struck again by how utterly far from home I am, and how homesick, and wonder what I am doing here. When I had the pads and the helmet, I knew. Now, I do not. I knew what I would find, hanging out with Kirby, 45 years later, and riding around with Coach and the guys. I knew I would see ferocity, faith, blind dedication to the greater thing that rested above us all, as if on an altar. For some, the blood of the Lamb Himself; for others, a football, and its allures, promises, temptations.

I just thought it would be fun. I thought I could go in, take the hits, share the pain, bleed the blood. But I thought I could also step away.

There was a lot to think about, on that staggering walk. Even before I was halfway across the field, I could hear Coach's lamentations, could see the lack of remonstration by the players: down 33–6, not an insurmountable score, and yet so many of them sitting or lying down, gasping, milking the sweet 15 minutes of halftime, an almost heavenly bliss—a tiny eternity—before they would all be summoned to go back out there and do it all over again.

Coach walked among them, instructing them, directing them, *coaching* them like crazy; offering little tips to the linebackers, to the O-linemen and to Shaun, who was hobbling around still holding his hamstring. "Isaiah, you got to be right up on the line; you're giving away your pass-blocking scheme." Poor Isaiah, who's never played offensive tackle in his life.

"Woodard! When that linebacker turns his hip, like this"—Coach demonstrates with a violent twist of his own—"you can plant and push off in the other direction."

Sharp-pained as if by a knife in my ribs, I deliver the ice to Shaun, who receives it gratefully, plops down on the Astroturf like a child summoned to naptime, rolls the tube of ice under his afflicted leg and lies there, arched, awaiting the slow relaxation that will allow him to recover just ahead of the melting halftime clock, so that he can go back out there again.

Luke, with his blackened eyes and gapped teeth, his scrawny arms and legs hanging slightly cattywampus as he favors numerous injuries, walks up and down the sideline in a delirium already, eager for the second half to begin.

Which, this being football, it does.

I'd play again, if healed. The addiction is too strong, and the bond, inside the bubble of those 60 minutes, too sweet. What's coming, however, is going to crush everything—will spread so many fractured pieces across the world that no one can foresee how, or if, the fragments might be put back together or assembled anew.

Does Coach know this, and is simply choosing to ignore and defy it—or is he truly oblivious?

We are already violating the governor of Texas's 50-person gathering ordinance, so that a thing that was once joyous and celebratory to us now feels to me illicit.

Still we play on. The third quarter begins. It is remarkably like pouring the men, young and old, into a meat grinder: 40–6, then 46–6. At one point Coach loses his shit even more than normal and is cursing at *our* offense. Again we're sending Kojo and our other receivers on impossibly long deep routes, even though the defense's pass rush is breaking through well before our receivers can get downfield. It seems to me like beating one's head against the wall.

Coach is berating the offense so loudly and shrilly that everyone in the stadium is just looking at him in a kind of daze; as if, like a blacksmith hammering against the anvil, his fury alone is enough to reshape the moods and emotions of all who happen to fall beneath the umbrella of artificial light that is his domain.

His fury is cyclonic; it drops the emotional barometric pressure of all who hear and gaze upon it. It's so profound that both teams are just standing there listening—our offense unwilling to snap the ball, and the Bison defense likewise uneasy, uncertain about lining up in position until that fury is spent.

Even the referees—ostensibly the authorities in this strange game, strange ritual, here at what seems possibly like the end of civilization as we know it—just stand there, almost as if with pity or compassion and some disbelief, as Coach unspools, winds himself out, shrieking his cautions and counsel, his insistence at those who will not yet heed or hear him. A jeremiad, and—there's no other word for it—*possessed*.

•

AFTER THAT, THE game slows, or our perceptions—beaten against the heated anvil that is Coach's brainpan—become slower. As if in a dream, I watch Luke, running alongside a wall of Bison blockers, trying to knife his way through them to find his way to the ballcarrier and the ball, his beloved. He runs with a wild death-grin, keeping pace, timing his thrust, then launching and, improbably, penetrating, wrapping his wiry arms around the powerful back's thighs, knocking the runner down, with Luke getting all tangled up in the clashing, as if he's just tackled the proverbial Mack truck.

Bouncing up dizzy, ditzy, grinning. *Why?*

•

WE END UP losing 59–6. Not the dreaded 100–0 shellacking that the other teams have been forecasting against us in the unmodulated swagger of their social media silos, but still, a trampling. The camaraderie here afterward is even briefer than it was for the Red Raiders' game. The Bison coach commends us for not quitting, says how any other team wouldn't have even gone out on the field. Coach nods slightly.

Coach gives the prayer, offering thanks to the one who gave his only son, so that we might have everlasting life.

I look down at my blue gloved hands. The webbing between thumb and forefinger is torn, revealing white palm. I have no idea how long it's been like that. Maybe the entire game. It makes no matter. I breathed their air, have been coughed upon by Kojo and now, after the game, by the elfin, battered, Shaun, who I think is "simply" dehydrated—so woozy he can barely stand—but who now like Coach and Kojo is hawking the dry cougher's hack, even during the prayer.

Why? Why am I not home in my bunker, eating venison from my freezer, carrots from my garden? Why am I so tempted by the brilliance of life, and the fantastic country out beyond the edges of the regular?

Why not? is surely the answer, or, *Because I am alive.* It is the natural condition of things. Wonder and denial are our twin identities. They make religion possible; they make life possible. They make life livable—more than livable.

Learning how to moderate them, of course, is the alchemist's trick.

Nobody gets out alive, and almost no one wants to leave early. The bad news is, we lost 59–6. The good news is, we lost 59–6.

We stagger, helping each other haul one another's gear toward the parking lot, where already sports cars are idling and rumbling. Players sit slouched in the front seats, the windows down, their stockinged feet propped up on the dash. The smell of pot rafts through the parking lot.

"Better not be any of y'all smoking," Coach says. He's listing, limping as if he's been out on the field: has absorbed every hit, has delivered every hit. Not beaten—never that—but humbled.

Little Shaun, who might or might not have already shared a toke with a couple of the Bison, suddenly his brethren, is coughing his dry cough again in a pretty much nonstop fashion.

"You all right, man?" Coach asks, putting a hand on his shoulder. Shaun nods. "I just swallowed some water wrong. Man," Shaun says, "I was so tired all night. I've never felt that way. I just had no energy."

Coach nods. "You better go get your blood checked," he says. Shaun just nods. "Yeah, yeah." But Coach makes sure he has eye contact, then says again, "Get it checked."

We drift off after that, the players with the rarefied and satisfied air of having competed, having given more than they might have believed they had—of having been tested, and acquitting themselves as best as they could, and better than anyone, themselves included, might have believed possible.

Theirs is an air of relief, of pacification—almost solace. The score is irrelevant.

I know the feeling. And how I miss it. What I would do, to have it back again.

In his dark tinted truck, Coach has a bag of DVDs that he burned from last week's Houston game. He's distributing them to the players for $2 a pop. On their way out, they stop by to pick one up, and I wait until everyone else has gotten one before I walk over and—feeling like a deserter, in my street clothes, and again like one engaged in some illicit and dangerous behavior—I dig through my billfold for two bills, there in the darkness at the edge of the parking lot street lamp, with Coach's features deep now within the dark interior of his truck. And all he says, when I hand him the $2, is "There you go, Cap'n Rick"—as if knowing, like a prophet, that our season is done. That we will not see each other in this capacity ever again. That it was as glorious and sublime as it was flawed, agonizing, and fleeting.

His eyes meet mine; he says nothing.

Our addiction.

10

DREAMS

I DREAMED AGAIN OF football, as I never do when I'm playing it—only when I've been away from it for a while. The dreams are never stress dreams of failure or vulnerability. They're always dreams of success: of being called upon to do my job, and doing it, and loving it. Last night's dream was wonderful. It was a game, not a practice. We were down by a lot, as usual.

It was late afternoon. I think it was the field in Georgetown, where we'd played the Capital City Bison, the first and only game I'd had to sit out. It was a new game, a redo, later in the season, still early spring. The field wasn't Astroturf, but instead the patchy worn turf of late winter heartbreak, and much trampled by all the previous games. But those places where players had not fallen were starting to green up again.

An Express player came limping off the field. As usual, we only had a few reserves left. And when I looked around, I saw that all of our bench players were lame and out of commission. It was up to me to take this faceless player's position. *Please don't let him be an offensive lineman—something like a left guard*, I thought.

"*Left guard*," the injured player rasped. The nature of his injuries was unclear, but he was severely discomforted. And I ran out there, across the humpbacked field.

It was The Rock, I realized now—we were playing in Brenham, and the huddle had already broken. The other 10 players were finishing lining up, so it was easy for me to find my spot on the line: the only vacancy, like an old-fashioned typewriter with the one key raised, mantis-like, above all the others. Not yet ready to hammer-strike back down into its nest among the myriad others: a tiny perfect gap there, where only I could fit.

Ernie is already over the ball. He motions me in next to him, and I slide in quickly, settle into a three-point stance as if I've been playing left guard all my life.

"Right guard," I correct the team—speaking to no one in particular, only clarifying that this was the position needed, not left guard.

Ernie nods, points to the defensive lineman directly across from me. He's monstrous: I feel like a flea. I'll do my best, but it's my great fear the giant directly across from me will run right over the top of me and disrupt the play, getting into the backfield immediately.

I don't know what the play is. I know only that I have to block him.

The ball's snapped, and I fire off the line, all enthusiasm and dream. And to my disbelief, we're standing him up, a double team, pass-blocking the giant—Ernie to my left, getting up under his shoulder pads and standing him up, and me hitting him on the right.

The giant is stood up; he's not going anywhere, and we're buying time, each precious melting second a great gift and bounty that allows the play, Coach's play, to develop into its natural design and desire.

This isn't so hard. This is awesome.

The ball's thrown over our heads and somewhere into the middle of the field, the scrum, where it's tipped, then intercepted by one of their linebackers.

Their linebacker, too, is a monster of a man, bulging and swollen with muscle, lumpen but powerful, and is wearing a Red Raiders jersey. He's coming straight down the middle again, and I release from my block and slide left, knowing I am the only one who can stop him from taking it in for a score. He has a gang of blockers deployed all around him; others of his teammates are rallying to him to help create "a flying wedge," long ago outlawed. The only hope I have is for him to keep coming straight on, so I can hit him low; and he keeps coming, thunderously. Be careful what you wish for.

I see his massive tree-trunk legs, his dangerous knees, but I drop down and hit him in his shins and wrap up tight. And though the impact of it upon me is significant, he begins to topple like a cut tree, and I wake up, my work as a backup offensive lineman finished. *Just do your job.*

Some mornings, as I'm just easing back into the bright light of the world after an entire night of sleep and dreams, I find myself wondering, briefly, not about Richard Sherman, but about the big guy who headbutted me so savagely. Who snapped my forehead so hard the back of my head went all the way back to my spine. As if he sought to extinguish me. Attempting to extinguish me.

He didn't. He was unsuccessful. I got out. I didn't want to, but I did.

EPILOGUE

MANY ARE SAYING WE live in a broken age, a time of great destruction, and that we are the architects of that devastation. The proof certainly is everywhere. So much is disappearing. The largest things are going away first—rhinos and gorillas, grizzlies, musk ox and bison—and vanishing also are the most intricately sculpted things that once and for a long time were so tightly fitted to the world. The enormous bears that leave in the marsh paw prints larger than a man's head; the salamander larvae and boreal toad tadpoles one can sometimes find inhabiting those water-filled prints, a month later.

I remember seeing these things, and the people, my beloveds, I have seen them with. My memory is coming back. It took about two years. When I began to spell words correctly again, and found my sentences and thoughts reconnecting, it was like climbing up out of a hole. As the bears themselves do each April, and the toads, and salamanders. For it is the nature of the world to try to heal broken things. To fit, once more. As if that is the current that flows beneath all life.

I don't think my addiction was, at its heart, any cliché about trying to recapture youth, or fear of aging. I actually don't mind getting older. Some days you're presumed to be frail or mentally reduced, but it's true also that some people are more patient with you, and pause in their hurried and harried lives to answer a question, any question, you might have. That the urge to help an individual of our own species is deep and strong within us, as if a map for such connections exists—still exists—within.

And on the field, the ritualized pageantry of the game, such connections—*team*—feels as powerful as they must once have done long ago—before they began to tatter. That on your team you exist like a red blood cell bobbing along in an arterial river.

I worry that in this memoir I have chronicled the addiction but not adequately identified its source: only that it exists. And now that I have been released from it—liberated, ironically, from the last hit I ever took, the one that snapped my head all the way back to my spine—I can see it better.

The wellspring and the allure—for me—is not valor or camaraderie, is not youth or finesse, is not speed or strength, but instead, the raw essence of beauty. As both an artist and a scientist, I have pondered the definition of beauty for a long time. The idea means different things to different people, but it seems to me its commonality involves the condition of fit; that the deepest beauty exists in relation to how it fits another thing, proximately.

The way one color is placed next to another. The way a certain curve relates to the space and other shapes around it. In nature, so much of the fittedness we call beautiful has taken eons to be achieved. The speckles on the side of a brook trout, with clear water shimmering across the spots that are the shape of the underwater gravel from which the fish was born. There is almost no one who would behold such an image and not call it beautiful, whether they know the ecology of the trout or the geology of the streambed. And the sight, the thing, no less beautiful whether ever witnessed by others or not.

A quarterback is generally required to have a hand width of at least 9¾ inches, to grip with strength and control the elliptical shape of the fully inflated ball. Once thrown, there is a beauty to the tight spiral of a ball rotating with speed on its journey to the waiting hands of the receiver. There is a way that the best receivers, running downfield and waiting for the ball to reach them, will not let the defender know the ball has been launched. The receiver will be looking back, watching the ball's approach, without appearing to be watching it come closer.

The receiver will wait until the last millisecond (all this happening at a full sprint) before reaching up and snatching the ball, the bullet, from the air, pulling it tight to his chest in the same movement and accelerating toward the end zone.

That, like so very much else in the game, is beautiful, but it is beautiful also when the same defender reacts just in time and twists to look back and sees the ball and taps it away at the last instant; or when both men catch the ball simultaneously and fight for possession of it even in midair, like two hawks battling over a fish.

On the field, everything conspires to fit itself to the logic of a universe that has been constructed only across the last 100 years or so, and can be witnessed for only one hour.

On the field, as in life, ugliness can appear amid the beauty, just as in life: the lineman who flinches before the snap and jumps offsides, like an actor dropped into a dream in which he does not belong. The bounce of a player's helmeted head on the Astroturf. Those things are not a fit, are not a part of the logic and intent of the game, which is to get the ball into the end zone, and to prevent the ball from getting into the end zone. There are blemishes. These are what hone the edges of beauty.

But the beauty is what is remembered, and is sought in each game. The beauty is what calls to us. We seek to fit it—to be a part of it—until we no longer can. And then we leave, and go searching for other beauty to which we may fit ourselves. And with luck, we find it; and I am lucky, for I have.

I was so lucky. That last hit knocked me out of one universe of beauty and into another, returning me to my beloveds: my memories of them, and my present-day presence with them, and my plans for a future in which we fit the world as it comes at us. Let us address those coming hours and years with passion, verve, creativity, strength, and keen attentiveness.

I have not heard from Coach in a long time. I hope he starts a gym. I hope he secures a reality show or a movie about his singular team, his singular fire. The world has an appetite for such charisma, such passion and paradox. I hope the Express hosts a charity game on behalf of stopping domestic violence, with Colin Kaepernick quarterbacking one team and Andrew Luck the other. Maybe I'll come out of retirement for that one and catch a swing pass out of the backfield from one of them, as long as it's a game of flag football. Maybe . . .

Stop it.

Right. It's over. I got lucky. There are so very many who do not.

ACKNOWLEDGMENTS

I'm grateful to Coach Barnes and the members of the Texas Express in the 2017, 2018, and 2020 seasons for supporting me not just as a journalist but as a teammate. I'm grateful to my family for their support of this strange foray, particularly my daughters, Mary Katherine and Lowry, and my partner, Carter. It could have been easy to not support me. And I'm thankful to my dad and Maryanne and brothers Frank and B.J., likewise, for never telling me that this might not be the most fully-thought-out idea. Might even be a really bad idea. It would have been easy to state the obvious.

Regarding the book's production, I'm grateful to Stephen Hull, Felicia Cedillos, Anna Pohlod, and Patricia Kot; David Evans, Don Redpath, and team; and again, to Carter, for extensive and much-appreciated editing.

Finally, I'm grateful to Kirby for his continued investment in any hijinks, anytime, anywhere, then as well as now. For not taking life too seriously.